SUSTAINING PRESENCE

A MODEL OF CARING
BY PEOPLE OF FAITH

EARL E. SHELP
RONALD H. SUNDERLAND

ABINGDON PRESS
Nashville

SUSTAINING PRESENCE
A MODEL OF CARING BY PEOPLE OF FAITH

Copyright © 2000 by Abingdon Press

This book is printed on acid-free paper.

Library of Congress Cataloging-in-Publication Data

Shelp, Earl E., 1947-
   Sustaining presence : a model of caring by people of faith / Earl E. Shelp, Ronald H. Sunderland.
   p. cm.
   Includes bibliographical references.
   ISBN 0-687-02589-3 (alk. paper)
   1. Church work with the sick. 2. Group ministry. I. Sunderland, Ronald, 1929-   II. Title.

BV4460.S53 2000
253—dc21

99-059061

All scripture quotations, unless noted otherwise, are taken from the *New Revised Standard Version,* copyright 1989, Division of Christian Education of the National Council of the Churches of Christ in the United States of America. Used by permission. All rights reserved.

Scripture quotations marked RSV are taken from the *Revised Standard Version of the Bible,* copyright 1946, 1952, 1971 by the Division of Christian Education of the National Council of the Churches of Christ in the USA. Used by permission. All rights reserved.

Scripture quotations noted KJV are from the King James or Authorized Version of the Bible.

Scripture quotations noted NEB are from *The New English Bible.* © The Delegates of the Oxford University Press and The Syndics of the Cambridge University Press 1961, 1970. Reprinted by permission.

00 01 02 03 04 05 06 07 08 09—10 9 8 7 6 5 4 3 2 1

MANUFACTURED IN THE UNITED STATES OF AMERICA

To 6,119 individual Care Team members, our colleagues, whose ministries of sustaining presence are described in this volume. Their loving devotion to their care partners daily inspires us and embodies the biblical ideals of care that shaped our concept of Care Team ministry

And to Ruth Reko, Director of Leadership Development of the Evangelical Lutheran Church in America, who challenged us to plant the Care Team model in other communities

ACKNOWLEDGMENTS

This book reports the biblical and theological tradition of the church in caring for members of congregations whose health-related crises are of such magnitude and intensity that they overwhelm the one-to-one pastoral ministries that are customary in congregations. It describes the Care Team ministry we developed in 1985, which has been refined as we participated in and observed the ministries Care Teams offer individuals and families with special needs.

Since 1985, these ministries have been offered by 6,119 Care Team members on behalf of their Christian and Jewish congregations to more than 3,000 people suffering from chronic, and often terminal, diseases or catastrophic disabilities. We acknowledge and thank the Care Team members, for without them this venture in ministry would be only an idea. They have embodied the highest ideals of pastoral care and, in doing so, have made a monumental contribution to the process of transforming a concept into praxis. In doing so, they have shared in creating Care Team ministry, testing its day-to-day application to families in need, and establishing a model that is being replicated nationally. The bestowing of a 1998 President's Service Award administered by the Points of Light Foundation recognizes the contribution the Care Team program is making to care of people who are chronically ill and disabled.

We acknowledge the signal contribution of Ruth Reko, who as Director of Leadership and Development of the Evangelical Lutheran Church in America, challenged us in 1994 to assist her to plant the Care Team model in other communities. Ruth introduced us to representatives of Lutheran nursing home and retirement institutions seeking a means of serving their member congregations. These efforts resulted in the initiation of Care Team programs in Dayton, Ohio; Columbia, South Carolina; Oshkosh, Madison, and Appleton, Wisconsin; and Stanwood, Washington. Based on these efforts, we have assisted agencies in Abilene and Corpus Christi, Texas, to develop Care Team programs for congregations in their communities.

We acknowledge also the many individuals and local communities who have replicated the AIDS Care Team program in more than 70 cities in more than 35 states. We celebrate the widening application of Care Team ministry for people with HIV/AIDS and other adults with special needs. This book is offered as a stimulus to such efforts.

Finally, we express our thanks to the Board of Directors of the Foundation for Interfaith Research and Ministry, whose affirmation and support encourages us to greater commitments, and to the members of the foundation's staff. We celebrate the professional manner in which staff members fulfill their own ministries to the Care Teams. Their devotion to their teams inspires Care Team members as they minister day-by-day to care partners and their families.

CONTENTS

PREFACE

Sustaining Presence was written in response to our growing conviction that substantial gaps existed in congregations' pastoral care of individuals and families with special needs—needs that are so intensive and so extensive that they overwhelm customary one-on-one ministry. While traditional delivery of pastoral ministry responds effectively to members' concerns, it often fails to meet the day-to-day needs of families struggling with chronic or terminal illness or catastrophic physical disability, especially when such families may need daily in-home support to cope at the most basic levels.

We describe how the notion of groups or teams of lay ministers—Care Teams—first arose in response to individuals and their caregivers stricken with HIV/AIDS, and subsequently was broadened to encompass needs related to other catastrophic conditions. We recognized that the onset of dementia placed particular burdens on family caregivers who, like caregivers of people living with AIDS, were called upon to provide twenty-four-hour care and support for their loved ones. No sooner had the AIDS Care Team program been replicated to respond to the needs of Alzheimer's caregivers than the model was further enlarged to support frail seniors living alone or cared for by family members, and extended still further to other frail adults, regardless of age.

The Care Team model enables congregations to provide pastoral support to members and their caregivers who may need in-home support two or three days per week, and in some instances, as frequently as daily. Few congregations are able to provide this level of care in the absence of a structured and finely tuned model such as the Care Team concept presented here as ministries of sustaining presence.

While we speak about gaps in congregational care of members with special needs, we acknowledge there have always been congregations that both perceived such needs and developed programs to address them. Two types of ministries have been used. In some congregations, what amounts to a "Care Team" of concerned members coalesces around the needs of a particular family, though often on an ad hoc basis that dissolves when the need is met. Other congregations may keep such a group in place and ready to respond to the next family emergency that demands more than the typical pastoral one-on-one mode of pastoral care. Nevertheless, it is our sense that such congregations represent a tiny minority of American churches. It is one of the purposes of this book to emphasize the value for all congregations of permanent structures that enable them to remain constantly alert and equipped to respond to the pain, loneliness, and need for community of individuals and families for whom traditional forms of one-on-one care are overwhelmed.

We find the term *presence* to be particularly apt in this context. A Care Team is a *sustaining presence* that pastoral care may take when a family is overwhelmed by chronic or terminal illness. The ministries of laypeople endowed with gifts of compassion and sensitivity are sustaining at points in families' lives when many have exhausted their own resources, are isolated and alone due to the ravages of catastrophic diseases or disabilities, and too often wonder if anyone cares. The presence of committed laypeople who provide support, and particularly opportunities for caregiver respite, is truly a ministry of sustaining presence that manifests God's compassion for those who are weak and heavy laden.

CHAPTER 1

CONGREGATIONAL CAREGIVING

This is an essay about the local church—that place where Christians gather to be spiritually nourished, and that community through which life is shared under the Lordship of the Christ. It is not necessarily about the universal church, nor the church institutional. Neither is it necessarily about denominations, doctrines, or histories. This is an essay about the Body of Christ in its congregational expression. More specifically, it is about caregiving.

Caregiving and churches go together. Like love and marriage, you can't have one without the other. To be church requires caregiving without specifying its form and content. A congregation's warm and caring people are often heralded as a leading reason that one should belong to one church rather than another. Being a caring community is of great, if not singular, importance to the identity and integrity of the church in either its local or universal expression.

Our focus on caregiving is not to dismiss as unimportant other aspects of congregational life. Congregations must be multifaceted communities of worship, study, evangelism, fellowship, mission, and care. Each attribute and activity makes a unique contribution to the identity and vitality of the whole. Although many of these features may have secular counterparts, which respond to a range of human needs and interests, the congregation's beliefs in and about God distinguish it from other forms of social organization and activity. It is not merely another secular venue at which people gather and engage one another;

it is a sacred space where the divine and human encounter is transformational.

For Christians, the Incarnation is a pivotal event in human history. The belief that God entered into intimate community with humanity through the redemptive life of Jesus means that the nature of this gathering of people born of God's grace must be the same as that of the One who brought it into existence. As the Incarnation denotes God's solidarity with humankind, so the faith community created by God must have solidarity with humankind. A congregation that does not acknowledge, respect, celebrate, embody, or express the compassion of God manifest in the Incarnation ceases to be church!

We are not suggesting that the church can or should be understood solely and fully in terms of its solidarity with humankind and the compassion it expresses. Such a reductionist approach would distort and impoverish the entity called by God to continue God's redemptive mission. Each feature of congregational life is an essential part of the full expression of community. Nevertheless, certain features may overshadow others in some congregations. For example, some churches are known for their great preaching pastors, rate of growth, physical facilities, music program, family program, or something else. There may be reasons for the personality and reputation of a particular congregation. Perhaps these distinctive characteristics merely point to certain strengths or gifts without implying that other aspects of community are subordinated, neglected, or absent.

INSTITUTIONAL AND CULTURAL IMPERATIVES

In a world where the community of faith must compete with countless secular attractions for a person's commitment, it may be prudent and effective "marketing" to highlight or build upon a congregation's particular strength. Just as believers have different gifts that function together for the good of the congregation, it is reasonable to suggest that individual congregations have gifts that complement the gifts of other congregations to more fully serve God's redemptive purpose. While acknowledging this richness, diversity, and fullness of gifts within God's providence, we wonder if a necessary feature of congregational life has withered and grown weak.

A congregation grounded in Christ and being transformed through faith and discipleship is defined as a community in which, among other things, its members care for one another. Caring for one another is not one option among many from which the church may select. It is not a feature of congregational life that may come into favor or be permitted to fall into disfavor. It is not superior to other expressions of God's redemptive will and neither is it secondary. Caregiving, a simple yet profound expression of concern and compassion, is a defining characteristic of God's community known as church. For Paul, the priority for caregiving among the congregation was clear. He admonished the Galatian Christians to "Bear one another's burdens, and in this way you will fulfill the law of Christ" (Gal. 6:2).

Caring for one another is not one of those biblical descriptions of community that seems limited or restricted to the first century, although there may be debate about the degree of care that is obliged. Acts 2:44-47*a* describes how those who were baptized following Peter's preaching related to one another: "All who believed were together and had all things in common; they would sell their possessions and goods and distribute the proceeds to all, as any had need. Day by day, as they spent much time together in the temple, they broke bread at home and ate their food with glad and generous hearts, praising God and having the goodwill of all the people." Rejoicing in God's grace and enjoying fellowship with one another at the table can be practiced more or less comfortably in the first century or the twenty-first century. However, the notion of possessing resources in stewardship for the good and benefit of any in need has been seen by some from Ananias and Sapphira (Acts 5:1-11) in the first century onward to extend unduly the meaning of community and the obligation of caring for one another. Despite these types of controversies regarding limits and applications, caregiving has endured as a central feature of Christian discipleship and Christian community in doctrine and, to varying degrees, in practice.

The impression one discerns from Acts 2 is that of a group of people who were disposed to share faith and life together, to be family related by belief rather than blood, and to be community bound by

13

commitment rather than coercion. To suggest that thousands of believers were intimate friends with one another strains the meaning of intimacy. Yet, it is difficult to imagine any member feeling abandoned or alone as the hurts of life came. The community to which they apparently felt called would have been in danger of dissolution if the isolating effects of suffering, guilt, fear, and grief were not overcome by the presence and care of members for one another. It must have been second nature for these people to turn to one another in a time of need. Perhaps the members were so sensitive to one another that they recognized and responded to a need even before the one in distress could call for care.

Turning to one's congregation to meet a need may be less likely today when self-sufficiency seems valued more than community and caregiving has become an occupation more than a gift. There may be few relationships marked by an intimacy that inevitably is forged as blessings and burdens are borne together on the anvil of life. The extent and strength of communal bonds in many congregations may be no greater than those found among a cohort of five thousand Lutherans surveyed about their beliefs, values, attitudes, and behaviors. Most adults reported having close friends, but only 4 to 14 percent in six age groups between 15 and 65 reported having three or fewer close friends who really cared about them. When asked how many of their five closest friends were members of their own congregation, 29 to 49 percent across age brackets said none![1] One should not draw many conclusions from this survey about Lutherans or about the status of relationships within congregations generally. Yet, the survey may provide insight into the status of congregational bonds from which caregiving must spring.

We were surprised in 1992 by the response of pastors and layleaders to our suggestion that a small group of their members could provide hands-on ministry with families caring for a loved one at home with Alzheimer's disease or another dementia. Few pastors whom we approached were aware of the number of families struggling with these forms of illness and incapacity. Fewer still could imagine a ministry by the congregation specifically for these families other than praying for them and perhaps taking communion to their homes.

This state of affairs may be fully understandable if the relationships and expectations among members of a congregation resemble more those of strangers or casual acquaintances than those among family. Congregations are to be communities in which their members care about one another and freely respond to each other's needs. Yet, there seems to be considerable evidence that members often resist calling on others for care, especially when the need goes beyond the common and generally effective one-to-one forms of pastoral care such as brief home, hospital, or nursing home visits; supportive phone calls or notes; or other forms of practical assistance at a time of acute need. In situations where the needs for care and support are long-term, related to disability or chronic illness, or intense, people seem to have become socialized to seek "care" and assistance in the marketplace, rather than among their faith communities. Caregiving for the chronically ill, and the ministry that is inherent to it, has become more of a commercial transaction than an expression of personal commitment or a characteristic of congregational life.

During times of increased vulnerability, it is reasonable to assume that people would seek assistance from others who are known to be trustworthy and are perceived to care about them. But our experience suggests, paradoxically, that instead, strangers may be hired to perform a needed service that mistakenly is referred to as "care." Care cannot be purchased. Care is an expression of a commitment, not an economic event. Care springs freely from a relationship of genuine concern that cannot be bought and sold. Care can only be a gift offered in love and received in gratitude. It is to the credit of many who provide a service that the service is provided in a sensitive and kind manner. A service provider may, in fact, grow to truly care about the person served; but such a commitment is not a precondition or necessary part of the exchange. Conversely, care appears to be an expectation and necessary feature of relationships among members of congregations.

There may be many explanations for the state of caregiving for members with special needs within modern American churches. Individualism and self-sufficiency are highly valued in contemporary American culture. Faith and religious practice in a culture dominated by individualism and self-sufficiency conceivably could sacrifice corporate worship and community on the altar of private devotion. Faith and spiritual growth, in such a setting, may be only weakly tied to the institutional mooring of the church. One consequence for members with a nominal connection to the congregation may be a feeling of insulation from the pain of others. A consequence for a congregation may be a lessened capacity to respond to the needs of members when those needs cannot be met in a pastoral call or other one-to-one ministry.

Some effects of individualism have been discussed by sociologist Robert Bellah and his colleagues in their classic volume *Habits of the Heart*. They observe that

> this is a society in which the individual can only rarely and with difficulty understand himself and his activities as interrelated in morally meaningful ways with those of other, different Americans. Instead of directing cultural and individual energies toward relating the self to its larger context, the culture of manager and therapist urges a strenuous effort to make of our particular segment of life a small world of its own.[2]

Being disconnected from others and fragmenting people into small homogeneous worlds or circles would appear to be logical consequences and sources of personal happiness in a culture that elevates individualism and self-sufficiency so highly. Ironically, however, Bellah and his colleagues found that their survey subjects felt bound together, if in no other way, in a common devotion to the American *ideal* of self-reliance and independence. Despite the language of individualism that permeates our culture and the great value placed on self-reliance, Bellah and colleagues found that Americans "do not imagine that a good life can be lived alone . . . [but] that connectedness to others in work, love, and community is essential to happiness, self-esteem, and moral worth."[3] This finding may help explain from a sociological perspective why congregations survive and why many people value congregational membership and participation. It does not explain, however, why relationships among members seem inconsistent with the "connectedness" believed crucial to a good life and putatively present in a congregation.

There may be other aspects of individualism and self-sufficiency that affect the scope and intensity of care that members will accept from their congregation. Shame and embarrassment about being in a

16

position of need may contribute to a reticence to accept care, and so also may a perception that a supportive response may be beyond the capacity of the congregation to provide. The relationships among the full membership may not be deep and strong enough to prompt members to make the required commitment of time and energy. Lest we risk being perceived as overly pessimistic, we hasten to celebrate and praise all forms and acts of care undertaken by a congregation and individual members. Visitation, prayers, and varying forms of practical assistance from transportation to casseroles during periods of illness, bereavement, or personal crisis suggest a meaningful connectedness at some level that includes some sense of responsibility for one another.

The presence and help given at these times are forms of care that surely comfort and encourage people in crisis. In fact, congregations tend to be very effective with this sort of short-term caregiving. An acute illness, hospitalization, or death generally triggers a caring response. The immediate need is met through practices and rituals that express the congregation's care and concern. But another crisis in another household may draw the caring response away to the new need. And unfortunately, the brokenness and pain of those left behind may be too easily forgotten and unattended. Tragically, it may be true in many congregations that the care stops with the casseroles. Congregations generally are not organized and members not trained to provide long-term care. Perhaps the clergy or a designated layperson will attempt to retain contact in these situations. Reports may be provided and prayers offered. But with the passage of time and the accumulation of other assignments, even these ad hoc efforts may wane and the feeling of abandonment may intensify. These generally are not willful failures of community. They are merely consequences of not having in place a ministry that specifically responds to the needs of the chronically ill or severely disabled members.

There are, indeed, gifted caregivers in every congregation who learn of individuals and families with special needs and seemingly offer the exact care that is needed. They lovingly bear the burdens of the whole congregation. The weight of the burdens, however, may become overwhelming. New needs may go unnoticed. Members may not bring their needs to the attention of the congregation. Help may be sought outside the fellowship of believers.

An elderly woman stopped at the church door following the Sunday morning worship recently. The service featured a major emphasis on caring for one another through a new form of ministry proposed to the membership. The pastor strongly endorsed the proposed ministry. An eloquent presentation was made by a guest preacher. The congregation was informed that several families could immediately benefit from the proposed ministry. Members were invited to express interest by placing their names on a roster as they left the sanctuary. The woman who stopped at the church door represented one of the families in need of the proposed ministry. As she passed, she noticed that only one woman had signed the roster, even though she was nearly the last to leave. She spoke of her disabled and homebound husband whose contact with his church was limited to the communion visits of the pastor. She told of his hurt and feelings of loss. She betrayed her pain and anger as she predicted that the members would not join the proposed ministry. Her words were, "not this church, not these people, they don't care." The one woman who signed the roster, it was later learned, had cared for her husband at home, faithfully and alone, during a long terminal illness without the assistance of her congregation. She knew from experience the weight of burdens being borne by other members. And she was willing to bear those burdens with them.

Not everyone is gifted for ministry in the world of the weak and weary. Their hearts may be touched by the plight of others. They may have compassion for people coping with distress. Yet, they may not be called or comfortable to become vulnerable themselves in the process of caring for others with special needs. This phenomenon was graphically portrayed among the laypeople with whom we worked in 1989. At the time there were approximately six hundred men and women caring weekly for adults stricken by AIDS. Their commitments to the people they served often required more than they ever imagined they could give to people they had known for only a short time. It was customary for the laypeople to serve their AIDS patients until they died. And then, because others were waiting with such intense needs and no one to meet them, they would go immediately to begin the process of bonding and loss all over again.

We began to see early indications that the number of children and newborns infected with HIV would grow. Unlike the single adults or adults with partners with whom we had mostly worked until then, these children were in family units that, as often as not, were quite unconventional. Normalcy for these children was different from the common family experience of the mostly middle-class white caregivers whom we coordinated. We began to invite these caregivers to embrace children with AIDS. We thought that the volunteers would eagerly care for this rapidly growing population of AIDS patients. Children with any affliction or impairment seem to evoke sympathies that adults with illness may not. To our surprise, many caregivers declined our invitation to enter the world of children with AIDS. Their refusal was not based on the challenges posed by the atypical family structures and multifaceted deprivation that tended to be common. Rather, the caregivers reported that watching so many adults suffer and die with AIDS was difficult enough; they just did not think that they could subject themselves to the numerous deaths that would surely be witnessed if they befriended and cared for the children. They were compassionate and gifted people, but most did not feel called or gifted for ministry with this special population of children. Ministry with these children was provided, however, by other members of teams who did not experience this reservation. We affirmed these decisions to serve and to not serve. A basic feature of Care Team ministry is the freedom of members to engage only in forms of ministry to which they feel called and with which they are comfortable and are competent to provide.

An important point to recognize from this experience is the anticipated effect upon the caregivers of an emotional attachment to children whose destinies were darkened by a then-lethal infection. Emotion has identifying power to draw people together. In the process of touching and being touched emotionally, people may be rendered vulnerable so that what happens to one party has some effect upon the other. Yet this is exactly what standing in solidarity with humankind may entail. In solidarity, it is not only the other's finitude, weakness, fear, and loss that is revealed, it is one's own. Not only may the pain of another be too great to bear for some, the prospect of one's own pain foreshadowed in the brokenness of another may be too threatening to confront. It may not be only personal discomfort with the condition of another that prevents one from caregiving; it may be an inability or unwillingness to accept one's own finitude and interdependence. The cherished values of independence and self-sufficiency, as well as their capacity to provide meaning to life, may be threatened in the presence of a child facing death or an adult reduced to childlike dependence by illness or adversity. Yet, it is just this world of grief, sorrow, affliction, injustice, and marginalization which God's servants are called to engage (cf. Isa. 53:3-12).[4] Obedience to God's call and will may involve giving witness to the divine love that creates, sustains, and suffers, even in the face of death.

CHALLENGES TO COMMUNITY

Personal, institutional, and cultural factors may converge to limit caregiving within and by congregations. The language of community, compassion, and care may be familiar; but the commitment and capacity to give content and life to these attributes of congregations seems in jeopardy with respect to situations where the needs for support are long-term or intense. The status of congregational caregiving may reflect, as well, powerful social and economic forces that are dramatically affecting the way people live and relate. Americans are a mobile people. Job opportunities and career growth increasingly are understood nationally or globally, rather than locally. Multinational corporations competing in a global marketplace routinely move employees from place to place or attract employees from one location to another. Long-term employer-employee relationships tend to be rare. Affluent people, especially those retired and freed from employment, choose to live where they wish for reasons of climate, cost, recreation, friends, or family. Deep roots in a neighborhood or community are becoming shallower. Long-term relationships among colleagues and friends, if they exist at all, may be sustained at a distance. Short-term, serial close relationships may be more the norm than lifelong friendships or employments of a past era.

Attachments to a particular church and congregation may be similarly transitory due to the twists and turns in one's life journey. There may not be sufficient time or interest while in a congregation to develop intimate relationships. The grief that comes when relationships of this quality are severed may prompt people to be reluctant to establish new bonds as they relocate from place to place. Significant events in life that are observed in a church and shared by its people may be scattered among churches. Few individuals or families celebrate all their major events marked by rituals and communal presence—births, weddings, deaths, anniversaries, baptisms—in a single congregation. Attachments to a particular church and congregation inevitably are weakened in this environment. Transience is more common than permanence in religious life as in secular life. The values of individualism and independence are perfectly suited to justify this style of life and flourish in this socioeconomic environment.

Priorities at work, home, and church may be at odds. Despite claims that technology has increased efficiency in many areas of life, many people do not have enough time in the day to earn a living, tend a family and home, and be a pillar of the church involved in many of its activities. Life is likely to be experienced less as an integrated whole than as a collection of movements that overlap or intersect, mainly because they are partial expressions of one person's existence. Accepting this manner of living as good or appropriate in adulthood requires socialization in childhood.

Andrei Simic discusses the apparent triumph of individualism and the social fragmentation that follows: "Nowhere is this more evident than in family life, with its deemphasis on corporacy and the orientation of its constituent members away from the household toward the external world, each with his or her own unique set of interests and concomitant social network."[5] As a consequence, the extended family becomes a loose network of nuclear families. A member's sense of responsibility for and connectedness to others is not nourished in an environment where one's group of choice is afforded greater value than one's group of origin. The fate of one family member may not necessarily concern the others. The source of security past generations felt from kinship and an attendant mutual responsibility is usurped by the belief that money makes one free and secures one's interests. A goal of parenthood is to help a child achieve independence, not rely upon, or necessarily cherish, given reciprocal ties and obligations between generations.

These parentally mediated social norms appear to be embraced unquestionably and their associated values deeply, almost intractably, ingrained. Seniors, for example, tend to resist "demeaning dependence" on their children, preferring to remain "their own persons" even if doing so comes at a time in life when the nurturing and sustaining company of kin would be reassuring, comforting, and prudent.[6] Simic concludes:

> It is significant that such folk aphorisms as "Stay active" and "Be independent" are so frequently heard in our country among the elderly. These maxims simply restate what are core values of our culture as a whole. Nevertheless, . . . in spite of their sense of alienation and ostensible loneliness, many of the elderly actually subscribe to the very world view that has contributed to their own sense of isolation. In effect, they are unwilling to forgo the reputed pleasures of individualism and independence to commit themselves to the kinds of intense reciprocity that typify family and other social relationships in more traditional societies.[7]

A kinship group, social group, faith group, almost any group other than an economic or psychological self-help or self-improvement group, is in peril in such a setting. To survive or flourish, it must counter powerful and sabotaging forces that threaten alternative values like reciprocity, mutuality, community, and selflessness.

Some churches seem willing to accommodate these trends and acquiesce to the triumph of these stereotypical American values and their social effects. Attempts are made to make church membership convenient and to make faith part, rather than the center, of one's identity. Attendance at worship on Sunday morning and casual friendships among members may be all that community can be or mean for people trying to *include* God in their lives. Faith and discipleship become individualized. For many, the nurturing and disciplining value of relationships may wane to the point of unimportance. Peggy Wehmeyer, religion correspondent for ABC News, may represent the 55 percent of Americans who do not attend public worship regularly as she comments: "I'm definitely on a spiritual journey, but my church is not the focal point."[8] The church and its members clearly are not a sustaining presence for Peggy Wehmeyer and others who agree with her statement.

When members of a congregation have only a nominal sense of belonging or feeling of mutual concern and responsibility for one another, a congregation's pastoral or nurturing care suffers. Most forms of care are relegated to and the responsibility of the ordained and lay paid staff. It is their job, as well as their calling. Care effectively becomes professionalized within the faith community, reflecting the commercialization of "care" in the secular economy. "Pastoral" ministry is restricted to the sacramental and professional functions of ordained people. Caregiving is demarcated as social ministry to the unfortunate or mission ministry to the faithless. Caring for one another or bearing one another's burdens falls to individual members who may care for one another on a one-to-one basis in times of crisis or short-term need through prayer, visitation, encouraging notes, covered dishes, and other limited forms of practical assistance. These expressions of concern, commitment, and kindness surely are comforting and supporting to those who receive them. Moreover, they are deeply appreciated as evidence of one's value in the community of faith to which one belongs. But when a need for care and support is longer term or more intensive, secular service providers tend to be sought by choice, if not default. The psychology of independence and individualism legitimizes one's turn to strangers for service, rather than to one's faith family for an exchange of gifts.

Caregiving within congregations has been hampered inadvertently in many churches as social, cultural, economic, and personal factors have transformed the meanings of community and discipleship. Members with hearts burdened by a particular need for the presence and care of God's people may discover that the congregation's menu of ministries does not provide an opportunity for that particular ministry. Too often secular charities become the venue where new forms of caregiving are developed and a member's gifts for ministry are transformed into volunteerism.

This was our experience in 1985 as we began to invite laypeople to embrace people with AIDS. The religious participants in the public discussion about AIDS were more known for their condemnation than their compassion, concerned more to reject than to reconcile. We could not identify an organized, hands-on congregational ministry to people touched by AIDS (patients, families, friends, medical personnel) in

23

Houston or elsewhere. As we entered the lives of these people to whom the scriptural description of the "poor" applies,[9] God's people were present as individuals and volunteers with a secular, and probably gay, social service organization, rather than as a ministry of the church. Their Christian witness of God's presence and care was unidentified. The countervoice their loving ministries constituted was not heard as certain preachers bellowed about God's punishment. When the compassion of members is not named as ministry, there is a risk that it appears the church doesn't care about this or that particular need.

Members with needs for longer-term or special ministries bear some responsibility when the congregation is not involved in their care. Their understanding of ministry may be limited, never considering to call upon their congregation to respond to a particular need. They may be persuaded by secularism and capitalism that care is a commodity requiring a commercial transaction or charity. Like the gifts of those who serve in secular organizations, their need for ministry may not be disclosed to a pastor or the congregation. These needs and opportunities for caregiving may not be known in a congregation, or known only to a few people. If known, existing structures and mechanisms of caregiving may not be responsive to a need. The pressure of other duties and the distractions of day-to-day life may not provide an opportunity to seek God's leadership to respond to longer-term needs in a creative and sustaining manner.

One might expect that small or rural congregations are more oriented to longer-term caregiving ministries. Where membership is counted in the low hundreds instead of many thousands, people ought to know one another. Where families have long histories of residency, the roots in the church should be deep and strong. Where members have been pillars of the church, active in many of its ministries and dedicated in its support, surely when dark times come, the people rally and provide sustaining care in whatever forms are required. Where this happens, there is reason to give thanks. God's people have resisted the isolating and depersonalizing forces all around them to preserve and protect key biblical concepts like community, solidarity, and discipleship.

Our experience suggests, however, that congregations which routinely respond to members with long-term or intense hands-on needs for care and support are the exception rather than the norm. Most of the

24

small congregations, prior to our work with them to develop more comprehensive and coordinated pastoral ministries, have done the best they can with one-on-one ministries. Size does not seem to be the determining factor. Similarly, in our work with congregations in small cities and rural communities, the same story was told. Certain members of the church knew of the caregiving needs of others, and maybe these folks did what they could to help. But the congregation as a people was not structured to more effectively serve in these situations. Members out of sight became members out of mind, beyond the thoughts and day-to-day care of a congregation, which formerly had been a great source of strength, nurture, comfort, and hope. The members professed to care, a profession that we took to be genuine and honest; but they seemed unable to imagine how caregiving could be anything other than those time-tested and largely individual acts of prayer, visitation, notes, and covered dishes.

Being in the inner circle of church leadership does not seem to improve significantly the prospect that one's care will be any different in a time of crisis. Equality of care, whether for a pillar of the church or holiday worshiper, may demonstrate that the congregation does not play favorites; but if equal care means no care, there is no reason to boast. We remember our dismay when a long-serving deacon in an affluent Baptist church requested help from our Foundation as he struggled to provide care at home for his wife with Alzheimer's disease. We called his pastor to determine if he was aware of the family's need and his interest to discuss a ministry that the congregation might implement to stand in solidarity with this member. The pastor invited Sunderland to discuss with the deacons how such a ministry could be developed. The deacons listened, empathized with the plight of their colleague, but in the end, decided there was nothing they could do! Fortunately, we were able to get another congregation with whom we share ministry to serve this burdened deacon. His hurt and bitterness about the response of his own congregation were great.

Even if it were true that shortcomings in care occur only for people who are members more in name or history than in attendance and commitment, abandonment in a time of need ought not be excused. These people may be members on the margin of congregational life, but the congregation may demonstrate greater concern for the hungry,

25

homeless, and lost who are not members through mission and evan-gelistic ministries than provide pastoral care for these "marginal" members of the family of faith. A "neglect" of any member weakens the witness of a congregation. A congregation's identity is distorted and its mission compromised when confessions of love and care are hollow statements.

God calls people to faith and community. Responding to God in love requires responding to God's children in love. Congregations in most instances are not gifted to meet all the needs of a member or family in crisis. But, without exception, congregations are gifted to be a sustain-ing presence in solidarity with broken people, bearing their burdens with them. There is hope for caregiving among God's people because God continues to sustain the community called church. We are excited about and in awe of the care that congregations give when their gifts for caregiving are discovered and nurtured. Our experience at watch-ing God's people come alive as they engage others in simple acts of kindness and care resonates with the conclusion of Bellah and col-leagues: "However much Americans extol the autonomy and self-reliance of the individual, they do not imagine that a good life can be lived alone. Those we interviewed would almost all agree that con-nectedness to others in work, love, and community is essential to hap-piness, self-esteem, and moral worth."[10]

A tragedy of contemporary life is that too few people experience community within a congregation or connectedness within a secular organization, seemingly by choice. Happiness is elusive and the bless-ing of mutuality is missed. Burdens are borne alone, and joys are bit-tersweet when celebrated in isolation. Congregations can and must be an alternative fellowship in which connectedness is experienced as community. They must be a people of the Incarnation in solidarity with humanity. They must give witness to the divine love on which they are founded and by which they are sustained. They ought not compromise their identity and mission by accommodating the isolating and deper-sonalizing effects of individualism and independence. They must, by their counterexample, give witness to the eternal value of intimate rela-tionships marked by grace and filled with love. By these and other means, the church will be community and caregiving will be com-monplace.

PURPOSE OF THE BOOK

We thank God for the love and care members spontaneously and selflessly offer to others. We are equally quick, however, to be the loyal opposition when the pastoral calling of the church and God's people is subordinated to other ministries and priorities. We are devoted to the church. We believe that local congregations, particular communities of faith and the people who constitute them, are a locus for and means of God's grace and redemption. Their multifaceted witness to God's love for humanity and all of creation, like the word and work of Jesus, invites people to faith and discipleship. One feature of this invitation that we consider crucial is the expression of God's compassion and solidarity with humanity through the humble service of God's people bearing one another's burdens. Through caregiving, the community God intends for the people of God may be more fully realized, confessions of faith and love by church members will have greater integrity, and the church can be a more authentic and compelling center in which life can be anchored and experienced more fully.

Our experience with church members who have borne the burdens of others suggests that the hearts of many of God's people are pierced by the pain of others. They have gifts for caregiving and a desire to express their faith in compassionate ministries. They properly perceive, in many instances, that they cannot provide all the care that may be indicated. But they are willing to be present to a person in distress and to do whatever is within their competence to be of help. Moreover, they derive a special feeling of spiritual and personal fulfillment from their acts of kindness and care because they minister in the name of and on behalf of their church.

Clearly we believe that caregiving has a leavening effect within a congregation. Through the special gifts of some members, the whole body of Christ is strengthened even as it identifies with people whose body or spirit has grown weak. In the chapters that follow, we examine the concept and practice of the pastoral ministry of the church and propose a metaphor of "sustaining presence" as a new way to articulate and express this characteristic of church life. Moreover, as an instance and expression of the pastoral ministry of the church, we will provide an apologia for the Care Team model of ministry that we created in 1985 and its several applications for specialized ministries to congregants and others.

In chapter 2 we argue that pastoral ministry is a function of the congregation as a corporate entity and not only the duty of ordained clergy. Theological and biblical justifications for this claim will be incorporated into analyses of relevant concepts, such as the call to faith and discipleship, the distinction between the pastoral office and pastoral roles, the "care" component of the pastoral role, the obligation to express gifts of caregiving, and the obligation of believers to receive care as the corollary of the duty to give care.

Based upon the developed understanding of the pastoral ministry of the church in chapter 2, we propose in chapter 3 that the defining feature of pastoral care is its sustaining function and the defining method of pastoral care is one of presence. We suggest that the pastoral ministry of the church can be comprehensively understood as a ministry of *sustaining presence*. In past decades, members with special needs typically were served by members of the adult Sunday school. These adult classes were the small groups in which relationships were formed and deepened over the passage of time. A class was a rapid response mechanism and the Sunday school structure provided a framework within which caregiving could be taught and modeled. This primary structure and means by which ministries of sustaining presence have been provided within churches has grown less vital and less effective for this task during recent decades, thereby creating a huge vacuum in caregiving.

Without a vital structure and means to provide ministries of sustaining presence, individuals within congregations are seeking avenues to express their gifts for pastoral ministry. The contemporary interest in and emphasis on small group activities reflects an awareness of a need for viable mechanisms of ministry and a desire to explore mechanisms to facilitate these interests. We explain in chapter 4 how the Care Team concept and model of ministry began in 1985 and has developed since then. We propose that Care Team ministries can make a significant contribution to the pastoral care and communal life of congregations. Based upon our years of experience, we present certain guiding principles for Care Team ministry and describe the organization and practice of Care Team ministry in general.

In chapters 5 through 7, we describe three forms of Care Team ministry designed to respond to families and individuals with special needs that a one-to-one ministry cannot meet. We present AIDS Care Teams as a pastoral response to people touched by HIV/AIDS, Alzheimer's Care Teams as a pastoral response to families caring at home for loved ones with dementia, and Second Family Care Teams as a pastoral response to frail seniors and younger adults burdened by disability or terminal illness.

There are others with special needs whom a Care Team ministry can assist. In chapter 8, we discuss the potential and capacity of congregations to provide more effective care of bereaved individuals through a multifaceted grief ministry that includes Grief Care Teams. We also review our experience in serving families with children who are disabled. These families constitute additional opportunities for ministry by specially trained members of Second Family Care Teams or Care Teams dedicated to the support of children that we prospectively have named Kids' Pals Care Teams. We conclude that the pastoral ministry of the church can and should improve in order to be more comprehensively faithful to the church's identity and mission. We suggest that the Care Team model of ministry is one means to actualize ministries of sustaining presence that has been demonstrated to be extremely effective in Houston and elsewhere.

Although we write as Christian clergy to the church, we acknowledge our debt to the Jewish tradition. We have learned much from our rabbi friends and from partnerships in caregiving with members of several Jewish congregations. The caregiving program that we promote and describe in this volume has been equally effective in Jewish and Christian life. The manner in which each tradition articulates God's will for human conduct reflects differing sacred histories, but the imperative to care for one another is similarly unqualified. One consequence that we celebrate from this common commitment to compassion is the cooperation that occurs in our program. Most Jewish and Christian Care Teams will serve anyone who seeks care. This, in our opinion, is as it should be because the care provided expresses the love of the one God for all of humanity

CHAPTER 2

PASTORAL MINISTRY

In *Ministry to Word and Sacraments*, Bernard Cooke commented on the enormous task to which he had set himself ten years earlier and wondered, in light of the massive and diverse amount of material concerning the origins and history of Christian ministry, if it was feasible to present a definitive text. The risk of "seeking justification for one's a priori views about that divine action or about the function of Christian ministry" was palpable. Cooke's inquiry was motivated by a desire to discern how we may minister to each other effectively, and what, if anything, is specifically "Christian" about the ministry that members of the church can undertake.[1]

Cooke joined a chorus of theologians who challenged the widespread notion that the pastoral function is limited to clerical "professionals."[2] A generation later, these voices have been heeded. As we enter a new millennium, most congregations recognize the proper role of laypeople, appropriately trained and supervised, in pastoral ministry. While the ordained pastor's care for individuals has usually been given a dominant emphasis, according to Charles Gerkin,[3] it is important to remember that the meaning of the term *pastoral* as it has been used within the Judeo-Christian tradition has always had a fundamentally communal connotation. That is, pastoral care denotes the care a *community* provides to its members. This fundamental recovery of emphasis, namely, that pastoral care is a ministry of the congregation, not of the clergy *qua* clergy, restores pastoral ministry to its rightful biblical and theological place, and rectifies a false perception that began in the second century, lasted until the Protestant Reformation, but then was reiterated in the twentieth century.

"PASTORAL CARE" IN THE EARLY CHURCH

While pastors and priests today exercise a central function, especially in pastoral care, the first century church emphasized the role of the *community* as the locus of the ministries that characterized its life. The ministries identified in Romans 12, 1 Corinthians 12, and Ephesians 4, including the care and nurture of members, were spread among all members of the congregation according to the gifts each had received (Rom. 12:6). At first, the day-to-day direction of each community's life rested on the corporate leadership of the *presbyterate*, which, according to Cooke, was less than a full-time occupation. The office of *presbyter* was overtaken gradually by the appointment of bishops *(episkopoi)* who assigned to deacons such community care as providing for the poor. Bishops increasingly assumed an "executive" role of directing the community. Their efforts to identify pastoral ministry as one of the episcopal functions gained ground during the second century as bishops arrogated to their office more and more responsibility for the ministries of the church. As power and authority were acquired by bishops, presbyters and deacons were assigned the day-to-day tasks as subordinate clergy, and the laity regressed into a passive role. The trend that emerged in the mid–second century was, by the end of the third century, a firmly established pattern: pastoral care, to use the twentieth-century term, had become an episcopal "office." It may have been delegated to presbyters and deacons, but there was no doubt that it was a manifestation of the bishop's role as the chief pastor.[4]

This arrogation of the ministries of the church to the respective clergy offices remained largely intact until the Protestant Reformation, and in the Roman Catholic Church until the reforms set in motion by Pope John XXIII through the Second Vatican Council. The Vatican Council in its key document, *Lumen gentium,* drew attention to the initiative and responsibility that laypeople should exercise by virtue of their baptism.[5] In the changes brought about in Scotland under the influence of

John Knox, the pastor (teaching elder, or dominee) assumed a teaching role with oversight of the lay ruling elders who bore the responsibility for the pastoral care of the congregation. In the Presbyterian Church in Scotland in the seventeenth century, lay elders often "labored fruitfully in the pastoral care and nurture of members," according to John T. McNeill.[6] When Presbyterian worship was proscribed in Catholic Scotland, worshipers met in secret locations that were disclosed when elders distributed the communion tokens that verified the holder was a member of the congregation. The distribution of tokens or certificates of membership was one occasion for this pastoral oversight.

The Wesleyan revival in England produced a similar pattern of ministry. Upon the establishment of a new Methodist Society, the earliest term applied to worshiping fellowships of Wesley's followers, layleaders were appointed over the Classes to which members of the society were assigned. At monthly Leaders' Meetings, the layleaders gave an account of their contacts with the families under their care. This pattern was repeated when Methodism gained its foothold in North America. Class meetings, the backbone of the earliest Methodist congregations, provided the basis for nurture of families. This identification of pastoral care as a ministry shared by ordained and lay members was perpetuated until the early twentieth century when there began a gradual reversion to the third-century model of a dominant clergy and a laity comfortable to leave the nurturing task to them.

THE PASTORAL OFFICE AND PASTORAL ROLES

Throughout the Jewish and Christian traditions, there is a strong emphasis on the peculiarity of the people of God as a community among other peoples. *Peculiarity* or *particularity*, is a usage of the King James translation of 1 Peter 2:9: "But [you] are a chosen generation, a royal priesthood, an holy nation, a peculiar people." It is noteworthy that in the Revised Standard Version, the latter phrase is translated "God's own people." This usage is followed by *The New English Bible*: "You are . . . a people claimed by God for his own." The self-understanding of the biblical communities is developed by Karl

Barth in *Church Dogmatics*. He insisted that the community was permitted, even commanded, to take seriously and to assert its uniqueness and distinction from other peoples. It is not the preservation of its own life that is at stake, but its "obedience to the will and work and Word of God." The claim of God that marks the community as a particular people propels it toward the fulfillment of this people's task: "To proclaim the triumphs of [God] who has called [them] out of darkness into his marvelous light" (1 Pet. 2:10 NEB). Once "not a people," they are now "the people of God." The uniqueness of the church springs from the act of God that constituted the church as a living fellowship commissioned to witness to this gracious act; it is directed not so much to the church itself, but to the world, which is the subject of God's love. This commission leads Barth, reflecting both Jewish and Christian images, to view the church as "an alien colony for the nature and experience of which there are no analogies in the world around."[7]

This particular people exists for all peoples; and its nature, function, and destiny are evoked by its task, *which also shapes the equipping process by which its members are prepared for their respective ministries.* The present form of the church's ministry developed in response both to the church's task and the equipment of its members for that task. Further, the church's task is integrally related to the structure and discipline by which the church's life is ordered and maintained. The church as the living fellowship of the people of God is called to exist in the world as a witness to God's steadfast love for humanity. It is called to perpetuate the work of Christ in seeking the lost, breaking down the barriers that divide people, and drawing all people to God. While the church's commission to engage in this work has an eschatological realization, it must also take place in the present. God wills that all people *now* should hear the good news in their own languages and know themselves to be claimed by it.

In the past fifty years this concept of the church's mission has led to two conclusions. First, if people are to hear the word God addresses to them, the words used to communicate the "good news" must be relevant to their existence in the (secular) world and, particularly, to each person's situation. Unless individuals grasp the meaning of the evangel for themselves, unless it speaks in terms that clearly are relevant to the daily stresses, decisions, and opportunities with which they are confronted, it is likely to be perceived merely as one voice among a cacophony of competing claims for attention. Second, while it is not bound or determined by them, the church must find its expression in relation to the forms and structures of society. The whole tenor of Scripture calls the church into a servant relationship to Christ and also to the world. The shape that its servant tasks take is not merely a question of listing additional areas of service by which it may fulfil its role as a servant people. The more radical question is how the church's basic service may be accomplished in new and bewildering situations. Should the approach be one of static mentality and rigid traditionalism, it cannot bring the church into a living encounter with the world, which leads to effective and relevant mission. This mission can only be accomplished effectively if the church and its members are clear about their call to ministry.

MINISTRY AND MINISTRIES

The call to ministry inherent in baptism, which may be termed the "general ordination" of all Christians from which specific ministries devolve, draws all Christians into ministry. Because ordination to the pastoral office sets aside clergy from the general ministry of the church, attention is drawn to the relationship of the roles of lay and ordained ministers. The ministries of laypeople are not defined in accordance with the roles of the ordained ministry, nor is the pastoral office defined with reference to the ministries of the laity. Both ministries are subservient to, defined by, and outcomes and expressions of the ministry of the church as the people of God. Only when the church's ministry has been defined can we proceed to examine particular ministries.

The ministry of the church is a commission laid upon all its members and is derived from God's act in creating the church and charging it with the task of witness and service. Since this ministry is a gift to the church, the church cannot of itself decide what that ministry is, though it has great freedom to decide the forms of ministry best suited to its ends. Indeed, the church bears the responsibility, in each age and in each location, to fashion its ministry in response to the circumstances in which it finds itself. Within the church's ministry, which all share, the members are differentiated according to the gifts of the Spirit. The ordained minister, for example, is set aside for the ministry of the Word and sacraments.

There is no first-century evidence for a set-apart ministry of Word, sacraments, and pastoral care as it has been defined by tradition. The New Testament community gave primacy to the ministry of the Word, and there were many special ministries that derived from this ministry. Those with special responsibility for this ministry did not have exclusive responsibilities for other special ministries, although they might exercise some general oversight. The New Testament concept of priesthood is corporate, a priesthood of the whole community. According to Alan Richardson: "The word *hiereus* (*sacerdos*, priest) is never used . . . of any priestly order or caste within the priestly community. All the members of the Church, men and women, are "priests unto God" (Rev. 1:6; 5:10; 20:6); their priesthood is in relation to the world outside the Church."[8] The church has limited freedom to decide the purpose of ordination. In recognizing ministry as a gift from God, and being committed to Christ's mission, the church allows for a continuation of the apostolic ministry of responsibility for witness to the Word. Its freedom to assign different functions to members is exercised under the authority of the Holy Spirit, whose gifts empower those whom the Spirit calls.

PROPHETIC, PRIESTLY, AND PASTORAL MINISTRY

The church's ministry traditionally has been defined as prophetic, priestly, and pastoral. These functions are expressed in the corporate life of the church, as well as in the lives of individual congregations. The threefold ministry has permanent validity to the extent that it corresponds to the threefold offices of Christ as prophet, priest, and king (servant).[9] There is an inseparable relationship between Christ, the ordained ministry, and the ministry of the people of God. Christ as prophet, priest, and servant works through a threefold function in order that the *laos* (the people of God) through their prophetic, priestly, and

35

servant roles may exercise the whole ministry of Christ in the world. This means that the ordained ministry exists for and within the ministry of the *laos*, and may not be considered in isolation from that ministry.

Beginning in the 1950s, this theology came to full flower in the Faith and Order and Life and Work conferences convened by the World Council of Churches and its regional working groups, and in theological and biblical studies that recorded these trends concerning the role of the laity and the ministry of the church. The emphasis grew that the ministry of the church in any given setting is an act of the whole congregation. That is, based on a renewed appreciation of the lessons that may be drawn from first-century congregations, one of the crucial tasks of any congregation is the equipment of the saints for the work of ministry. Ministry is shared by all members, and one of the central tasks with which the church is charged is giving "cash value" to the identification of the whole people of God as God's servant people. Thus, Hendrik Kraemer pointed out that the New Testament emphasizes *diakonia* as a ministry of the whole membership, because the church as a whole stands under the same token as its Lord, that is, "servantship."[10] The services of clergy and laity are both aspects of the same *diakonia*, each in its own proper sphere and calling. Richardson emphasized that the early church regarded baptism into the church as ordination to the ministry of the church: "There are no 'lay' members of the Church who are without a ministry in it; the Church is a ministerial priesthood of the laity or people of God. We must not allow the development of a special order of *diakonoi* to obscure the truth that the whole community and every individual member of it were a ministry which participated in the one ministry of Christ."[11]

Lesslie Newbigin warned that the laity and clergy, as two manifestations of the church's ministry, belong together and should not be placed against one another. Commenting on the meaning of 1 Peter 2: 9, he stated:

One of the tragic facts of Christian history has been the obscuring and distorting of [the] great scriptural doctrine of the royal priesthood of the whole church, firstly by a clericalism which practically confined the priestly character to a professional ministry, and then by an understandable but lamentable counter-distortion which tried to assert the self-sufficient priesthood of every individual apart from the organic unity of the priestly body of Christ.[12]

The examination of the relationship between clergy and laity, which emerged anew during the 1950s, addressed the issue from a historical perspective, for example, noting the impact of Patristic and medieval concepts of ministry on the twentieth-century church. Thus, J. A. T. Robinson observed that under Constantine, certain privileges granted by the Roman Empire to heathen priests were extended to the clergy of the Christian church. It is ironic that the line between clergy and laity was first drawn by the secular government of the day! It was firmly established well before the twelfth century, when the lawyer Gratius could refer to the clergy and the laity as two sorts of Christians.[13] Theologians such as Newbigin, Cooke, and James Fenhagen have suggested that this dichotomous image has been fostered for various reasons by clergy and laity alike. Newbigin noted that modern Protestantism is as fertile as ancient Catholicism in producing new and vigorous varieties of clericalism! If, however, a servant concept of ministry is recovered, a vibrant and creative opportunity emerges, based on Scripture and echoed by Hans Rudi-Weber, who suggested that the laity are not the helpers of the clergy so that the clergy can do their job, but the clergy are the helpers of the whole people of God so that the laity can be the church.[14]

CLINICAL EDUCATION OF CLERGY IN THE TWENTIETH CENTURY

Despite calls for reexamination of the relationship of lay and ordained ministries within the ministry of the church, other stirrings in the United States were at odds with these voices. Beginning in the 1930s, change was dramatic and the pace accelerated, due largely to the development of specialized training of clergy for the pastoral role, first in mental hospitals then spreading to general hospitals and other clinical settings. The development of the clinical pastoral training movement as a specialized mode for training clergy and seminarians for pastoral care and counseling functions was modeled on the emerging profession of social work. Clinical training for professionals in the social sciences served as a catalyst for social change within Protestant churches. Clinical pastoral training (later, clinical pastoral education or CPE) became the doorway through which clergy entered the growing clinical professions. They now had their own clinical training process, standards for certification in pastoral skills, and the ability to participate, more or less as equals, with other practitioners in the burgeoning fields of health care and treatment of the mentally ill.

The impact was felt in congregational pastoral care as CPE students entered parish ministry, and culminated with the emergence in the 1960s of a new professional group of certified pastoral counselors. It is ironic that as clergy achieved this new professional status, the pastoral care of the congregation appeared more and more as a task reserved for a specially trained clergy. During the Civil War, one of President Lincoln's banes was his discovery that some northern merchants with sufficient means were able to buy their way out of the army by paying mercenaries to take their place. It may seem a painful analogy, but lay members in many twentieth-century congregations began to regard their pastors as mercenaries: those paid to fulfill the pastoral responsibilities of a laity freed thereby to adopt a former, more passive role. This was expressed, for example, in the typical response of lay members who felt they were not receiving adequate pastoral care from their (male) clergy: "What else do we pay him for!"

Beginning in the mid-1960s, there was widespread acceptance of a clergy-dominated model of pastoral care and the restriction of laypeople to informal "friendly visits" (as opposed to any formal incorporation in congregational pastoral care). This was challenged by pastoral theologians who urged a return to a biblical precedent, which emphasized the role of the congregation as the locus of pastoral ministry and the duty of clergy to equip members for ministry. Sunderland's model, *Equipping Laypeople for Ministry*,[15] provided a means to achieve this goal. It adapted the concept developed by the CPE movement that pastoral functions are learned as people are assigned to make pastoral visits subject to the supervision of their learning process. The clinical training of laypeople assumed that clergy were familiar with the supervisory process, or would need to be trained for this role. The growing emphasis on the role of laypeople as a vital aspect of the congregation's pastoral ministry led in turn to reemphasis of the biblical themes of baptism; gifts of ministry and the call to ministry at the bidding of the Holy Spirit; and the congregation as a community of people of faith.

THREE STRANDS OF PASTORAL MINISTRY

Pastoral ministry as congregational activity incorporates three interrelated theological strands: baptism and its obligations, the gifts or *charisms* of the Holy Spirit and consequences of the Spirit's presence in baptized individuals, and the interdependence of ministries affirmed in the New Testament (Rom. 12:4-8, 1 Cor. 12:12, Eph. 4:15-16). Each of these three strands is constituted of many threads which, when bound together, contribute to the strength of the cord that binds congregations together in ministry, including loving and compassionate nurture of members.

Baptism

Baptism provides the theological basis for every aspect of pastoral care. Baptism lodges Christians within the community of faith, identifies us with the death and resurrection of Christ, signs us with the presence of the Holy Spirit in our lives, and calls or ordains us to ministry. Incorporation into the community of faith places us under the community's discipline, including its care and nurture. Max Thurian and Geoffrey Wainright, reporting for the World Council of Churches Commission on Faith and Order study *Baptism, Eucharist, and Ministry,* stated:

[Christian theology interprets Ezekiel's prophecy (36:25-28)] as announcing baptism: "I will sprinkle clean water upon you, and you shall be clean from all your uncleanness. . . . A new heart I will give you, and a new spirit I will put within you . . . (gift of the Holy Spirit) . . . [I will] cause you to walk in my statutes and be careful to keep my ordinances (life in faith). . . . and you shall be my people, and I will be your God" (becoming part of the Church). . . . Baptism—as a sharing in the paschal mystery—implies a confession of sins and a change of heart; the recipients of baptism are pardoned, cleansed, justified, and sanctified by Christ, in the power of the Holy Spirit.[16]

One consequence of baptism is the obligation to follow Christ, that is, to manifest in one's life the attributes of life in Christ (Matt. 16:24; Mark 8:34, 10:21; Luke 9:23, 18:22; John 10:27, 12:26). Oscar Cullmann emphasizes that "God sets a man within, not merely informs him that he is set within, the Body of Christ"[17] (1 Cor. 12:13 and Gal. 3:27-28). We are made one in Christ as we are engrafted into the community of God's people, the church.

In stating that "the ministry of the church is exercised by every man, woman, and child who bears the mark of baptism," James Fenhagen underscores the importance of the relationship between baptism and a believer's call to ministry.[18] Fenhagen subsequently amplified this conviction, stating that the laity of the church are called by virtue of their baptism to share in the ministry of the gospel, even suggesting that the term *layperson* should be abolished altogether in reference to the ministry of the church, "in order that we might emphasize the interdependence inherent in our baptism. . . . To speak of total ministry in the church is to speak of a ministry of all the baptized, each dependent on the gifts of the other."[19] That is, baptism and ministry are inextricably linked: baptism is the ordination to ministry for every member of the household of faith, and ministry is an obligation, not an option (as distinct from the secular notion of lay "volunteers").

The Gift of the Holy Spirit and Gifts of the Spirit

Adopted as children of God at baptism, Christians receive the gift of the Holy Spirit; are born to new life and made members of the Church, the Body of Christ; and are restored to a place in the covenant with

God (2 Cor. 1:21-22; Eph. 1:13-14). With the indwelling of the Holy Spirit, Christians are gifted for ministry. The task of the Spirit is to bind members of the household of faith with such bonds of love that the community expresses in members' communion with one another that spirit which was in Christ Jesus. This mighty work is complete only when members not only build each other up in love, but extend that response as neighbors to all who are vulnerable, as exemplified in the parables of the good Samaritan (Luke 10:29-37) and the last judgment (Matt. 25:31-46).

The presence of the Spirit is accompanied by bestowal of *charisms,* that is, gifts of ministry. Paul emphasizes that all do not have identical gifts (e.g., Rom. 12:4-8 and 1 Cor. 12:4-13; see also Eph. 4:7-16). Christians are to employ the gifts each has been given in the service of Christ, "from whom the whole body, joined and knit together by every joint with which it is supplied, when each part is working properly, makes bodily growth and upbuilds itself in love" (Eph. 4:16 RSV). The gifts are many and varied because, when manifested in ministries, that is what the body requires in order to be fully operational. Their purpose is fulfilled when all gifts are coordinated and used in the service of the whole body. It is for this reason that if there is one gift that supersedes others; it is the gift of love, which builds up the body. Love is not jealous, conceited, or proud, but rejoices equally in the gifts of others (1 Cor. 13). Cooke proposes that we are faced with both the possibility and the need to pay renewed respect to the action of the Holy Spirit in the community, particularly to the "Spirit's charismatic designation of Christians for special ministerial roles." Further, he reminds us that since the discernment of spirits involves the whole church, the entire community must participate in the discovery of the gifts (charisms) granted to individuals or groups for the sake of the church.[20]

Among the gifts recognized by the earliest Christian communities was the gift of compassionate service that was manifested in the care of members of the fellowship. Growing out of the images of Jesus as servant and shepherd, Cooke terms this ministry "the gospel ideal of shepherding service."[21] It had become clearly established in Christian communities by the end of the first century. Victor Furnish concurs, suggesting that the greatest contribution Paul made to the church undoubtedly was his impressive demonstration of how the gospel and

41

the Christian ministry are fundamentally and absolutely inseparable. Paul "saw that 'the truth of the gospel' (Gal. 2:14) must manifest itself concretely in the life of the Christian community and in the individual lives of Christian believers wherever they are in the world."[22] Furnish adds that, like Jesus, Paul established a pastoral model he expected his congregations to follow (1 Cor. 12:26; 2 Cor. 11:29; Gal. 6:2, 10). Paul's pastoral ministry, no less than his missionary activity, was rooted in the character and meaning of the gospel to which he was committed, including the indelible image that members of the community are to "bear (share) one another's burdens, and so fulfill the law of Christ" (Gal. 6:2 RSV). According to Furnish, Paul's nurture of the congregations he established is an overlooked aspect of the apostle's ministry. Expressed in today's terms, congregational nurture includes

> strengthening the fabric of the Christian community, giving guidance and support to its members as they confront perplexing moral choices, providing leadership as the church formulates its response to pressing social issues, comforting the sick and the bereaved, and giving counsel and aid to those in any kind of need.[23]

Paul understands that among the charisms, the shepherding and nurturing ministries for which these gifts equip members occupy a central place:

> That one's service to Christ involves serving others is brought out clearly in the discussion of Romans 14 about the "strong" and the "weak" in the congregation. Each member of the community should "walk in love" toward every other member . . . [Rom.14:15]. When one *"thus serves Christ,"* Paul concludes, one "is acceptable to God and approved by men" (v. 18). *Diakonia,* then, is one of the signs of life in the body of Christ, and when it ceases to be a vital force, both Christian community and the praise of God likewise fail.[24]

The New Testament leaves no doubt that Christians are accountable for the ministries to which they are called (cf. Rom. 14:12, 1 Cor. 4:2). The congregation should therefore exercise diligence in their training and oversight. Attention was drawn to this matter by Vatican II, which promulgated the *Decree on the Apostolate of the Laity* urging that Christians should prepare themselves painstakingly for their respective ministries: "For the advance of age brings with it better self-knowledge, thus enabling each person to evaluate more accurately the talents with which God has enriched each soul and to exercise more effectively those charismatic gifts which the Holy Spirit has bestowed on all for the good of others" (#30).[25] In drawing attention to this concern, Richard P. McBrien notes the imperative that underlies the Vatican decree, which stated that from the reception of these charisms or gifts, including those which are less dramatic, each believer has the right and duty to use them in the church and the world for the good of mankind and for the upbuilding of the church. This means, notes McBrien, that baptism and confirmation empower all believers to share in some form of ministry, the specific form of which varies in accordance with the gifts of the Holy Spirit.

Interdependence in the Body of Christ

The Holy Spirit is a gift to the church. The Spirit was bestowed on the disciples and their company when they were gathered together. One work of the Spirit is that of creating and nurturing the community, which should be of one mind and one spirit (Phil. 1:27), and so manifest the love of Christ toward one another that all may believe (e.g., John 13:34-35). The Spirit's presence is disclosed in the hospitality that is a mark of the community, the life of which is manifested supremely as its members gather for the eucharistic celebration of the Lord's Supper. It is noteworthy that the Roman Catholic Church, by incorporating laypeople into the eucharistic celebration, emphasized the unique relationship of the Eucharist with the congregation's pastoral nurture of its members. A Lay Eucharistic Minister cannot bring Holy Communion to Mrs. Robertson, confined at home following her stroke, without that celebration becoming the context for a pastoral visit with the homebound member. Lay ministers receive the elements of the communion service at the altar during the celebration in the sanctuary, and prior to the close of worship with the benediction are sent out by the pastor and congregation to carry the elements to members unable to attend worship in the sanctuary. Homebound members are thereby reminded that they are members of the gathered community of faith, a community manifested where two or three are gathered in the Lord's name. This setting in which eucharistic participation and pastoral nurture are joined emphasizes the indissoluble bond that links baptism and eucharist with the community's obligation to care for one another and build each other up in love.

Another aspect of the community's call to nurture its members is expressed in the notion of hospitality, a practice that is prominent in the Judeo-Christian tradition. Israel was reminded that God's people were once aliens in an inhospitable world. That remembered experience should prompt Israel to be hospitable to the stranger and the alien, as well as to the "poor" among them. Hospitality was enjoined upon the early church by Paul and Peter (Rom. 12:13, 1 Tim. 3:2, 1 Pet. 4:9) and is one of the central motifs of Christian life. According to Parker Palmer, it is the one word above all others that indicates how we are to live in community, and, especially, to care for one another: "That is what Jesus called for—hospitality to the sick and the hungry and the imprisoned without demanding that they become our friends or grateful allies; hospitality is simple recognition of our unity with them. . . . Every hospitable act is an outward and visible sign of our inward and invisible unity."[26] Thomas Ogletree uses similar images to call for openness to the unfamiliar and unexpected in our most intimate relationships, an openness that takes regard of our differences and social locations that mold perceptions and value orientations toward others and that transcends barriers that separate us from them.[27] Stanley Hauerwas uses the story of *Watership Down* to dramatize how a community is formed and its individual members grow together as they learn to rely on and value each other's capacities. The members of the community learn that it is on these traits that their lives depend: "Such a community depends on the ability to trust in the gifts each brings to the group's shared existence."[28] To be a disciple is to be a part of a new community for which the Gospels are "manuals" for the training necessary for membership.

This emphasis on mutuality is present in Paul's thinking. *Charismata* were granted primarily for the edification of the community, not for individual enjoyment. According to Robert Banks, "it is precisely through seeking to fulfill the needs of others . . . that various members of the community will come into a greater experience of the gifts" (1 Cor. 14:12), one group of which is directed toward the psychosocial well-being of the community. "Important here are the gifts which have a pastoral orientation, for example, practical 'helps,' 'acts of mercy' and the pastoral gift itself."[29] Banks understands Paul to imply that participation in the community centered primarily around fellowship of the members with God and with one another, expressed both in word and deed. This concern is reflected in the Johannine epistles, for example: "Little children, let us love, not in word or speech, but in truth and action" (1 John 3:18). The redeemed community demonstrates concretely the "already-experienced reconciliation" that ought to characterize a community, the gifts and fruits of the Spirit being instruments through which this is expressed and deepened. The focal point of reference must always be a set of relationships, the most profound communication being God's communication of God's nature through one another.[30] John Patton also develops this theme:

> God is the author of community, creating it as an expression of human relationality . . . [which is] brought into being through human action, empowered through relationship to God. Through their vocation of caring for the earth, human beings learn to care for one another. . . . The purpose of Christian community is not only to experience relationship, but also to experience relationship in order to empower ministry.[31]

Patton cites Edward S. Casey's linkage of caring to remembering, or keeping the other person in mind. The process of remembering links ministry, community, and caring. Casey draws on the relationship between memory with the Greek *merimna*, that includes elements of care, solicitude, anxiety, and sorrow, stating that remembering is caring for the one whom we remember. Thus, Patton concludes, "care and community are obviously related . . . , but it is memory that brings them fully into relationship."[32] God has covenanted not to forget us: "How can I give you up, Ephraim! . . . My heart recoils within me, my compassion grows warm and tender" (Hos. 11:8).

Jewish scripture holds memory, community, and care in a tight relationship. As God's creation, Israel is reminded over and over that

45

God's creatures were created for community, one of the most fundamental aspects of which is their care for one another. The Torah refrain
that becomes part of Israel's liturgy, "You shall love your neighbor as
yourself," (Lev. 19:18) is set in a series of *mitzvot* that emphasizes the
nation's responsibility to care for the poor and the sojourner (vv. 10,
34), and the deaf and blind (v. 14; see also Deut. 10:18, Ps. 146). God's
instruction to care for widows, orphans, and aliens in the community
is set in the context of "doing justice" (Jer. 7:1-7). Israel is to care for
the disenfranchised and vulnerable because God's people are to
express in their relationships with the poor the tender loving care with
which God looks upon them. Terrible punishment will be visited upon
Israel for failure to judge with justice the cause of the fatherless or
defend the rights of the needy (Jer. 5:28). Micah expresses what each
of the prophets experienced: that to be holy as God is holy is to do justice, love kindness, and walk humbly before the Lord (Mic. 6: 8). The
prophet imagines a redeemed community—not just of Israel, but one
that includes all peoples—gathered on Mount Zion and including all
whom society has overlooked or cast aside (4:1-7). It is not surprising,
then, that the community of faith also has been perceived as a refuge,
a safe place in which the poor—those who have been disenfranchised,
the frail who have no one to speak for them—can gather with security.
It is the place in which those who have been cast out from the family
to which they had looked for nurture are assured by the community of
faith that they are named and welcomed as *family*. This family, far
from being exclusive, joyfully welcomes its newcomers, for it is the
community that is the foretaste, the first fruits, of the people claimed
by God as God's own (Pss. 133, 147, Isa. 61:1-4, Jer. 31:7-9, Amos
9:13-15; see also Matt. 23:37 and 1 Pet. 2:10).

Moreover, as the parable of the last judgment (Matt. 25:31-46)
declares, invitation into the family of God is determined more by
one's response to the poor than by other criteria: the expression of
love for the neighbor manifests the nature of the servant community.
Schubert Ogden comments on a suggestion that we are to give bread
to others, not to bear witness that they do not live by bread alone but
that we do not, and adds that we bear witness not only that we do not
live by bread alone but also that they do not either. In this sense, servanthood consists in being signs of the good news that care for others

is witness to the belief that they also are given God's love and possess the possibility to be free themselves.[33] Christians are accustomed to using the term *witness* to refer to verbal presentation of the gospel. William Clebsch and Charles Jaekle went so far as to claim that unless the challenge to faith is presented verbally, acts of compassion may be rendered, but they cannot be represented, as *pastoral care*: the Name must be *named* before an act can be described as ministry.[34] But naming the Name is not indispensable. According to Ogden, what is indispensable is what Matthew 25 says is indispensable! We will apparently not be asked on judgment day whether we believed in God. We will be asked how we acted in the face of the immediate needs of our neighbors. We should expect that what holds good on judgment day is expected of us now.[35]

SERVANTHOOD

The theology of servanthood is rooted in baptism, in the gift and gifts of the Holy Spirit, and in the people of God as a called community, the three formative elements that underlie the call to ministry. The image of servanthood as capturing the essence of what it means to be a member of God's community is rich in symbolism. When love of God is expressed as love of neighbor, the church as a company of servants becomes a sign to the world of that community into which it is God's will that all should enter. A servant theology, so basic to the biblical witness, compels the servant to live as an exemplar of loving service and the community of servants to live as the first fruits of the society so created. In New Testament terms, God's community must conform to the character of servanthood embodied by Jesus. Matthew's depiction of the last judgment (25:31-46) is a case in point. The author of the first gospel either placed the parable at the close of his account because the oral tradition so remembered it, that is, it was seen as having special emphasis because it closed out the sayings of Jesus; or its location at the close of Jesus' ministry indicates it was remembered and valued as summarizing the nature and quality of membership in the community of faith. Surprised when called to enter and possess the kingdom, faithful servants seemed not to perceive the basis of their invitation—they had served the Lord unknowingly throughout their lives. Servant ministry was so deeply grounded in them that it was of the very essence of their beings. Their compassion and concern for others was expressed in deeds of love so unostentatiously that they did not make the connection.[36]

This theology of care that is so basic to the whole tenor of Scripture, however, is lived out in the secular world, the influence of which continually impinges on the church's life. The "care-response" is not exclusive to the Christian community, of course. Martin Buber captures this "being for others," or "being there" for others, stating that selfhood is fully realized only in the presence of another; it takes presence to become a self.[37] One of the most profound ways this presence can be realized is in our care of one another. Indications are that caring for one another is not an innate human trait, but may be learned very early in life in the context of familial relationships and reinforced in wider societal contexts, particularly those of religious communities. More generally, the ideal of caring for one's fellow human beings may be correlated with the influence and example of Judeo-Christian values upon community mores that elevate care as a "good." Yet even in religious communities, care may receive lip service when attendance at worship becomes perfunctory and a congregation abandons ministry functions to an overburdened professional staff. This image is captured in down-to-earth terms by a cowboy philosopher: "A body can pretend to care, but they can't pretend to be there."[38]

What prompts one to "be there" is of interest to Robert Wuthnow, who examines the motives that underlie the caring responses people make to others' needs. Throughout the nation's history, Wuthnow suggests, there has been a constant emphasis by clergy, educators, and others that the biblical injunction to share one another's burdens was expected of all. "Variously interpreted, the biblical tradition teaches compassion as a duty of divine law, as a response to divine love, and as a sign of the Judeo-Christian ethic."[39]

Despite the explicit warning that sharing one another's burdens is an injunction, not an option, congregations are still prone to invite members to volunteer for this or that activity. In secular circles, the term *volunteer* denotes nonprofessionals whose service activities supplement the activities of full-time professional staff workers. The term thus differentiates lay (volunteer) services from those of professional social workers, licensed counselors, nurses, and clergy. A layperson who joins a volunteer department in a hospital, nursing home, or hospice, for example, is likely to be welcomed with open arms, especially as institutions reduce staff budgets. But volunteers may withdraw their services just as readily as they were offered, and properly so—individuals' time allotments for voluntary services may be reduced or eliminated as they assume other family, social, or work-related responsibilities. Further, whereas professionals undertake service functions as vocational choices, with the tangible rewards of payment for services, the functions of volunteers are usually secondary to vocational choices and other personal responsibilities. More important, the designation of people as volunteers implies an inferior, optional role that, in a Christian context, is refuted by Scripture.

The question of whether the term *volunteer* may be applied validly to the functioning of laypeople within the congregation's pastoral care ministry hinges on a theological question: Is that service activity a voluntary commitment that may be withdrawn at will, or is it a ministry that is entailed by virtue of being a member of the community of faith? Despite the theological argument that the term *volunteer* has no place in the vocabulary of the Christian community, it still receives wide acceptance. When Sunderland was requested to write the article "Pastoral Care of Volunteers" for the *Dictionary of Pastoral Care and Counseling*, the request was based on the assumption that no congregation could exist without the volunteered services of committed laypeople. Sunderland argued that the term *volunteers* should be included in the proposed text only if its irrelevance to congregational ministry was emphasized.[40] We are called (conscripted) to care for one another, not invited to "volunteer"!

THE CALL TO FAITH AND DISCIPLESHIP

First-century Christians did not "volunteer" for ministry, since ministry was never perceived as an option. Paul emphasizes that we are *called* into ministry by the presence of the Holy Spirit in our lives (Rom. 1:1-7, 8:28; 1 Cor. 1:1-9, 7:21-24; Col. 3:15; 1 Tim. 6:12; James 2:7; 1 Pet. 1:1-9, 2:9, 21-23, 3:9). One of the characteristics of early Christians, noted by others in the communities of which they were a part, was the manner and depth of their love for one another. That is, as one aspect of profession of faith in Christ, life in Christ was (and was expected to be) manifested in Christlike care of one another. "Bear[ing] one another's burdens" (Gal. 6:2) consisted not only of *saying* the right words, but of physical care (Acts 2:44-46; 4:32-35), including healing and sharing of resources. The U.S. Council of Catholic Bishops noted that Jesus established the church "to bear witness to God's Kingdom, especially by the way his followers would live as the people of God: 'This is my commandment that you love one another as I have loved you' (John 15:12)."[41] The power that makes this possible is that engendered by the presence of the Holy Spirit in individual lives and in the congregation as the gathered community to which baptized members belong.

However, God's people are not to live solely for themselves. God's will is to draw all peoples to God, and the church has a specific responsibility to press this mission. Thus, while there is a primary obligation to care for each member and family, the care of individuals and families beyond the congregation's membership is also a divine imperative. There are ample biblical injunctions from the instructions to Israel to recognize the claim of the alien in the midst, to the Samaritan who placed an unknown traveler on his donkey and took him to a nearby inn. The claim of people who are chronically ill or disabled upon the compassion and nurture of the congregation is sharp and clear. Failure to respond with love expressed in prophetic word and hands-on love is a denial of our identification as a servant people of a just and loving God.

RESISTANCE TO RECEIVING CARE

Societal responses to the needs of people and communities who are suffering are usually spontaneous and unreserved. Yet it is one thing to experience the call to loving and compassionate response to people whose life situations force them to accept the care of others; being comfortable with receiving such help is often a very different matter. The nature of the helping relationship often is clouded by human traits that render a task that seems simple and straightforward into a complex and difficult process that includes both mundane, practical problems of convincing pastors and layleaders of the value and utility of the model, and more complex, psychosocial barriers that people erect between themselves and their congregations that offer pastoral ministry.

The problem revolves around such issues as how care is offered and accepted and the inhibition that so many people feel about "being in need," being "needy," and "accepting help" from others. This reluctance to acknowledge one's need of support contraverts a fundamental biblical image, namely, that the Christian fellowship—the congregation—is the primary locus of nurture for its members, who are constituted a new family as the people of God (Eph. 2:19) who build one another up in love (Eph. 4:16); are servants to one another in love (Gal. 5:13-14); help one another carry (life's) heavy loads (Gal. 6:2, 10); look to one another for encouragement (Phil. 2:1); exercise forbearance and charity toward one another (Eph. 4:2); are generous and tender-hearted toward each other (Eph. 5:32); and let their bearing toward one another arise out of their life in Christ (Phil. 2:5).

The authority for such ministry is Jesus himself, expressed movingly in his farewell discourse to the twelve. After he washed the feet of each disciple, Jesus asked: "Do you understand what I have done for you? . . . You call me 'Master' and 'Lord,' and rightly so, for that is what I am. Then if I, your Lord and Master, have washed your feet, *you also ought to wash one another's feet. I have set you an example: you are to do as I have done for you*" (John 13:12-15 NEB; emphasis added). Jesus clearly places an equal emphasis on receiving ministry as well as giving care. Paul states that the gift given to some to be of help to others (Rom. 12:8), results in love for one another that breeds "mutual affection" (12:10; also 12:13, 15). When Paul identifies the gifts of the Spirit, he reminds the Corinthians that there must be no sense of division in the body, so that "all its organs might feel the same concern for one another. If one organ suffers, they all suffer together. If one flourishes, they all rejoice together" (1 Cor. 12:25-26 NEB). In 1 Corinthians 13, he speaks of the royal gift of love—a love that soars

51

beyond mere sentimentality to incorporate their mutuality in the Body of Christ. He reminds the congregation that their generosity of spirit demonstrated in their willing service of others in the household of God is not only a contribution toward the needs of God's people; more than that, "it overflows in a flood of thanksgiving to God" (2 Cor. 9:12 NEB). As noted above, Paul admonishes the Galatian congregation to bear one another's burdens and so fulfill the law of Christ (Gal. 6:2).

Despite this biblical injunction that calls members of the congregation to care for one another, the reality may be quite different. Resistance to receiving help is exacerbated by the degree to which the terms *need* and *help* are perceived negatively. Alan Keith-Lucas suggests that if we assume that each of us has some degree of innate tendency to grow, that is, to move forward, to make constructive choices in the direction of self-actualization, the person who confronts a life crisis may be likened to a trolley that has stalled. One reason for stalling is that the road ahead may be too rocky or too steep, or the trolley is stopped by a barrier. Second, forward motion may be obstructed as if by a strong spring of negative feelings, guilt, fear, or despair that makes any further movement difficult, even impossible. In this case, the more forcefully a helper tries to push the trolley forward, that is, urge or even try to force the person to receive the offered help, the more that effort only results in the spring becoming more tightly compressed![42] Keith-Lucas acknowledges that the analogy of person with trolley is imperfect, but it may assist us to understand why some people who seemingly would benefit by our help are unable to accept it. American individualism is manifested in a reluctance to accept offers of help, even when such help may lift some of the burden created by an individual's or family's situation, for example, chronic illness or disability. *It is as if the very offer of help becomes a barrier to accepting help.* Yet, in receiving care from fellow members of the household of faith, we accept and receive God's grace. In even stronger terms, *to refuse such ministry is to decline God's offered grace.*

Unfortunately, the American frontier mentality reinforces the value society places on becoming and remaining autonomous and independent, with the corollary that to *need help* is to have failed to be properly self-reliant. In this light, needing help is the antithesis of strength and self-reliance, to be avoided at all costs. It is unfortunate that these traits appear to be reinforced by a reference in Acts that has become a widely accepted adage. Luke records in Acts 20:17-38 that in anticipation of his journey to celebrate Pentecost in Jerusalem, Paul called the elders of the congregation in Ephesus to meet him in Miletus. As shepherds of the Ephesian congregation, he reminded them of their responsibilities to care for one another and bids them to help the weak, remembering the words of Jesus: "It is more blessed to give than to receive" (v. 35). Such an instruction not only has no other biblical support, but strikes at the heart of the whole tenor of scriptures that stresses the mutual nature of life in Christ. The Judeo-Christian community is essentially one of a corporate relationship in which human need is simply the opportunity for members of the community to respond with compassion. Yet Acts 20:35 has become a widely accepted truism that affirms the person who offers assistance, but devalues the subject of that help. Consequently, many people unhesitatingly respond compassionately to fellow citizens in crisis, lavishing aid wherever it is needed, but may have difficulty receiving the "charity" of others. When forced by their circumstances to receive help, they nevertheless often do so at a cost to self-esteem and may experience hidden feelings of antagonism. It is part of this tragedy that care and nurture so fundamental to membership in the Body of Christ is confused with the current perception of "charity" and its corollary "welfare," with their notion of haves and have-nots, or worse, of the fortunate versus the unfortunate.

The biblical sense of "mutual responsibility and interdependence" that bonds God's people to one another in caring relationships is manifested unambiguously by Jesus. Images that present those *needing help* as less worthy and those in a position to care being in some measure worthier, are entirely absent from Jesus' ministry, whether in personal meetings with the "poor," or in his teaching. Examples include his conversation with Bartimaeus (Luke 18:35-40), Zacchaeus (Luke 19:1-10), the incident of the woman accused of adultery when Jesus squats with her in the dust (John 8:2-11), and the Parable of the Lost Son (Luke 15:11-32). Jesus responds to each individual at his or her point of need without implying an inferior-superior quality to the relationship or that he was more blessed than those who received his care. Indeed, he said, a person's need created the opportunity for God's grace to be revealed. Both giver and receiver are blessed in such a transaction. Whereas *help* has become a four-letter word that consistently receives bad press, the helping process as properly perceived is a mutual relationship. Both the helped person and the person offering help bring gifts to it; and according to Alan Keith-Lucas, its success or failure may depend as much on the former as the latter. In contrast, many therapeutic theories that promote achieving independence emphasize just the opposite, idealizing the goal of individual autonomy to the point that individuals are motivated to become unconnected, that is, un-dependent.[43]

There is a more basic concern than avoiding the notion that to receive help is to be stigmatized, namely, that underlying the concern to safeguard and strengthen the autonomy of the person needing help is the issue of where *power* resides in the relationship. The pejoratively perceived terms *need* and *help* too easily imply that power is wielded by those who give care, since the recipients of care, or *care partners* (we use this term to refer to those who receive care) are no longer able to manage activities of daily living without some support! If that in turn adds to care partners' deepening sense of loss of control, the relationship may detract from, rather than strengthen, their ability to receive support with grace while maintaining dignity and self-esteem. The alternative is to ensure, as far as possible, that power issues are dealt with as *authority* issues. When authorization of the care relationship is granted by the one who *receives* care, he or she retains control and enters the relationship on an equal footing with caregivers. When this is established at the outset, the focus can be shifted to the mutuality of the relationship and can emphasize that each brings gifts that are offered to the other. Care providers learn all too well that to care means to enter into the situation of those requiring help knowing that they are unable to change the circumstances. But that does not mean they are powerless to do anything. Their primary purpose is to be present as fellow members of the household of faith, manifesting in their sustaining presence the community that draws both together; experiencing in themselves the care partner's vulnerability; willing to enter her or his world of anxiety, pain, or helplessness; and participating in that suffering, sharing that pain. Henri Nouwen, noting that the word *care* has its origin in the Old High German *kara*, meaning to lament, to mourn, to be present in the other's suffering and pain, suggests that

To care is to be compassionate and so to form a community of people honestly facing the painful reality of our finite existence. To care is the most human of all human gestures, in which the courageous confession of our common brokenness does not lead to paralysis but to community. . . . The great mystery of care is that it always involves the healing liberation, redemption and conversion, not only of the one who is cared for but also of the one who cares. When both come together in common vulnerability, then both experience a new community, both open themselves to conversion, and both experience new life as grace. . . . Care only becomes real in a mutuality in which those who care and those who are cared for are both aware of their wounds and open for the healing gifts to each other.[44]

Keith-Lucas places his exposition of the helping relationship in the context of Christian theology. He suggests that the offer of care can best be phrased as a "statement" the carer makes, not simply in what is said, but as a gesture that is conveyed in words, feelings, and actions. It can be conveyed in the form of three sentences:

"This is it."

"I know that it must hurt."

"I am here to help you if you want me and can use me," or more succinctly, "You don't have to face this alone."

These sentences are comprised of three elements, according to Keith-Lucas: *reality, empathy,* and *support,* which are always necessary in any helping relationship. Like a three-legged stool, the entire process falls if any one element is absent. *Reality* refers to the acknowledgment by both the caregiver and the care partner of the real life situation that has to be confronted, for example, diagnosis of a chronic illness, and for the family caregiver, the burden of hourly care, month after month, of a loved one who is no longer able to manage activities of daily living. *Empathy* is the ability to know, or imagine, what the other is feeling, and, as it were, feel with him or her without becoming caught in that feeling and losing one's own perspective. It is both a strong and a strengthening emotion; formally an *act*, it is an act based on *feeling*.

Empathy can open the door to giving and receiving *support,* which can be material, psychosocial, and most often, spiritual. Support can be offered in a variety of ways. The mere fact of being present may be sufficient, but physical support can take many forms.[45] Keith-Lucas sees images of a triune relationship between reality, empathy, and support—necessary to each other and incomplete without each other—that are shadows of the Christian Trinity. God the Creator as the author of "reality" is the One who proclaims, "This is it!" or "This is the way things are!" But biblical history, from a Christian perspective, suggests that this reality was not enough: We cannot by our own will face reality and change in relation to it on our own. An act of empathy was needed, and there is no more characteristic or total act of empathy than that described in the Incarnation—a God who became man and yet remained God, and who, in effect, says: "I know you are hurting. It matters to me that you hurt. I care." Third, the name given to the Spirit is Comforter—derived from *cum,* with, and *fortis,* strong—one who is strong for you, or who says, "In this difficult and painful place, you are not alone. You don't have to face this alone, for I am here at your side."[46] The important word is *here*. It assures care partners that caregivers will be unshaken in their desire to be present and to support them, "no matter what." Thus, our ministries of care are to embody the care of God, who loves to the uttermost. However hesitant we may be to equate our "little bit" ministries with God's care for humankind, the parallel holds: we are to love as God loves us!

CONCLUSION

We turn once again to the biblical revelation for the model on which this quality of human relationships is founded. James Wharton points to the manner in which the Hebrew scriptures tell of God, who wills relationship with Israel and all humankind. God's "choice" makes God vulnerable to the possibility, with its suffering, that Israel—and humankind—may choose to ignore, even rebel against, God's choosing to be related to this people. So deep and so intimate is God's involvement with Israel that Scripture

speaks of God being "angry" or "grieved" or "pleased" when things go one way or the other. That is vulnerability, the surprising vulnerability of one who chooses to be so intimately involved in the story of others that what happens in their lives, for good or ill, becomes part of that one's own story. The vulnerability of God disclosed in the biblical story goes deeper than "compassion" (in the sense of "suffering with") . . . [At the heart of this vulnerability to Israel's story] is God's free gift of relationship to people who are not in a position to demand it, or to expect it, except on the grounds that God has offered it, obligated himself to maintain it, and renewed the offer again and again.[47]

This is manifested in God's covenant relationship with Israel. It is what binds Israel to God in community, and it is the model for the congregation's replication of this relationship between God's people—the congregation—and its members. The love that God graciously shows us is to be manifested in our love toward the neighbor, "and the love of neighbor that participates in and reflects God's love of one's neighbor *is* the love of God."[48] The parallel is clear: in its care for each member, the community is to reflect God's care for the community—an image captured in the words of Jesus: "I have given you an example, that you also should do as I have done to you" (John 13:15 RSV). This is precisely the point at which the person who offers care is vulnerable to the other, not only in being invited into the other's pain and daring to be present at whatever cost, yet, in some instances, having to accept that another may decline the offered gift, or indeed, having the feeling "I am not the person who can serve this other and another should step forward."

Dietrich Bonhoeffer reminds us that our own human efforts in serving others are always "pen-ultimate" in relationship to God's saving acts.[49] Our ministries are always "second to the last," for the last word is always God's. Wharton picks up the same theme, protesting against our assumptions of self-importance, reminding us that we are at best stewards, not proprietors, of even the initial motivations that stir us to care. The resources to care for others, he suggests, are things to pray for, and to celebrate when they are received—for we know from the outset that we cannot manufacture them! If we are clear about our own deep need for God's ministry, at best we may learn just how little and how much any minister, lay or ordained, may presume to offer a human other:

The only serious indication that someone has been "helped" through our ministry are the signs, not always perceptible to us, that the other has discovered his or her weakness as a perfectly adequate basis upon which to undertake ministry to others. . . . The biblical word about ministry does invite us to celebrate, in very practical ways, the love of God that liberates us from, and therefore for, the people for whom God gives us to care. It is our freedom we celebrate, as well as theirs, when the relationship of ministry discloses signs that God's gift of freedom has been accepted and is being shared.[50]

Wharton concludes that "every penultimate indication of human healing in response to ministry is a God-given sign of the wholeness for which God intends us. To undertake ministry on such grounds is an exercise not only in faith and love but also in hope—hope for oneself, for the other, and for the whole human experiment: It is designed to be the most liberating, authentically serious, and joyous calling on earth."[51]

CHAPTER 3

MINISTRIES OF SUSTAINING PRESENCE

Sharing life's joys and burdens is part of what it means to live in community. The joys and burdens of everyday living, however, tend not to be marked by ritual or ceremony; and they tend not to be the subject of significant community interest. Routine experiences with work, family, school, social groups, and church are the ordinary ingredients of life with their associated pleasures and disappointments. These experiences often are the subjects of conversations and important subtexts of relationships among people, but they lack that dramatic quality that signals something unusual or extraordinary that warrants special attention.

CONGREGATION AS A CONTEXT FOR CAREGIVING

Birth, baptism, marriage, and anniversaries are examples of common events that evoke special recognition. These milestones in life tend to be joyous occasions for the people directly involved and for others who care about them. Associated celebrations and rituals are invitations to a community of concern to gather and share in the joy of the moment. Similarly, significant loss, disruptive illness, and death are common events that draw people together to share their sorrow and find strength in the company of others. Most people do not come together at these times of happiness and sadness unless they were previously connected to one another by some form of link or bond

59

grounded in shared experience. Indeed, these shared observances may contribute to the formation of community and they certainly strengthen community; but they tend not to be the source of community. The source lies in the stories of people whose lives have become woven together over time as faith and doubt, happiness and sadness, gain and loss, success and disappointment that constitute biographies are experienced, known, and shared with one another.

Sharing and caring are dispositions and traits that are expressed generally as short-term and episodic phenomena. Christenings, baptisms, weddings, and anniversary parties generally are brief observances that invite recognition and participation, even though the planning process may be detailed and lengthy. Acute illnesses, terminal phases of diseases, and funerals similarly are relatively brief but unwelcome intrusions into daily life. These are coercive events that demand some form of personal and communal response. In both types of circumstances, the time required to share the blessing or burden with those principally affected typically is short. The disruption to one's routine or the investment of one's time to express compassion tends to be limited. Witness is given to meaningful personal relationships and to the ties that bind the community. Then, life goes on. Celebrants are left to bask in the afterglow of the party. People in sorrow are left alone to cope with their distress or to rebuild their lives.

While we do not wish to diminish the value of these forms of sharing life's joys and sorrows, we suggest that communities, especially communities of faith, have long-term obligations of care and support. Some of these long-term obligations have been met structurally. Congregations typically have programs that provide for the education and nurture of children, support and strengthening of marriage, and mechanisms to respond to relatively short-term needs associated with illness and death. Through church-related denominational hospitals, nursing homes, residences, relief and service agencies, individual congregations have a role in responding to many long-term needs that are beyond the capacity of one congregation or one person to meet. The care and support provided through all of these programs and resources demonstrate a love for humanity expressed through the combined and organized efforts of many.

Sharing and caring, accordingly, become part of the story of the church in both its universal and congregational forms. These characteristics and functions are basic to the identity of the church as God's community and Christians as God's children. The church is formed by God to care for humanity through acts of mercy, service, and prophetic preaching, and to demonstrate human solidarity through community. Being part of a Christian community means, among other things, loving and caring for one another, including those burdened outside the membership.[1] It is a basic belief of Christianity that life takes on meaning through such love and care. As Milton Mayeroff observes, through caring "I *live* the meaning of my life."[2]

One's autobiography, according to sociologist Robert Wuthnow, is constructed in part around stories of caring and being cared for. Stories help define perceptions of communities of which one is a part. They do not define so much the rules of caring as they give witness to the reality and possibility of caring. As such they are gifts that provide instruction, hope, and encouragement. We can identify with the actors and the compassion revealed in the stories. Through the stories, we can imagine ourselves as giving and receiving care. We can discover hope for living because such narrated compassion seems within our human reach to give, as well as being a gift to receive when we are in need.[3]

Love and compassion are central to the Christian gospel. Wuthnow correctly observes that when acts of compassion and kindness are related to the biblical message, they take on a larger meaning and an added historical and sacred significance.[4] They become part of God's story of relationship with humanity. They become part of the identity and witness of God's people called the church. The stories speak to the character of God, as well as the character of the person who shows compassion or care. To the extent that these stories of compassion and care are part of a congregation's life, the congregation sustains an orientation to caregiving and the priority of persons.

The New Testament presents life in Christ as a compassionate life lived together as community (Phil. 2:1-4). Henri Nouwen interprets compassion in a compelling manner by drawing upon the parable of the sheep and the goats in Matthew 25:

Compassion asks us to go where it hurts, to enter into places of pain, to share in brokenness, fear, confusion, and anguish. Compassion challenges us to cry out with those in misery, to mourn with those who are lonely, to weep with those in tears. Compassion requires us to be weak with the weak, vulnerable with the vulnerable, and powerless with the powerless. Compassion means full immersion in the condition of being human.[5]

In and through community, accordingly, God becomes present as burdens and joys are shared, for both are part of the human condition.

Presence and compassion, sharing and caring are more than just familiar terms to God's people. They are words rooted in the gospel. They define for God's children the character and conduct of the community to which they are called to be members. They summon and prescribe a response to situations of joy and sorrow like those identified above. Whether the need for care and support is short-term or longer-term, the community must be present as a sign that God is not absent. The presence and care that is offered, in whatever forms taken, reveal that by nature as well as by calling we are stewards of each others' lives.[6] The task before us is to learn how to care for one another and be responsible to one another in a manner that is obedient to God.

DEFINING FEATURE OF PASTORAL CAREGIVING— SUSTAINING

How to care for one another is a question of interest to students of any caregiving relationship. Bookstore shelves are full of texts offering insight and advice about how to establish and preserve meaningful relationships. People in the helping professions similarly have at their fingertips a seemingly limitless library to help them conceptualize their roles and improve their practices for the benefit of those who seek their care. Pastoral psychologists, practical theologians, and pastoral care practitioners have drawn upon the conceptual and moral resources within theology and secular research to assist clergy and laypeople as they seek to give care within a Christian context. The quantity and diversity of this literature demonstrates that there is no univocal guidance within sacred or secular disciplines about these matters.

Comprehensive concepts and rules of conduct that are universally accepted and applicable seem beyond reach. The complexities and contingencies of human relationships and conditions of human existence are too vast for singular description and unqualified direction.

Caregiving and the relationship between the parties, nevertheless, are too central to social existence and the moral life to be unexamined. Images and models have been used to offer insight into the nature and character of caregiving.[7] Such an approach is familiar to any student of Scripture. Although God and God's care of humanity may be beyond full comprehension, certain aspects of God's nature and providence are suggested by the terms *father* and *shepherd* in the New Testament. Additional terms like *creator, spirit, lord, servant, covenanter,* and others fill in but do not complete the picture of God and God's will for human conduct.

Images, models, and metaphors provide an important heuristic service. They can illustrate certain features of caregiving relationships, personalizing and bringing the relationship to life. They can communicate perceptions and expectations about the respective roles of the care partners. One advantage of applying an image, model, or metaphor to a caring relationship that is dynamic and interpersonal is that the image, model, or metaphor is suggestive without necessarily being prescriptive. It does not prescribe what is right or good in a particular circumstance. Rather, it provides a way to understand the relationship and inform the conduct of the care partners. With respect to pastoral caregiving, we propose that it is fundamentally a "ministry of sustaining presence." *Sustaining* and *presence* each denote key elements of pastoral caregiving relationships. First, they are defined or distinguished by their sustaining nature. Second, presence is the defining or distinguishing method of giving care. In order to support this claim, more should be said about caregiving relationships, in general, and with people burdened by illness, in particular.

Caring relationships, from a theological perspective, are grounded in God's love and seek the growth and well-being of the care partners. Confusion about this matter is common. Too often, the *need* takes on an all-consuming focus, rather than God, who is present and who brings people together in the midst of need.[8] This misunderstanding about the foundation of caregiving also leads to another confusion.

People tend to think that their task in a situation of need is to *fix* the problem by satisfying the obvious need. Then their work or care is finished.

This notion is inconsistent with the nature of caring relationships, if God's role in covenant with humanity is a model to be emulated. God seeks to embrace and empower people to realize the divine purpose in and through covenant relationship. God does not control us, deprive us of responsibility for our conduct, or protect us from the consequences of our actions. Rather, God enters into relationship with us and calls us to faithfulness. The prophet Micah has defined faithfulness: "to do justice, and to love kindness, and to walk humbly with your God" (Mic. 6:8). Faithfulness is not shown by sacrificial offerings (Mic. 6:6-7). It is shown by a lifestyle of "active concern for the well-being of all the people of God, but particularly for the weak and underprivileged among them—the poor or any whose status offers no ready advocate in the society."[9]

Walking humbly with God entails support of and care for the weak, however they are described. This attitude of faithfulness to God is manifest concretely in acts of service offered freely, without condition, and without expectation of repayment. Walking humbly with God lies "in attending the will and way of God."[10] As God seeks justice and mercy, the "humble" journey with God in this course. The journey is set for individuals and the community of faith as a whole. Pastoral caregiving is a duty of the congregation expressed through the gifts of its members. It is a process of valuing people and investing in their growth before God.[11]

Nurture and care contribute to growth. Care is more a way of relating to someone that develops over time than it is concrete acts of service. Nurturing relationships that engender growth among the parties emerge as mutual confidence and commitment deepen. A level of comfort results from the process of caring and receiving care. Care partners become at ease with one another and at home in the world. They experience their need for one another as a kind of stewardship or trust, not as power over the other.[12] The particular outcomes of circumstances being negotiated cannot be known. They are relatively incidental to the quality of the care being expressed. Through the concern being expressed now, the value of the other is demonstrated. Our interest in the outcome is shown by the care given now. The process and the outcome are interconnected; the relationship or process is the outcome in the making.[13]

One is sustained through the relationship with and care of trusted others to grow in one's own time and way toward whatever intermediate or ultimate ends life incorporates. Caring, therefore, is essentially a process of sustaining a person while outcomes develop. The well-being of the other is the desired goal, and one's conduct within a caring relationship promotes this end. Comfort with this perspective of caring depends on being clear about whose good and autonomy has priority. If one truly values the other in his or her uniqueness, then the temptation to control or take charge of the other may be more easily resisted.

Nel Noddings refers to the relationship of one giving and one receiving care as *engrossment*, which emphasizes reception of the other into one's self in order to see and feel with the other. She illustrates the concept by the manner in which people typically respond to a crying infant. The first response is "something is wrong," not an interpretation of the cry as a signal that the baby is hungry, wet, or feverish. The reaction to the cry is "I'm here" followed by an offer of comfort "everything is all right." This seemingly instinctual offer of comfort comes before analyzing the situation and developing a plan of action. In Noddings' words, "We do not begin [caring] by formulating or solving a problem, but by sharing a feeling."[14] We agree and add, by being present.

Caring for another, entering into that person's experience, seeing and feeling the world from his or her place, respecting and valuing the personhood and autonomy of the other informs what care means and the manner in which care is given. Caring for another may exclude certain goals that are not goals of the person receiving care. Genuine care, in a key sense, requires "letting go" of the other to realize his or her identity and purpose. Caring for others includes sustaining them as they grow to their maturity and well-being in whatever pleasant or painful forms they take. Accepting one's limits as a caregiver is a basic condition for having the freedom to offer care and to personally grow through the relationship of care. Milton Mayeroff correctly observes, "I do not try to help the other to grow in order to actualize myself, but by helping the other grow I do actualize myself" (emphasized in the original).[15] Caring for another reveals an interdependence and mutuality between the care partners. Scripture refers to this form of caring or bearing of one another's burdens as servanthood. With servanthood, each party is vulnerable, each has need for the other, and each is incomplete without the other.

Bearing another's burden typically occurs in a context in which care and concern for the misfortune of another are expressed. For example, sickness, pain, suffering, or threat of death are occasions in which one experiences some loss of control over one's life or becomes less self-sufficient. This threatened state and accompanying loss present an opportunity for others to help, thereby compensating for some of the loss of control. Through another's presence and acts of care, the person is enabled to regain some control over life and circumstance. Caregivers, accordingly, not only symbolize relief and protection, they confer it through their support and nurture. The caregiving relationship is a joint venture, a process, wherein resources are marshaled to defeat the threat and the individual learns to live with the limitations it imposes, or to accept its realization. The person experiencing loss or threat ought not be excluded from designing and executing the plan of care. If excluded from this process, the sense of impotence and lessened value only increases. But, if made part of the process, the person feels respected and the bond between caregiver and recipient of care strengthens as trust and confidence increase. These critical moments of threat and loss, whether of short or long duration, can be seized as opportunities to learn about life and death and to learn that life entails responsibility to make hard decisions in small events and even in matters of life and death.

These are times of uncertainty and potential danger. Suffering may be relieved by the support and nurture of caregivers, who impart a certain meaning to a situation in which meaninglessness seems the only explanation. The opposite may also result. The receiver of care may help caregivers to discover meaning in what otherwise appears senseless. How this is done for particular situations and people cannot be specified in advance. It must be discovered and experienced as a new dimension of a dynamic relationship marked by contingency. The temptation is to resort to performing specific tasks as a substitute for the intimate encounter with weakness and uncertainty, which may be more stressful. Giving and receiving support and nurture or care, in the more robust and respectful sense advocated here, may require more energy, creativity, and personal risk than merely doing good deeds.

To people experiencing adversity, the presence of caregivers provides assurance that they are not excluded from the human community in which care and concern are mediated. In the shared experience of sickness and suffering, the weak and strong are bound together in an interdependent, sustaining alliance. Rather than being abandoned, the sick and suffering are a central concern. Their importance is elevated, rather than diminished. Whatever forms support and nurture take, they aim to certify the value placed upon the person receiving care and the character of the community. The relationship among the care partners is a joint endeavor in pursuit of identifiable goods and avoidance of identifiable evils. It is a relation initiated or redefined by threat or agony. It is a relation in the shadow of uncertainty and potential danger.

If the duties of relationship during periods of illness or adversity were defined in terms of and derived from the parties' respective strengths, their mutual obligations would end when strength and capacity wane. But this limitation is contrary to experience and Christian tradition. Hence, our emphasis on *sustaining* as a defining feature of caring relationships. Relationship and care may endure, even deepen, when the parties are powerless to achieve a desired goal. An emphasis on *sustaining* allows for strength and weakness. It does not imply or endorse any notion that the parties' duties to one another are tied to strength alone. It suggests that embodied weakness can be present to a weakened body in a preserving and affirming manner. It calls attention to faithfulness and loyalty (covenant) in the face of uncertainty and degeneration. An emphasis on *sustaining* liberates the parties to seek a preferred outcome, while preserving their bond and mutual care if another outcome results. An emphasis on *sustaining* does not suggest expectations of one another that are impossible or unreasonable. It allows for fallibility and doubt.

Caregivers can provide few guarantees. They can promise to be available and to sustain by every reasonable and worthy means. They can journey with one in need into an unknown that may be dangerous. All parties assume some risks through and some responsibility for the process and its conclusion. The alliance or relationship is one of relative strength and weakness. The parties embrace life as it is and attempt to achieve whatever good is possible, perhaps in the presence of the inevitable. The unthinkable may become actual, and life with no prospect of meaning—or death—may come. Efforts to help may fail or even produce undesired results. The truth that human strength and will are finite may be reluctantly forced upon us. In these circumstances, the care partners are called to decide what is important within life, to recognize what dangers exist, to decide what certain goods are worth, and perhaps to end up choosing among evils.

Care that is sustaining is liberating and empowering. We are not suggesting a fatalism in caregiving, rather, we are urging a disposition to care that is infused with compassion. Such care sustains through the mutual commitment and perseverance of the care partners, even if accompanied by intermediate or ultimate losses of unspeakable depth. Comfort and consolation, even joy, may flow from the faithfulness of the relationship, and thereby the care partners find security even amidst threat.

Compassion is a mode of relationship and a redemptive form of power that is not controlling and cannot be coercive. According to Wendy Farley,

> Compassion is power to bring to life what is broken by pain, to bring to justice and redemption what is twisted by brutality, to free creatures from the torment of self-absorption and enliven them for care and delight and creativity. . . . Compassion . . . wears the disguise of weakness; this is its folly. But this is a folly that respects the uniqueness and beauty of every creature and opens a space for each one to delight and work and create for itself and in community with others. *It is through the disguise of weakness that compassion gives to creatures their own strength* [emphasis added].[16]

Compassion sustains and fosters healing or completion. Farley makes this point powerfully:

> Compassion is the incarnation of divine love as redemptive power against the domination of evil. It is directed against the tyranny of suf-

fering and sin to redeem humanity not *from* their historical, natural existence but *for* responsibility and joy within this existence. . . . Compassion is evoked by a concrete event or situation of suffering and is responsive to the possibilities of redemption available within it.[17]

A congregation is an incarnation of compassion. Its members are called to embrace suffering "not as professionals who know their clients' problems and take care of them, but as vulnerable brothers and sisters who know and are known, who care and are cared for, who forgive and are being forgiven, who love and are being loved."[18] Care is not something that the strong give and the weak receive. Care is mutual, just like compassion is mutual within relationships. Brothers and sisters in the Body of Christ have the privilege and burden to be with us when we are most vulnerable. Their presence and care have power to sustain people broken by travail.

Stanley Hauerwas correctly observes that our capacity to care may be tested as illness or suffering persists. Our willingness to be present and sympathetic may fade as the time of illness or disability grows longer and early optimism and good humor turns into despair or bitterness. Our initial sympathies may wane as we begin to feel that being compassionate year in and year out asks too much of us. Our sense of connection may lessen as our world expands and the person who needs our sustaining presence contracts. It is little wonder that people with chronic illness report that their condition often leads to the alienation of former friends.[19]

But it is both the identity and the calling of God's people to do just that—be steadfast in compassion, overcome alienation, and have company with the stranger year in and year out. Hauerwas concludes, "Only a community that is pledged not to fear the stranger—and illness always makes us a stranger to ourselves and others—can welcome the continued presence of the ill in our midst."[20]

By remaining part of the community, an acutely or chronically ill person experiences compassion and care that acknowledges his or her value as a child of God. The continuing relationship and engagement of the congregation with people suffering illness is a powerful reminder of our common vulnerability, dependence upon one another, and ties that bind us together as a family of faith. These forms of pastoral care are relationship centered, oriented toward healing (completion), and redemptive in purpose. From this perspective, the person has priority over the problem, and the relationship has priority over the solution. William Oglesby observes:

> Many of the problems of life are insoluble on their own terms: lost opportunities do not come again; death may be postponed but not avoided; decisions that offer pain, however made, cannot be escaped. In the biblical sense triumph comes not in the altering of the externals, although at times this is needed; rather the true success comes in the transformation of the person in a relationship of love and forgiveness so that s/he is able to deal creatively with any situation (cf. Phil. 4:13). So it is that presence is more important than programmed solution as the person discovers the basic meaning of "I will fear no evil for thou art with me" (Ps. 23:4).[21]

Compassion and care require being with someone in pain or suffering, and being with someone in these circumstances has a sustaining effect.

DEFINING METHOD OF PASTORAL CARE—PRESENCE

Support, nurture, and care that respects the personhood of others empowers them to grow toward their own end. They are sustained or empowered by the faithful presence of others with no agenda other than the growth and personhood of the person receiving care. As noted above, the character and content of the caring relationship are more important than the outcomes of activities. From a Christian perspective, caregiving is incarnational because it is a means by which God is present and active in the world. Mighty acts or divine interventions are not God's method of caregiving. Rather, it is through human presence to the poor, sick, hungry, and sinful that God becomes present (cf. Matt. 25). Through acts of love and compassion, the Incarnation of God continues in history.[22] God's abiding care and redemptive purpose are revealed in the sustaining presence of God's people who respect personal autonomy and freedom.

Human autonomy and freedom may be expressed by refusing offers to be present. The image of Christ knocking at the door which must be opened from within is a powerful reminder of this truth (Rev. 3:20). Unless the door is opened, relationship cannot be established or renewed. If an opened door is closed again, relationship is interrupted. Freedom to open or close the door to the sustaining presence of others is a condition of caregiving that must be accepted, if caregiving is to have the required moral quality. Nevertheless, it is part of a congregation's identity and mission to cultivate a disposition and readiness to be present with those who suffer life's hurts when the door is opened. It is the nature of a congregation to be a sustaining community whose ministries are a sustaining presence.

Presence is basic to caregiving. It includes being with someone in some way, not necessarily only being physically present. Presence gives recognition and expression to the dignity and worth of those who suffer. It is a symbol of goodness, kindness, hope, and, most important, grace. Through presence and mutual care, the relatedness or interdependence that is fundamental to human existence is maintained and enhanced. One participates with another, each fully giving of oneself, each sustaining the other, each contributing to the other's growth.

Stanley Hauerwas writes that the story of Job's friends who sat with him illustrates the power of presence and its sustaining nature: "most of us are willing to be with sufferers, especially those in such pain that we can hardly recognize them, only if we can 'do something' to relieve their suffering or at least distract their attention. Not so with Job's comforters. They sat on the ground with Job doing nothing more than being willing to be present in the face of his suffering."[23] Presence is a sign that an event or circumstance does not separate one from human contact. He continues:

> Because of God's faithfulness we are supposed to be a people who have learned how to be faithful to one another by our willingness to be present, with all our vulnerabilities, to one another. For what does our God require of us other than our unfailing presence in the midst of the world's sin and pain? Thus our willingness to be ill and to ask for help, as well

as our willingness to be present with the ill is no special or extraordinary activity, but a form of the Christian obligation to be present to one another in and out of pain.

Moreover, it is such a people who should have learned how to be present with those in pain without that pain driving them further apart.[24]

We may feel that our presence contributes little or that it is useless. We are programmed to understand *help* as completing a task or doing something measurable or tangible. This view of presence is inconsistent with its sustaining nature. Presence shows solidarity. It brings hope and help to discover new directions to people in despair. It conveys consolation and comfort to those who suffer. The challenge that caregivers face is to "learn how to be patient and endure the suffering" with those for whom they care.[25] Such patience, and the faithfulness and loyalty that it implies, is at the heart of all care. Acts of kindness may be small, completely ordinary, and even enjoyable. Caring is not necessarily difficult or exceptional. It is a natural part of life that reveals our need for one another in good times and bad.[26]

There may be occasions when caring for one another is not enjoyable, ordinary, or consisting of small acts of kindness. Devastating illness, the intensity of one's needs, or the unrelenting nature of a person's condition may test a caregiver's faithfulness and decrease the joy that should come through being a sustaining presence. Caregiving may become a burden in these circumstances. One's ability to stay the course alone may be exhausted. Feelings of resentment may develop and fatigue may become overwhelming, both accompanied by feelings of guilt. These situations, in particular, cry out for the presence and care of others. If relief is expected from one other person, the danger exists that this person, too, will be overcome by the level of care required. The sustaining effect of the additional care may be lessened, if not lost, and the joy of caregiving for the other may dissipate under the burden.

Situations where the presence of more than one caregiver is warranted may seem exceptional, but they are not. Nearly any intense or chronic illness that impairs one from fully caring for oneself requires the presence and care of another, if not many others. Caregivers, whether family members or friends, generally become aware over time that they cannot "do it all" alone, despite a desire to provide full care and not to *bother* others with the problem. A coordinated and shared caregiving response in these circumstances, much like the way large families are perceived to have cared for one another in times past, is indicated. Caregivers realize, often reluctantly, that the sustaining presence of others is needed, even if this requires a more formalized method of caregiving wherein no single caregiver is responsible to provide all the care. Kindness becomes *institutionalized* for the benefit of those needing care and for those providing the indicated additional care. Participants in the process should understand their own limitations and realize that each provides discrete forms of care that are part of a multifaceted presence that sustains. Seemingly small expressions of kindness or care make a large, collective contribution to relieving the burden of others. One's value and place in the community is demonstrated by the presence of others. Each party gives something of value to the other. Each has an opportunity to grow.

Presence is testimony that one's experience of suffering does not separate one from God's community of care and concern. Presence, "communion with the sufferer," to use Wendy Farley's phrase, is a "balm to the wounded spirit . . . [that] mediates consolation and respect that can empower the sufferer to bear the pain, to resist the humiliation, to overcome the guilt."[27] The presence of God's people manifests redemptive power sufficient to prevent evil, pain, or loss from gaining ultimate victory (Rom. 8:38-39). This presence, according to Farley, demonstrates that "nothing separates God from the world, but suffering can be a veil that hides this loving presence. In the midst of suffering, compassion labors to tear the veil."[28] God's compassionate presence is manifest in the presence of God's people.

The phrase "I am with you" (Gen. 26:24) and its variants are a powerful statement of God's faithfulness to humanity, especially at times of hurt, loss, fear, and agony. The significance of this divine affirmation is captured by William Oglesby:

In such a fashion the Lord God speaks to Abraham, to Isaac, and to Jacob. It is the word that is given to Moses in preparation for the deliverance of the children of Israel (Exod. 3:12). It is the sustaining presence that continually enables the prophets to bear witness to the righteousness

73

of God. It is the meaning of the affirmation in Psalm 23, "even though I walk through the valley of the shadow of death, I fear no evil; for thou art with me" (v. 4). The word reaches its fulfillment in the coming of the Messiah, whose name is "Emmanuel," "God is with us" (Matt. 1:23) and moves toward the "holy city" where the dwelling of God is with men. "He will dwell with them, and they shall be his people, and God himself will be with them" (Rev. 21:2, 3 RSV).[29]

Presence—what a powerful and comforting image! Whether expressed as "I am your shield" (Gen. 15:1), "Do not be afraid, for God has heard the voice" (Gen. 21:17), or "Rest assured, do not be afraid" (Gen. 43:23), it is *presence* that gives the reassuring word substance. "I am with you" as an expression of care from God does not portend a fix for one's problems. Rather, "I am with you" is a word of grace that has power to overcome estrangement, weakness, failure, pain, or loss. It is an invitation to a relationship that can endure through the dark valleys of life. It is a word of assurance that one does not bear burdens apart from the presence of God.[30]

The abiding faithfulness of God's presence is not and cannot be a substitute for human faithfulness to one another. Michael Lodahl notes that whether in giving Israel the Torah following the Exodus or in anointing the life and ministry of Jesus of Nazareth with initiating and sustaining power (Luke 4:18-19*a*, Acts 10:38), "the deepest aim of divine liberation is to enable responsible human action. If that is a legitimate reading, then a premium is placed not so much upon the activity of God, but upon that of human beings."[31] Through the faithfulness of God's people in loving one another, the sustaining presence of God is revealed (1 John 3:23-24).

Like the life and work of Jesus, a ministry of sustaining presence is a form of servanthood. It is a pastoral ministry characterized by vulnerability and participation in the lives of the people served. It entails entry into the experience of another. It is open to God's grace and redemptive purpose. It is based in a relationship of love and care modeled after the love and care of God for creation. It echoes God's pledge that "I am with you" from which suffering people may derive consolation, comfort, courage, and hope to enter into an uncertain future. It gives priority to relationships and the autonomy of the persons involved. It accepts limitations, is noncoercive, and nurturing. In short, pastoral caregiving, whether offered by an ordained or layperson, has potential to sustain people amidst their suffering—this is its defining feature or characteristic. The care and support provided is achieved through various forms of presence expressed most commonly through tender acts of kindness, including the act of simply being present to broken humanity as demonstrated by Job's friends. Ministries of sustaining presence are oriented to the experience of God's presence and discovery of God's will in the presence of broken humanity. Ministries of sustaining presence give witness to the relatedness of human existence. They draw together the weak and the strong in recognition of the stewardship that each bears for the other. They are a sign of God's love and presence in the midst of despair manifested by the sustaining presence of God's people. Ministries of sustaining presence are incarnational in that they are sufficiently open to God that, in a more or less fragmentary way, God's divine power becomes manifest in them.[32] Ministries of sustaining presence are pastoral ministries, whether offered by ordained or laypeople, because they are nurturing ministries of being with and for others, just as God is faithfully with and for humanity, patiently present, vulnerable, and cherishing the need for humanity as a kind of trust that respects and honors human freedom.

NOSTALGIC MEMORY OF PASTORAL CAREGIVING

It seems to us that ministries of sustaining presence have been offered primarily in American churches through the structure of adult Sunday school classes. Without formal instruction, special prompting, or novel organization, when the burdens of a class member became known, other members mobilized to sustain him or her through the difficult time by whatever means were appropriate and as they were able. Whether the crisis was major illness, death, family trouble, financial hardship, or the lesser threats that are common to daily life, care for one another was expressed through prayer, phone calls, encouraging cards and notes, visits, meals, help with routine tasks, and other concrete forms of assistance that relieved some of the burden. These interventions typically were short-term and not very demanding on the responding class members. At other times, the depth of interpersonal commitments were challenged by long-term crises that only grew worse.

Perhaps most adults over age forty within American Protestant life could cite example after example of a Sunday school class surrounding members and their families with love and care during a time of need. Without their care being labeled, they were providing ministries of sustaining presence in whatever form and content the situation required. Their loyalty was steadfast, their presence was reassuring and comforting, the effect of their care was sustaining. The institution of Sunday school was, in many instances, both a means of religious education and an instrument of pastoral care. Indeed, we suggest that the *educational aspect of Sunday school included the pastoral care that members shared with one another and through class outreach or mission ministries.* As tenets and doctrines of faith were translated into ministries, as conduct was guided by basic beliefs of servanthood and discipleship, abstract religious lessons took on content, were tested, and internalized. People were continuously transformed. They grew in faith and discipleship as they experienced the grace of life in community, collectively the community of the class, the congregation, and the family of God. Seldom was a question raised about whether a class should respond to a member's need. Seldom did the members have to coerce one another to share in the care that was required. The culture of the class was such that when there was a need, there was a spontaneous response experienced as a sustaining presence.

The class was more than a gathering of adults to study the Bible. It was a training school for pastoral care. The members learned each other's stories through regular attendance at Bible study and monthly class meetings, usually in the home of a member around a covered dish meal. The class was a training ground in which new members to the church were incorporated into its fellowship.[33] Longer-term members would introduce new members to others, provide information about the congregation, and model Christian discipleship. By watching the members care for one another and through participation in other ministries of the congregation, new members learned not only the culture of a congregation, they learned how to care for one another. Members were mentors to one another for a variety of ministries. The gifts of each were a resource from which all could learn. And the collective memories of the class became histories of the congregation, perhaps not always accurate in every detail, that revealed the character and heart of the people through their relationships with one another in good times and bad.

Personality conflicts, cliques, and jealousies were not totally unknown within the classes, or within the full congregation for that matter. It should be remembered that, after all, they were classes of imperfect people. Yet despite the imperfections, the members strove to understand God, live by faith, and love one another. The Sunday school structure was the primary means by which the congregation's pledge to be present to one another was fulfilled. Teaching these lessons and learning these skills began at birth for children of *churched* parents. The observation of William Clebsch about Sunday schools in the nineteenth century appears true today:

> For thousands upon thousands of American children the earliest sorties beyond the family into a social group . . . [have] been enrollment in the church nursery, kindergarten, Sunday School, or the parish day school. Through the Sunday School's orientation to character-building the child became an integer in an extrafamilial group that elicited rudimentary political, social, and even economic activities. Thus religious education sought not so much to teach as to enlist, not so much to impart information about Christianity as to evoke loyalty to the church or to the Sunday School class.[34]

The careful reader will have noted the use of the past tense in these remarks about the ministries of sustaining presence by adult Sunday school classes. We may be challenged, even criticized, for implying that adult Sunday schools are waning or that caregiving within contemporary classes is less spontaneous, generous, sustaining, or admirable. This is not the point that we wish to make. Our point is more positive. The small group of an adult Sunday school class was, naturally and spontaneously, a primary and extraordinary instrument of pastoral caregiving. There are congregations today with vital Sunday school organizations where adult participation is significant and serves

77

their members through thick and thin. Unfortunately, there is considerable evidence that this mechanism for pastoral caregiving may be in irreversible decline. Moreover, the exceptional care that they offer may not extend routinely beyond the membership of the class, thus leaving church members who are not members of a class outside the scope of the congregation's care. It might be suggested that the professional or paid staff of the congregation know and respond to the needs of these members. But it is literally impossible for clergy to provide this intensity of care, even if the needs are known. Moreover, few, if any other, ministries within congregations have demonstrated the capacity for multifaceted caregiving as well as the Sunday school class.

This overview of pastoral caregiving, indeed, may be nostalgic, as the heading of this section states. Perhaps our memories as Southern Baptist and United Methodist clergy are more generous about the past than reality would support. Alternately, our assessment of the current status of adult Sunday school may be too pessimistic. The truth about Sunday school and congregational caregiving may lie somewhere in the middle of these two possibilities. Nevertheless, it is irrefutable that enrollment and participation in adult Sunday school is in decline in nearly every major Protestant denomination in America. From the mid-1980s through the mid-1990s, total Sunday school enrollment has declined in the Evangelical Lutheran Church in America, Lutheran Church—The Missouri Synod, The United Methodist Church, Christian Church (Disciples of Christ), The Episcopal Church, and United Church of Christ. The Southern Baptist Convention and Presbyterian Church (U.S.A.) denominations report a slight increase in total enrollment, but the Presbyterians report a decrease in adult enrollment.[35] Moreover, in many congregations, the number of members who participate in any small group activity is a fraction of the congregation's membership.

We are cautious about drawing too many conclusions or inferences from these reports. Data from one denomination may not be fully comparable with data from another. Not all congregations in each denomination report Sunday school data. Few denominations are able to document Sunday school attendance by age group. This imprecision may mask an even more dramatic decline in adult attendance that is partially offset by children and youth enrollment. Moreover, nearly all denominations report enrollment, rather than attendance. There may be a wide gap between the two. This disparity and decrease in Sunday school enrollment may be offset, also, by adult participation in surrogate religious education activities like short-term or special classes, Bible study groups away from the church campus, or prayer groups for which attendance is not reported to denomination offices. But even if these alternative small groups are abundant, it is fair to question whether they offer, as Sunday school classes did, the sort of open-ended, longer-term, and more interpersonal experience that gives rise to caring for one another in the form of bearing one another's burdens.

Religious educators and church growth experts surely interpret these data from their own perspectives to assess the strength of contemporary congregations and denominationalism. Our lament is based on the threat to congregational caregiving a weakened adult Sunday school program may portend, particularly if our assumption is correct that adult Sunday school classes have been the primary means of ministries of sustaining presence. The notion that adults uninvolved in a Sunday school small group provide these ministries with a comparable spontaneity and dedication seems questionable. People are more likely to know one another and grow to care for one another through frequent and sustained contact common to small groups like Sunday school classes. Apart from small groups, intimacies are more difficult to establish, information is less shared, and feelings of responsibility to another are less formed. Attendance at worship without participation in one or more small groups comparable to a Sunday school class probably does not create the sort of bond and relationship for which people will sacrifice the time and energy to bear the burden of another, despite biblical injunctions to do so.

There is another reason to expect that worshipers will not fill the caregiving gap. Fewer people seem to be attending worship services regularly. In 1993, 45 percent of Protestants and 51 percent of Roman Catholics reported attending church within the last seven days, according to a Gallup survey. In contrast to these self-reports of church or synagogue attendance, Hardaway, Marler, and Chaves' actual count of attendance in 48 Catholic dioceses representing 38 percent of Catholics showed a weekly attendance rate of 26.7 percent. Head counts for Protestant attendance showed a comparable difference.

Weekly attendance is 45 percent by self-report, but approximately 20 percent by actual count.[36] The prospect that weekly worshipers can take up the caregiving slack looks even dimmer as more recent data are reviewed. According to a Gallup poll in 1996, 38 percent of adults said they attended church or synagogue in a given week, down from 43 percent in 1995. This is near the all-time low of 37 percent recorded in 1940 and far from the high of 49 percent reported in 1955 and 1958.[37]

The trends in decreasing attendance at worship and Sunday school may be ominous for the church's caregiving. Perhaps the church is less at the center of people's lives. As observed in the first chapter, one's closest friends may not be fellow congregants. More and more members of congregations appear to be strangers to one another, if there is a relationship between attendance and familiarity. This may mean, as well, that comparatively few members have the sort of relationships, nostalgically described above, that evoke an intensely caring response in adversity. It seems that for many, according to C. Kirk Hardaway and Penny Long Marler:

> regular church attendance is increasingly difficult, even for those committed to it. Sunday morning is no longer *sacred* time: job responsibilities, sports leagues, family outings, housework, and many other things get in the way of traveling to a church building for worship at a scheduled time. And if you happen to miss church next weekend, will anyone know if you slept in, comforted a sick child, left town on business, or decided to have brunch at the Hyatt? Church attendance is increasingly a private matter, and it is correspondingly easier for each of us to maintain an idealized image of ourselves as regular attenders when in fact we may only manage to attend church two or three times a month at the most.[38]

Taking note of these data, trends, and impact on community may lead to despair regarding the vitality of congregations. The mission of the church in all of its expressions would appear to suffer as attendance, and the commitment it implies, wanes. Such pessimism may be premature and unwarranted. There do not appear to be wholesale closings of church doors. Fewer people in attendance may not be resulting in fewer ministries. A smaller proportion of members may be carrying a disproportionate share of the church's work, a phenomenon that would not appear new and that most pastors know very well in small and large congregations.

It could be argued that little has actually changed during the past several decades in rates of actual attendance in worship and Sunday school, especially if higher rates of attendance are interpreted as exaggerated self-reports of socially desirable behavior. The change being described may be no more than a heightened preoccupation with numbers as the salient measure of member commitment and congregational health. As Donald A. Luidens remarks regarding church growth promoters, "The cult of aggregate data leads inexorably to the corollary that bigness is a sign of faithfulness . . . numerical decline is tantamount to death."[39]

Smallness does not necessarily equal death. Many congregations with a small engaged membership are quite vital communities of worship and discipleship. An inability among members to think that someone else will undertake a given ministry may provide additional motivation to be involved in many of the church's ministries. Familiarity and intimacy among members, which may be more likely, may predispose members to be more willing to share one another's burdens. Thus, one can hold onto the belief that community is not lost, even when aggregate numerical measures of strength decline over time or regular participants are relatively few. It may be that the fellowship and intimacy are more apt to flourish in such circumstances. This may be one of the virtues of small congregations. Alternately, within congregations with a large number of participating members and ministries, fellowship and intimacy probably develop in small groups. Relationships may deepen, and care for one another may be centered in these small groups.

In order for a congregation to remain vital, independent of size, it must meet the needs of the people who turn to it. George Gallup identified six basic spiritual needs of Americans that churches should address in one form or another. These are (1) the need to believe that life is meaningful and has a purpose, (2) the need for a sense of community and deeper relationships, (3) the need to be appreciated and respected, (4) the need to be listened to—to be heard, (5) the need to feel that one is growing in the faith, and (6) the need for practical help in developing a mature faith.[40] There is no single method by which these basic needs can be met for all people. For that matter, there is nothing particularly novel or surprising about this list. In fact, it could be argued that these needs are not particularly spiritual. People who eschew anything spiritual probably would agree, with the exception to the explicit reference to faith in items 5 and 6, that these needs exist for all people, whether or not they value religion in any form. As ministries and activities are examined, congregations might consider the extent to which they help to meet these needs. Hopefully, congregations can and do respond to these needs, as people variously experience them, through their ministries and activities.

Three of the six needs identified by Gallup are related to the quality of relationship among members of a congregation. The need for a sense of community and deeper relationships reflects reported feelings of separateness. Mobility, divorce, family fragmentation, radical individualism, and other phenomena of contemporary life undermine community and deep relationship. Nevertheless, the yearning for connectedness and feeling that someone cares about what happens in one's life remain powerful needs to be met in some context or another, by some group or another. The congregation can be such an inclusive and caring community. Declaring it as such, however, does not make it a reality. Community requires commitment and participation. Relationships that are meaningful require certain measures of selflessness, even sacrifice, as a testament to the value of each member of the community. A desire to feel cared for in community has as a corollary a duty to care for others. Such an experience of community, of belonging in a family of faith, can be realized in both large and small congregations. In either case, a sense of community and deep relationships is likely to spring from participation in small groups where people can become sufficiently familiar with and loyal to one another over time to develop strong, intimate relationships that stand the test of time and human trauma.

The need to be appreciated and respected also relates to a quality of relationships. It is a basic belief among Christians that the most humble act of servanthood is as worthy as any other. Moreover, there is no hierarchy of favor among God's children. All are equally loved by

God. Each is specially gifted by God for service. Grace is not more generous for one than for another. These basic beliefs and others define a community where the life and personhood of each member is valued. The community called church is by definition a fellowship of mutual respect. Each is called to respect the freedom and uniqueness of the others, even as God respects the freedom of humans to accept or refuse God's invitation to deeper relationship. The quality of care and concern for one another that flows from these defining characteristics of community go a long way toward meeting the need to feel appreciated and respected.

The need to be listened to, to be heard, is not met by people who do not care enough to take the time to listen to another's story. The need to be heard is consistent with the need for community and intimate relationships and the need to be appreciated and respected. If one lives apart from community and the affirmations associated with relationships, it is not likely that the gift of hearing one's story will be received. Of course, someone can be paid to listen while one tells the joys and sorrows of life, but *hearing* one's story is different. Hearing, not just listening, requires a bond, a commitment to the growth and well-being of a person that causes one to listen empathically—to hear. Hearing is not geared toward a quick fix or impatiently looking for an opening for a polite dismissal of one's burden or joy. Hearing, if Job's friends are a model, requires being a sustaining presence to another even if a word is not spoken. The community and relationships that predispose people to this level of caring ought to be common characteristics of every congregation.

Sunday school classes have fostered and still may foster this type of community and relationship. There may be something about Bible study as a basis for being together that helps members translate the precepts of Scripture into a lifestyle, a manner of relating, and an orientation for looking at life. An invigorated Sunday school program or alternative small group structures are ways to respond to the needs to belong, to be valued, and to feel care. For some members, small groups may be substitutes for Sunday school or Bible study. They may create possibilities for people with special gifts and interests to meaningfully relate to one another in common service. Robert Wuthnow suggests that small group innovations constantly arise within churches. So-called special purpose groups may entice disaffected or minimally involved members to become more active. Wuthnow speculates that these new groups seem to run on fresh energy, rather than draining resources from existing programs. They can reflect and project a vision of what may be possible. They can be grounded in spiritual values, while adopting secular strategies and techniques. They may have the strengths of a limited mission, a membership of like-minded people, collectively reflect a wide range of interests and embody great diversity, and require a limited time commitment. Wuthnow argues that special purpose groups are a valuable way of sustaining religious commitment. As these groups have risen in prominence, churches have been revitalized.[41] The congregations in which they are anchored provide their identity and charter.

Beginning in the next chapter, we shall begin to describe one such alternative small group ministry called Care Teams. Care Team ministry can provide a structured response to the needs of members and neighbors burdened by chronic illness, disability, or terminal disease. They can be a key feature of a congregation's life as community, as well as constituting a servant ministry to members and others. Our experience since 1985 demonstrates that through varying forms of care and support, the members of a Care Team are a sustaining presence for individuals and families overwhelmed by health-related needs. It is equally true that this ministry of sustaining presence can make a significant contribution to the vitality of congregations, as well as addressing those basic human needs to belong, to be valued, and to feel care.

CHAPTER 4

CARE TEAM MINISTRY

W hat we began in response to one person in 1985 has evolved into a national congregation-based caregiving movement that is focusing attention on the needs of chronically ill and severely disabled people. At the time, we were not intending to be visionary. We were not even mindful of the implications of what we were doing for the pastoral ministry of congregations. These broader issues were not a conscious concern as we considered how to care for the immediate and overwhelming needs of a young man during his last days of life with AIDS. Yet, as we cared for this man and then others, the significant possibilities for the method of caregiving we initiated gradually became clear. The story of the creation of Care Team ministry begins as does any good story—with a person.

PRAXIS PRECEDED CONCEPT

Jay was a gifted young Ph.D. candidate in philosophy who started work as Earl Shelp's research assistant in 1983. His duties were routine—bibliographic research, evaluating source documents, reading page proofs, and other tasks. Spending time with him and talking about subjects scholarly and mundane was always enjoyable. As the relationship developed, Jay told his story. He grew up in Texas. His parents were divorced. His father married again. His relationship with his mother, who remained single, was closer than that with his father.

While not estranged from them, he was ambivalent about the degree of intimacy he wished to have with either of them. His brother was a troubled man. Jay wanted to make his own way in life. His education was financed largely by grants and scholarships. He looked forward to teaching medical ethics and philosophy. He was a relatively quiet person who enjoyed his coworkers in the university library, but chose not to surround himself with a large circle of friends.

Jay was a jogger. He ran regularly to stay in shape and to relieve the stress of graduate studies and work. For days he seemed to be short of breath, feverish, and unable to complete his usual exercise routine. Thinking that something was wrong, but never imagining that it could be anything serious, he visited the campus physician. A physical exam and chest X-ray later, Jay was referred for admission to the hospital. The preliminary diagnosis was AIDS. Devastated and numbed by the physician's words, Jay called Earl. After a pleasant exchange that did not betray the true reason for Jay's call, Jay asked if Earl could take him to the hospital. The request seemed improbable—he looked to be in the peak of health—prompting Earl to ask what was wrong. The response was as chilling as it was straightforward: "The campus doctor thinks I have AIDS." Earl replied, "I'm on the way."

AIDS became personal. If Jay's disease followed the usual course at the time, his life expectancy suddenly was reduced to six months of persistent and rapid decline—alone! This was an unacceptable prospect. Shelp shared Jay's diagnosis and prognosis with Sunderland. We agreed to help Jay however we could. In order to prepare to keep this pledge, to understand more fully the natural history of AIDS, and to anticipate the full range of needs of a person with AIDS, we began to spend time in an AIDS outpatient clinic and with hospitalized patients. We were struck by the depth of the anguish we observed. We were embarrassed by the lack of an identified ministry of God's people in the lives and by the beds of people affected by AIDS. We decided to pursue two courses of action simultaneously: first, personally to care for people dying with AIDS to demonstrate God's abiding love for them and to prepare ourselves to care for Jay, and second, to write about the meaning of the HIV/AIDS epidemic for God's people.

Misinformation about AIDS and stereotypes about people with AIDS were rampant. We began to write articles and books in order to provide factual information about the disease, to show more accurate portrayals of the people burdened by it, and to identify some of the challenges this new epidemic posed to faith communities.[1] Our relationships with people touched by AIDS (patients, family members, physicians, nurses, social workers, and friends) helped us, in ways not previously recognized, to understand the meaning of compassion, faithfulness, discipleship, community, redemption, and grace. The lives, stories, and intense needs of men and women we met in the clinic were like magnets that drew us ever closer to these people who had been mostly ostracized, condemned, and abandoned to die apart from the comforting embrace of family, friends, and God's people.

One young man whose story we included in our first book stopped coming to the clinic. We discovered that life for him was no longer a blessing. AIDS had frightened away his family and friends, taken his strength, sight, control of his bowel and bladder, and finally, depleted his will to live. Amidst these losses, his sense of dignity remained strong. He chose to die on his terms, rather than to endure a prolonged terminal phase that would further exhaust his companion caregiver who was already exhausted. We learned that George was confined to his bed, refusing food and most offers of water, and waiting for the peace of death. A hospice nurse visited every few days, but his day-to-day care for comfort was left to his companion at night after work. George was alone all day. His companion was up all night, night after night, doing what he could to comfort George, crying out in grief in the solitude of their apartment so no one would know their secret, and numbing his pain with scotch.

This tragic cycle repeated day after day. Death was elusive. Fatigue and despair were abundant. Because our teaching assignments prevented us from assisting during the day, our offers of help were confined to evenings and overnight stays. We took food and shared the evening meal with George's companion. We had conversations with George about subjects he chose. We heard their stories, feelings, and fears. We kept watch in George's room in order to reassure him when he became restless. We bathed him and changed his diapers. We dressed his brittle lips. We prayed silently. We let his companion rest so that the remaining time they had together would be more meaningful. We were a sustaining presence. But George had daily needs that could go on for two or three weeks, and we could not maintain this schedule unaided indefinitely. We turned to friends, some clergy and some laypeople, inviting each to spend a night on a rotating basis until George died. Our number grew to six. We did not realize at the time that we were forming a pioneering ministry that we would subsequently name AIDS Care Teams. We simply were doing what God calls us to do—befriend and bear the burden of people who satisfied the scriptural definition of the *poor*.

After George died, our special ministry group of six turned to the needs of other patients during their final days. So many were dying alone that we could not keep up. Some of our prophetic pastor friends permitted us to make special presentations about AIDS to their congregations. We reported the facts as they were known. Through stories, we introduced our audiences to people stigmatized, feared, rejected and broken by disease. We invited congregations to honor their identity and mission as God's people to befriend and defend people devastated by a new retrovirus. We challenged them to sponsor an AIDS Care Team of at least 12 adult members who would respond as they could to the multifaceted and intense needs of the dying. Their time commitment would not be overnight. Rather, we suggested that they devote two to four hours a week to the ministry, serve in pairs, and coordinate their service. No individual would be responsible for the total care of a patient or expected to do anything that was uncomfortable. We pledged our continuing support as Care Team members entered the world of people with AIDS. Our personal experience and confidence in the faithfulness of God's people led us to expect a positive response in some congregations, even though limited to a relatively few members.

The concern generated by Jay's diagnosis in April 1985 had extended by December to embrace other people affected by HIV/AIDS. What began as loyalty to a friend had been transformed into a pioneering ministry grounded in faith and motivated by love. Our personal effort to care for people with intense, even extraordinary, needs without being consumed was becoming a model for ministries of sustaining presence for people with HIV/AIDS and a prototype for caring for people with other chronic or terminal illnesses. At first, we had no well-defined protocol to care for the dying. Our long-term planning consisted mostly of looking at our calendars for the next several days to determine who would be with which patient or at which church meeting to invite others to ministry. Because AIDS evoked fears of infection and transmission was linked to behaviors judged immoral by many, our calls for compassion and servant ministry were controversial. Our efforts on behalf of people with AIDS often were ignored, rejected, or condemned. Nevertheless, the depths of despair and anguish of people with HIV disease continued to draw us closer. We persisted despite an ambivalence that ultimately hardened into resistance from our institutions located in the Texas Medical Center.

Our personal ministries and those of the first AIDS Care Teams that joined us were "lean and mean." Paperwork essentially consisted of a name and other limited information on an index card. Patients were matched with a Care Team and ministry began. The waiting list grew longer every day. We were learning by doing the best we could. Our mistakes with patients were quickly forgiven. We were discovering a new method of ministry that responded to the desperate needs of men and women caught in the mortal vise of a new disease. The infrastructure of an interfaith ministry was being put together as new needs were identified and responses fashioned. We had little time for deep reflection on our experiences and ideas, nor were we implementing any master plan. There was no time to develop a robust concept of AIDS ministry—that would come later. We merely recognized a need, decided that meeting it was not someone else's responsibility, considered how we might provide some relief, and invited others through publications and personal presentations to embrace people with AIDS as an expression of faith and discipleship.

CARE TEAM CONCEPT

Jay's misfortune started us on a path that has led to greater appreciation for the capacity of God's people as congregations to manifest community and to compassionately embrace people in extreme distress. AIDS Care Teams and subsequently Alzheimer's Care Teams and Second Family Care Teams have been a sustaining presence on behalf of their congregations to thousands of people coping at home with disability, chronic illness, or terminal disease. Care Team members have stayed the course, learned creative ways to meet needs great and small, and demonstrated that the people they serve have not been abandoned by God or God's people. They have befriended and defended God's children from all walks of life rendered vulnerable by disease and disability. Care Teams have become a primary means for caregiving, sharing the burdens of others within and beyond their congregations. These small group ministries effectively fulfill the community and relationship-building roles once provided by Sunday school classes as they respond to the needs of people to belong, to be valued, and to experience care.

As more and more congregations and members accepted our invitation to care for people affected by AIDS, we began to realize Care Team ministry was an effective response to people whose needs for care and support overwhelmed one-to-one care, whether by a family caregiver, friend, or fellow congregant. We observed the success of the first Care Teams and heard the consistent stories from men and women dying with AIDS of how the presence of these compassionate and dedicated people had restored hope and contributed to their sense of peace. We listened again and again to Care Team members report their joy from caregiving even as they witnessed death after horrible death. Only then did we pause from organizing and coordinating to analyze why Care Teams worked so well. As we began to understand this, the Care Team concept was formulated. The key seemed to be that Care Team ministry provided caring men and women a structure within which to exercise gifts for special relationship and caregiving as a ministry of their congregations.

In the first years of the epidemic, we met many people of faith attending to the diverse needs of people with AIDS in the clinic and in homes. Some were people with simple explanations of how faith formed their commitment to people with AIDS. "Even the lepers were loved by Jesus" was a common response. Others were people more prone to introspection and reflection. Although their statements tended to be more theologically sophisticated, at the core they said "This is what God calls me to do." Their ministries were exhibited in their secular work as social workers, nurses, home health aides, or volunteers in one of the newly created AIDS service organizations. Nearly all of the people we met in caregiving roles chose to be in AIDS service though their light often was hidden from public view. Their confessions of love that grew out of faith were drowned out by opportunistic preachers pronouncing judgment and condemnation.

The church was not absent during the first years of the AIDS epidemic in the United States, but its sustaining presence was camouflaged and muted within secular organizations. Many of the people who became members of the first AIDS Care Teams grasped the opportunity for their faith-based ministries to be claimed and publicized. This was one reason for the effectiveness of the Care Teams—people with diverse gifts for caregiving had these gifts validated by the church and the exercise of these gifts was efficiently and effectively coordinated. The main difference between the care common to a Sunday school class and an AIDS Care Team was the relationship of the recipient of care to the congregation. Sunday school classes tend to care for one another, family members, or other members of the church. AIDS Care Teams were caring for people who generally felt unwelcome and abandoned by the church when they needed the sustaining presence of God's people. Yet as we came to know them, we found many to be people of faith.

A second element of the Care Team concept that emerged as we reflected on our increasing experience was the value and wisdom of sharing the burden of care in situations where the needs are intense or prolonged. AIDS, like other chronic and degenerative diseases, deprives people of their abilities to maintain their independence and erodes control over lives and circumstances. These losses may come slowly or quickly, compounding one problem upon another. Most people resist and do not require custodial care. They benefit greatly from basic and simple forms of assistance that enhance their independence and self-esteem. They frequently may need varied forms of assistance. When all needs are identified, meeting them is too much for one caregiver to attempt without risking physical, emotional, and spiritual exhaustion.

Care Teams are an excellent response to these situations because the needs often are appropriate for laypeople to meet, can be met by limited time commitments, yet are so frequent as to warrant the involvement of several people in order to not overburden individual caregivers. At the outset this structure and process were practical concessions to the magnitude of the needs we encountered and our limited capacity to provide care. As we reviewed our methodology, we concluded that it was also theoretically and theologically sound. A team approach to caregiving, like the care a Sunday school class provided its members, is a community response to needs not adequately met by familiar one-to-one visitation, prayer, encouragement, and practical assistance.

A key aspect of the theological strength of the Care Team concept is that a Care Team's ministries are part of the congregation's pastoral ministry. Each Care Team may function in relationship with others and receive nurture from professional staff outside the church membership. Nevertheless, each Care Team is accountable to the congregation and draws its life from the congregation. A team may serve fellow congregants or provide a mission or outreach ministry to nonmembers. *A Care Team ministry signals that a congregation is dedicated to be a community where relationships have priority and caregiving is a defining characteristic rather than an afterthought or ad hoc activity.* The ministry gives witness to the congregation's mission and interprets its life within the faith tradition of the congregation. Care Team members are called to the ministry and commissioned by the congregation to serve on its behalf.

A practical advantage of anchoring this intensive and more comprehensive form of pastoral caregiving within the total ministry of the church is commitment. The congregation bears responsibility for the ministry's strength and continuation. The commitment of team members may be for a set term, for example, of one year; but it may be open-ended. Call to another ministry, changes in one's personal life, relocation to another area, or other changes often result in a decline in team membership. The congregation's commitment to Care Team ministry is then expressed through recruitment drives, promotion to new church members, and recognition of the Care Team during prayer, announcements, or anniversary observances.

Another strength of the Care Team concept is cohesiveness among the members. Care Team members drawn from the congregation typically have more in common with which to create bonds than people whose primary reason to be together is interest in a particular disease,

92

cause, or need. A shared faith tradition that shapes beliefs and instills values that engender concern and compassion for others helps team members who may not know one another very well at all to relate to one another, respect and care for one another, develop a collective identity, and fulfill their responsibilities to the congregation, the team, and the people they serve with care and integrity. Sufficient relationships and bonds exist to function as a team sharing the blessings and burdens of ministries of sustaining presence.

The final features of the Care Team concept critical to its integrity are supervision and nurture. The first Care Teams embraced a population that evoked fear, anxiety, and risk for social rejection. There were concerns about risks of HIV infection or infection by a long list of other viruses and bacteria. There was uncertainty about individual and team capacity to be present to so many people as they died. There was a range of feelings and moral judgments among team members about the sexual or drug-use behaviors by which the people they served came to be in a situation of need. Patients who became infected through blood transfusion, organ transplant, or birth to an infected mother did not bear this moral burden. There were risks, as well, that Care Team members would experience a similar form of social ostracism because of their relationship with people touched by AIDS. These issues were clear to us as we recruited the first congregation-based AIDS Care Teams. Addressing them factually, respectfully, and nonjudgmentally was a prerequisite. Orienting Care Team members to their ministries in a world of AIDS was a critical first step.

Orientation had to be followed by training and supervision. Supervision essentially is a pedagogical device by which knowledge is imparted and the learner's skills are honed. Ideally, this occurs in a nurturing relationship between supervisor and trainee. Sunderland's expertise as a supervisor in clinical pastoral education contributed greatly to the Care Team concept. AIDS was new. The natural history of the disease was being learned by clinicians before their eyes. The psychological, social, emotional, financial, interpersonal, and spiritual aspects of AIDS similarly were being observed. We knew that it was impossible to train people to address needs that could not be foreseen. Care Team ministry as we were doing it, and the Care Team concept we constructed to undergird it, had to have a clinical method of training in order for it to be effective. Care Team members would learn in the same way as other students in the helping professions learn. They would learn by doing under supervision.

With six to twelve people sharing in the care and support of a person with AIDS, communication and coordination were required. Forms of care taken for granted with other diseases had a different significance with AIDS. Recurring guidance about infection control had to be given. Information about the complications of AIDS was required so that Care Team members could understand what they were observing and experiencing. Negative and cruel social reactions to patients broke the hearts of team members. Being present with so many young adults during periods of wrenching deterioration and death evoked profound feelings of loss and grief, anger and rage. Spending time and providing assistance on a rotating basis meant that information had to be transmitted from one Care Team member to another in a timely and accurate fashion. Levels and descriptions of care were frequently revised as a patient's condition changed, usually for the worse. Care Team ministry necessarily was flexible and responsive to changing needs and circumstances. Concerns about what to do and how to do it were constant. There were no experts in AIDS caregiving or AIDS ministry. We and the Care Team members were learning as we served and sharing personal lessons with the others.

The circumstances of patients and the Care Team method of ministry required regular meetings of team members. Meetings provided opportunities for building relationships among team members, reporting on patients and the care being provided, sharing feelings, talking about how their ministries informed and shaped faith, receiving timely information or instruction to respond to new needs, monitoring member relationships with patients, and maintaining prudent boundaries, and much more. Monthly meetings of the team were safe gatherings where members could have their ministries supervised by us and one another. The supervision that is pivotal to the Care Team concept is nurturing rather than judgmental. The goal is to enhance the skills of members, contribute to personal growth, and affirm their ministries of sustaining presence. The integrity of the Care Team concept is grounded more in the priority of supervision and the nurture of team members than any other operational feature.

The Care Team concept, in essence, is an enhanced and intentional representation of community and caregiving described nostalgically in chapter 3. Care Team ministries are not designed to replace the educational or caregiving ministries common to Sunday school classes where they exist. Rather, the concept provides a foundation for a form of servant ministry that meets needs for care presently unmet by congregational caregiving. The ministries supported by the Care Team concept complement customary forms of pastoral caregiving. This ministry of sustaining presence embraces those members the severity of whose health-related conditions has removed them from active participation in the life of the congregation. Care Team members can establish relationships with families, become a sustaining presence through care and support appropriate to the needs, and demonstrate that a family separated from the community by illness or physical deterioration remains a valued part of the community. Even in congregations with relatively strong Sunday school programs and other caregiving ministries, a Care Team can respond to special needs that no other pastoral ministry addresses. We shall describe in greater detail in subsequent chapters how the Care Team concept has restored relationships and provided valued ministry to families caring for loved ones at home with dementia (most commonly Alzheimer's disease), frail or disabled adults, or AIDS.

We were not surprised when we first introduced AIDS Care Team ministry to pastors that none could identify a member diagnosed with AIDS. As noted above, only a few of the AIDS patients we met were active members of a congregation. Occasionally a pastor knew of a family with a relative who had been diagnosed with AIDS or had already died. The ministries that seemed obvious to them were prayer and visitation when requested by the patient. An open-ended ministry of presence that included significant hands-on caregiving in the homes of the patients never occurred to them. Yet, when we introduced the idea of just such a ministry, it made sense. The main difference between our proposal and the readiness of pastors to organize members to respond to significant illness was the nature of AIDS as an infectious, fatal, and stigmatized disease. The "nuts and bolts" of Care Team ministry were nearly identical to the ad hoc types of extended and intense caregiving that periodically occurred within the membership when crisis or disability befell a family. While we could rejoice when the congregation mobilized to care for these families, we were saddened that these ministries were the exception rather than the norm. Few families coping with chronic illness, disability, or terminal disease at home were offered this intense level of pastoral care. Moreover, these ministries tended to be reactive and sporadic rather than proactive and constant. In order to provide more consistent ministries in these current situations and to meet future opportunities for ministry, steps should be taken now.

It is increasingly recognized that chronic conditions are the leading causes of illness, disability, and death in the United States. Of almost 100 million people in the U. S. with one or more chronic conditions, more than 40 million people are limited in their daily activities such as bathing, dressing, eating, walking, and other personal care activities. An even greater number has difficulty with instrumental activities of daily living such as preparing meals, shopping, using the telephone, managing money, taking medications, doing light housework, and other measures of living independently. Contrary to popular belief, relatively few of these people live in nursing homes. Care of the chronically ill tends to be provided in place, in other words, in the home of the impaired person. The services typically and most commonly needed emphasize assistance and nurture, not cure, and may be provided competently by laypeople.

It is unfortunate, if not tragic, that there is no effective system to meet the nonprofessional needs of people with chronic conditions in the U.S. As a result, much of the practical or nonskilled care that is commercially available is fragmented, inappropriate, and difficult to obtain. A congregation's Care Team is a compassionate and suitable response to these psychosocial and spiritual needs. A Care Team's ministries may truly be the sustaining presence that enables people with chronic or terminal conditions to remain more safely and comfortably in their homes with the support of a caring community. Care Team ministry, like secular, nonprofessional, and informal caregiving by family, friends, and community organizations, inevitably will have even greater contributions to make to the independence and quality of life of people with chronic conditions in the future, particularly as the population ages and proportionately more people become impaired.[2]

Current needs for basic assistance are staggering. The prevalence of unmet need for assistance by people 65 and older for bathing is 36%, eating 31%, transferring from bed or chair 40%, using toilet 37%, mobility indoors 34%, and dressing 37%. The prevalence of unmet need for help with these tasks for adults under 65 is even higher at 40%, 45%, 55%, 45%, 38%, and 41% respectively. The consequences of no assistance are not surprising for both age groups: individuals do not bathe due to fear of falling (60% and 63%), do not follow special diets (25% and 46%), fall while moving in or out of a bed or chair (58% and 49%), do not get to the bathroom or be changed often enough (58% and 49%), are unable to fill prescriptions or buy needed medical supplies (25% and 37%), and miss doctor or other medical appointments (29% and 53%).[3] It is reasonable to assume that some, if not many, of these impaired people are members of a congregation. Similarly, it should be noted that much of the assistance needed with these basic tasks that able people take for granted could be provided by trained laypeople such as Care Team members.

The sustaining presence of caregivers contributes greatly to the welfare and well-being of the people they serve. Perhaps existing health problems would not be exacerbated, costly treatments could be foregone or lessened, and unnecessary pain and suffering could be avoided. People with chronic conditions supported by an informal network of family and friend caregivers surely fare better than others living alone or without adequate support from any source. The level of unmet needs identified above suggests that the demand for caregivers is high and destined to increase. The presumption that family members will provide the needed care may not be valid. The supply of lay caregivers is shrinking due to decreasing birth rates, family networks getting smaller while consisting of more older than younger family members, employed women no longer available to be the unpaid family caregiver, and marriage and birth of children at later ages. The impact of these sociological and cultural changes on the pool of potential caregivers will become more critical during the next several decades. In 1990, the ratio of potential caregivers for an elderly person was 11 to 1. This ratio is projected to decrease to 10 to 1 by 2010, 6 to 1 by 2030, and 4 to 1 by 2050.[4]

The magnitude of the need by adults for the type of care commonly given by a Care Team is daunting. This gap in the nation's care of the chronically or terminally ill is large and has serious potential consequences for people struggling to remain in their homes. The challenges to provide basic and decent care stem from several causes including an aging population, medical care oriented to out-patient treatment, reduced governmental funding for social services, and the socioeconomic and cultural shifts described above. Congregations clearly do not have the human or financial resources to resolve these systemic challenges in caregiving. Nevertheless, the magnitude of the need is not a reason for congregations to neglect being part of a solution by sponsoring caregiving ministries, especially for members. These ministries can constitute a safety net beneath members and neighbors whose needs for basic assistance are unmet. When individual members make a bite-size commitment to be community and surrogate family to people with special needs, a harvest of blessings for caregivers and care partners is reaped. The Care Team concept defines and facilitates a ministry of sustaining presence that validates a congregation's identity and mission as a community of care.

A CONTRIBUTION TO PASTORAL CARE AND COMMUNITY

Care for one another within a congregation is not an option if the church is to be faithful to its identity and mission. The Pauline epistles contain insight and instruction regarding the nature and character of Christian community.[5] Paul uses the metaphors of family and body to develop his understanding of church membership. All members of the community are related in faith as family through Christ the son to God the father and one another (Gal. 4:4-6 and Rom. 8:14-17). In Christ, believers become brothers and sisters who relate as adult children in intimate and mature relationships "doing good to all" (Gal. 6:10 RSV; cf. Rom. 15:14, Rom. 16:2, 2 Cor. 7:15, 1 Cor. 15:58, Philem. 2). They are bound together in love such that "if one member suffers, all suffer together; if one member is honored, all rejoice together" (1 Cor. 12:26 RSV). The love that defines and unites the congregation is more than an attitude or emotion. It entails intentional and concrete acts of service (1 Thess. 1:3, cf. 2 Cor. 8:24, Rom. 13:10). Paul's use of the metaphor of the body also is instructive. The community is an organic whole and its proper function requires the involvement of every part or person. Each member has a unique role, yet each is dependent upon all the others (Rom. 12:4-6, Eph. 4:12, 15-16, 1 Cor. 12). The unity of the body is a reality to be acknowledged rather than a potential to be realized (1 Cor. 1:10, Rom. 15:5, Phil. 2:1-2, Eph. 4:3).

Unity and love among the members of the community are critical for Paul. Disorder and schism within a community occur from disagreement or failure to care for one another (1 Cor. 1:12, 11:21), and are works of the flesh (Gal. 5:20). Each member receives from God's grace (1 Cor. 1:4ff., Rom. 12:6) gifts for service to God and the common good (1 Cor. 12:7, 1 Cor. 14:12, Rom. 12:6). A member's gifts, therefore, are concrete expressions of God's grace. They are defining features of community life. Their manifestation protects and preserves the community which is both context and means for the edification of the members. Those gifts that contribute to the growth of the community are given highest importance because they fulfill the needs of others.

Community is pivotal to Christian identity and discipleship. For Paul, participation in the community or fellowship demonstrates a person's reconciliation with God and other persons. The gifts and fruits of the Spirit are instruments through which reconciliation is expressed and deepened. The importance of community and the relationships it entails ought not be overlooked or minimized. Robert Banks emphasizes this point noting that the focal point for the early Christians was neither a book nor a rite, but a set of relationships. The centrality of relationship is demonstrated in recognizing that God's loving purpose and presence were not revealed primarily through the written word and tradition, mystical experience, or cultic activity, but through encounter with and care for one another.[6]

Caring for one another must occur for the church to be the community that God wills. Through relationship and care, the presence and love of God are revealed and community is achieved. The precise forms of care are less important than the witness they provide to the priority a congregation gives to people and relationships. Care Team ministry is one means by which a congregation may demonstrate its obedience to the law of Christ by bearing one another's burdens (Gal. 6:2). Care Team ministry is not and ought not be the only form of care-giving in a congregation. But it may be the best form of ministry in sit-uations where the need for support is longer-term, intense, or overwhelming. Rather than neglecting people with this level of need or responding in an ad hoc and inconsistent manner, a congregation's Care Team ministry signals its commitment to be a sustaining presence at a time of special need. The unity and solidarity of the community are protected and sustained as Care Team members serve on behalf of the full congregation. The Care Team concept and its ministries of sus-taining presence strengthen community through their focus on people whose special needs tend to be overlooked and relationships estranged by disease or disability. It makes good the congregation's pledge to be present through darkened and tumultuous passages of life. It brings people into meaningful caring relationships in the context of God's love which, at root, is the strength of any congregation.[7]

The term *Care Team* appears to be gaining wider currency to describe cooperative services by members of congregations or others involved in organized community service activities that may be more or less re-lated to a congregation. Most of these efforts are provided by custom-ary one-on-one volunteer programs. Although we celebrate any activity undertaken alone or in cooperation with others to attend to human needs, such efforts do not meet the criteria for Care Team ministry as we define the concept. Programs that assign individual volunteers to a nursing home, hospital, or other facility where some form of need exists may not meet our criteria for Care Team ministries. They merely com-plement the volunteer programs of the respective institutions.

We were approached several years ago to consider managing the volunteer program of a hospice on a contract basis. The idea of the hos-pice management was that we could draw people from congregations with whom we had relationships, train and supervise the volunteers, and thereby relieve the hospice of a legal requirement that they were consistently finding difficult to meet. We declined the invitation to mask a volunteer program as ministry. In addition, programs that address only one need are not Care Team ministries. For example, delivering meals-on-wheels is not Care Team ministry as we have defined it. Neither this need-specific nor institution-specific service program satisfies our theologically and ecclesiologically grounded definition of Care Team ministry.

It is not appropriate to dilute the meaning of Care Team ministry or diminish the contribution it makes to a recovery of pastoral caregiving to the chronically ill within congregations by characterizing other forms of volunteer-based helpful acts as Care Team ministry. These forms of service do not grow necessarily out of the life of a congregation or implement the congregation's mission. They are related to faith traditions only to the extent that some participants may be recruited from congregations or the volunteers meet, if at all, in a church building. These volunteer programs masquerade as or mimic pastoral ministry properly defined. As noted by William Clebsch and Charles Jaekle, "On many occasions, works of charity, of welfare, of education, of the binding up wounds, . . . and so forth, have come to be closely associated with the Christian ideal of love for the neighbor,"[8] but such helpful acts, however admirable, are hardly Care Team ministry. The risk to designating any and all community service activities as Care Teams is that the longer-term, more intense needs to which Care Team ministries respond may lose focus and priority. Little will have been gained among congregations if the opportunities to enhance their pastoral care is dissipated by similar sounding but essentially secular volunteer programs. The Care Team concept supports caregiving ministries, not volunteerism!

PRINCIPLES FOR CARE TEAM MINISTRY

A Care Team provides an infrastructure for a form of caregiving that enriches and strengthens a community of people with a faith-based sense of responsibility for and to one another.[9] Being a sustaining presence through the joys and sorrows of life seems perfectly ordinary for a people whose lives are governed by a commandment to love one another. Little special notice is taken when a community of this character does what it is called to do (cf. Luke 17:10). Considerable notice is taken, however, when the community falls short of this standard of conduct or defaults in its care altogether. The oft heard question, Why isn't the church doing something about this need? is as much complaint as declaration of the church's loving nature. Neither the church nor a congregation can attend to every need, and no congregation should feel obliged to respond to manipulative or disingenuous calls for action. Rather, we are arguing that care is a fundamental value and defining characteristic of congregations. Although care is at the core of community, the precise form that care should take cannot be prescribed apart from a particular need.

Care Team ministries are responsive to needs that tend to be long-term, intense, or overwhelming and amenable to the involvement of laypeople. It is impossible to predict the exact presentation and scope of needs, since they emerge from a variety of losses and are set in the unique contexts of individual lives. One strength of Care Team ministry is its capacity to respond to diverse needs even as they change over time. Flexibility in caregiving is a virtue in dynamic situations of illness. Flexibility and responsiveness, however, require direction if optimal outcomes are to be realized. Rules either prescribe or proscribe certain conduct as right or wrong. Clearly there are actions that are morally right and wrong in caregiving, which ought to be followed. In the main, however, most Care Team ministry occurs in situations where the standards of right and wrong are more pragmatic. Does a particular intervention provide aid and comfort or not? Care Team members tend to do the best they can, given the circumstances. Our experience is that they perform nobly.

Caregiving is a dynamic process within a dynamic relationship. Principles of conduct are more general and fundamental than rules. This is a strength. Principles provide general guidance or direction toward worthy ends without specifying what conduct is mandated or allowed in a given instance. We propose five basic principles for Care Team ministry. These principles collectively set the moral foundation for the relationships that are established and the forms of care provided in response to particular needs. A proper interpretation and application of these principles requires an accurate and wise assessment of each situation. For this reason, good judgment is perhaps the single most important virtue for Care Team members, with compassion and sensitivity close runners-up.

The first principle is that *the Care Team's mission is compassion.*

Care Teams serve people coping with acute or chronic disruptive impairments. The sustaining presence of Care Team members not only contributes to a higher level of function, it elevates a care partner's self-esteem and confirms that person's dignity. According to Wendy Farley, "Compassion is a mode of relationship and a power that is wounded by the suffering of others and that is propelled into action on their behalf. Compassion resists suffering rather than tries to justify it. It resists suffering by offering whatever comfort, healing, or empowerment it can within the confines of a particular situation."[10]

The second principle is *genuine respect for the autonomy of persons.* This principle reminds Care Team members that they are guests in the home of the person being served. Their role is supportive and nurturing, not controlling or manipulative. They recognize and respect the values, judgments, and choices of competent people, even when they disagree or think that judgments are mistaken. Respecting a person's autonomy acknowledges his or her capacity and right to make decisions and to pursue the good life however that person defines it.[11] Respecting the autonomy of persons means acknowledging their right to self-determination. The use of *genuine* in our statement of the principle emphasizes, if even implicitly, that respect may require a Care Team member not to interfere in or disvalue certain choices, behaviors, beliefs, or values of a person served merely because they are different from or contrary to one's own. Respect requires more than verbal assent to a proposition.

The third principle has two parts—*respect for one's own personhood* and *freedom to withdraw without guilt.* Respect as an action guide is bi-directional. If respect is to have moral force, it must extend to oneself as well as to a suffering person. This may seem self-evident but it warrants emphasis in caregiving relationships. Caregivers tend to have sympathy for the plight of the people they serve. Their needs have an urgency that calls forth a caregiver's compassion. A caregiver may feel obliged to subordinate feelings or disregard values, understandings of the good, and notions of right and wrong in the course of serving another. But disregarding one's own personhood undermines the integrity of the caregiving relationship, which involves all parties in giving and receiving care. Respect for one's own personhood may require a Care Team member to terminate a relationship because continuing would compromise or violate his or her personhood. Withdrawal in these circumstances ought not induce feelings of guilt or failure. Rather, it should be interpreted as an affirmation of personhood and autonomy, both as expressed by the Care Team member and the person receiving care.

The fourth principle is *security in one's faith and morality grounded in faith*. Care Team ministry is faith in action. Faith is personal. Scripture, reason, tradition, and experience may inform faith; but in the end, one's relationship with God is an individual construction. It is a foundation for one's commitment to and compassion for others. It is the soil in which a Care Team member's caregiving relationships take root and grow. But one person's experience of God is likely to be different from another person's experience. Caregiving relationships are more likely to reach intimacy and be strong when caregivers are secure in their faith and open to spiritual growth that may entail change. Caregiving experiences may challenge a Care Team member's beliefs and moral judgments. Confidence in one's faith and morality will help a Care Team member through these times of stress. Conversations about God, faith, and morality easily occur among people who feel comfortable and secure with one another. The experience of caregiving will be enhanced if a Care Team member is able to participate openly and honestly, without expecting concurrence with one's own faith or morality.

The fifth principle is *a commitment to justice as a limit to self-righteousness*. The parable of the Samaritan suggests that need is the relevant criterion for care in situations of physical harm or decline (Luke 10:29-37). Nothing else is known about the identifying characteristics of the man set upon by robbers. It was his physical need, not his race, religion, lifestyle, age, gender, type of disease or trauma, or other factor that apparently prompted a caring response by the Samaritan. There is no suggestion that his need is greater than another's or that he is more worthy of care than another. Rather, his particular need and the Samaritan's knowledge of it are sufficient to cause a demonstration of what it means to "love your neighbor as yourself." Being "neighbor," "showing mercy," or having compassion is a basic standard of discipleship. Meeting this standard does not give one reason to feel superior to others. No matter how much one serves or cares for people in need, still others go without. Justice requires similar treatment for similar cases. A commitment to justice acknowledges the claim of others for care, even though providing care is beyond one's capacity. Recognizing the scope of need, the value of people with need, and their comparable claims for mercy (care) weakens a propensity to feel or think that one somehow deserves special consideration, recognition, or praise for the care that one gives. Being a sustaining presence (being neighbor, caring, having compassion, showing mercy) is no basis for self-righteousness. One is merely being disciple, utilizing one's gifts of grace, sharing the burdens of others, fulfilling the law of Christ.

ORGANIZATION AND PRACTICE OF CARE TEAM MINISTRY

Care Team ministry offers congregations a structure to care efficiently and effectively for people with special health-related needs, which develops the members' caregiving gifts as they provide social, emotional, physical, and spiritual support. Each detail of Care Team ministry cannot be presented here. However, the main components and procedures will be reviewed as orientation to the following chapters, which describe three types of Care Teams—AIDS, Alzheimer's, and Second Family. Reasons for these designations will be identified later. Here we provide content that is common to each specialized form of Care Team ministry.[12]

Care Teams may vary in size. Experience has taught us that teams with at least 12 members and 2 coleaders tend to be stronger over time. Team members may be divided into smaller ministry units assigned to the care of one person or family. We refer to these ministry units as mini-teams. Some Care Teams have been as large as 60 members. A team of this size presents certain challenges, as well as opportunities. Viability, however, tends not to be one of the challenges. Viability becomes a critical challenge if the team size contracts to 6 or 8 members. A basic premise for Care Team ministry is that care is shared among the team members. A team of 14 members enables a team to be in the home of a care partner each day, if necessary, without asking any single member to serve more than one time per week for a few hours. The team leaders typically determine whether the care that is indicated may be provided by one team member alone or two members serving together.

Care Team leaders are responsible to stay informed of the type of service each member is able to provide and when each member is available. This knowledge enables the team leaders to covenant with care partners regarding which needs will be met and when care will be offered. Team leaders assess the needs of people who ask for care, determine if the needs are appropriate for laypeople to meet, and coordinate the service of team members. Team leaders also convene the monthly meeting of the team. These monthly gatherings must be given a high priority by all team members in order for the team to function at an optimal level of efficiency and effectiveness. Team meetings provide opportunities for fellowship and bonding among the team members, continuing education and training, individual reporting of ministries and discussion, spiritual reflection, care of one another, and other activities that contribute to the growth of team members and the team's ministries. The team leaders are motivators, coordinators, and communicators. It is important for the leaders to meet regularly with the congregation's clergy to provide status reports on care partners, to receive requests for ministry from the clergy, and to request pastoral involvement with the team or a care partner as needed. Team leaders typically serve a one-year term after which another member assumes the role.

We have referred above and elsewhere to *care partners*. We use the term to designate the people served by a Care Team. They are not merely passive recipients of care and support. If caregiving is to be an experience that reaches its potential, it will be mutual. The parties to the relationship will both give and receive. Although the relationships may become quite close, it is a basic canon of Care Team ministry that caregiving ought not be consuming. Boundaries and limits must be set and respected. Attachments must be close enough to sustain commitment and distant enough so that team members are not immobilized when the relationship ends.

Although Care Team service is a ministry of a congregation, teams do not necessarily serve in isolation. Our organization, the Foundation for Interfaith Research and Ministry in Houston, Texas, promotes and supports Care Team ministry in three counties the size of a small state. Professional resources are provided to each congregation that becomes a partner in our interfaith caregiving network. One of our staff is assigned to each Care Team to provide comprehensive care and support of the team. The assigned staff member effectively becomes adjunct staff to the congregation, supervising and nurturing the team's ministries, helping team leaders to assess needs, drawing resources from the community to enhance the team's ministries, and reporting to the clergy. Finally, if a Care Team has sufficient resources and commitment to serve people who are not members of the congregation, our staff will present referrals from community social service agencies, hospitals, and other organizations in touch with people in need of care.

There are many nuances to Care Team ministry that go beyond the purpose of this book. Understanding that Care Team service as a ministry of the sponsoring congregation, minimal size, basic responsibilities of team leaders, priority of team meetings, caregiving as a mutual activity, and value of a partnership between a congregation and a central, coordinating organization should provide sufficient background for the subsequent chapters on AIDS Care Teams, Alzheimer's Care Teams, and Second Family Care Teams.

CUMULATIVE EXPERIENCE WITH CARE TEAM MINISTRY

This chapter began with a description of some of the events that led to the formation of the first Care Team and subsequent invitations to congregations to join our ministry with people touched by AIDS. When we began to reflect on the experiences of those first AIDS Care Teams, we imagined that this method of caregiving could renew congregational caregiving by embracing individuals and families with intense needs associated with a diagnosis or condition other than AIDS. Our first effort to make the concept more inclusive was in 1989. We thought that congregations could provide more comprehensive pastoral care of members by revising the model to support a GenCare Team. The term *GenCare* was a neologism created by combining *general* and *care;* a general care team became a GenCare Team. Four congregations began a GenCare Team ministry as part of the pilot project. All four disbanded within 26 months. Our analysis of the experience led us to two conclusions: (1) GenCare or general care needs were too nonspecific for people to be motivated or feel called to this particular ministry, and (2) requesting and accepting hands-on, in-home ministry was uncomfortable for many church members who were coping with significant health problems.

We began to look for a single condition, like AIDS, that produced specific, clear needs among patients or caregivers so intense that offers of assistance would likely be more readily accepted. Also, we looked for a condition that affected enough members of a congregation to evoke interest, understanding of the intense need, and a willingness to try to help. We chose Alzheimer's and other demential diseases to test whether Care Team ministry could serve others as well as it served AIDS patients. As with AIDS, Alzheimer's is a chronic, progressive disease that is ultimately fatal. Patients and their caregivers tend to become more isolated as the dementia progresses. Care is usually provided at home until the patient's condition deteriorates to a point where custodial care is required. Primary caregivers become increasingly exhausted physically, emotionally, and spiritually. Moreover, we could find no congregation that provided any form of consistent supportive ministry to members caring for loved ones at home with dementia. We began to promote Alzheimer's Care Team ministry in 1991. The first Alzheimer's Care Team was formed in 1992. Alzheimer's Care Team ministry is now an established part of our multifaceted caregiving ministry.

Encouraged by our new success with Alzheimer's Care Teams and the continued success of AIDS Care Teams, we returned in 1994 to the GenCare Team concept. We knew that the needs for Care Team support among frail seniors were great and would grow as the population ages. We knew, as well, that the presence and participation of seniors in church activities tend to decrease due to physical decline and other reasons (for example, lack of transportation). Often these faithful pillars of the church feel abandoned and forgotten as contact with the congregation dissipates. Family members who might be expected to provide basic care and support may be distant or dead. Contemporaries in the church may be similarly impaired such that their peer group may not be available or able to meet needs. Moreover, we knew that isolation from one's congregation was not limited to seniors. Younger adults with chronic impairments or overwhelming caregiving duties for a family member generate comparable needs for assistance and similar feelings of abandonment.

We observed that AIDS Care Team members and Alzheimer's Care Team members functioned and saw themselves as surrogate and extended family to their Care Partners. They were a second family to the people they served. We decided to reincarnate our proposed GenCare Team ministry as Second Family Care Team ministry. We thought that this designation built upon the metaphor of the church as family. The term *family* had theological and affective appeal. People could understand the "job description" of Second Family Care Team ministry because of their caregiving experience in their own families. The team would be a "second family" because, in most instances in which they would serve, biological family members were not available or were overwhelmed by the load of care. In addition, church leaders were becoming more aware of the number of members who were frail (mostly seniors), disease- or trauma-impaired (generally younger adults), or unusually burdened by the care of a loved one at home. Most clergy felt that the congregation could and should be a sustaining presence. Second Family Care Team ministry offered congregations an opportunity to expand their pastoral care in a way that did not duplicate one-to-one ministries if they existed, such as Stephen's Ministry, parish nurse ministry, or ministry to the homebound, hospitalized, or nursing home residents. Our Second Family Care Team ministry project is now the largest and fastest growing form of Care Team ministry.

We are inspired by the ministries of more than 6,000 laypeople that we have been privileged to observe from 1985 to June 1999. These dedicated men, women, and children have served on 110 AIDS Care Teams, 60 Second Family Care Teams, and 26 Alzheimer's Care Teams based in approximately 200 Christian and Jewish congregations that span the theological spectrum. They have been a sustaining presence to 1,850 people with HIV/AIDS, 361 people with Alzheimer's or another dementia, and 490 frail seniors and others. We began to count their hours of service in Care Team ministry in September 1988. In eleven years (September 1988—September 1999), Care Team members have reported more than 800,000 hours of ministry. We are convinced that this record is only a preface to the story of Care Team ministry as it is written in Houston and elsewhere in the nation. These quantitative measures capture the magnitude of the ministries that we have been blessed to share. A better measure and witness to the singular importance of these ministries is the testimonies of Care Team members, care partners, and church leaders whose lives have been enriched and souls have been refreshed through these caregiving relationships. In small congregations and large, Protestant, Catholic, and Orthodox, white, African American, and Hispanic, we have witnessed a renewal of community, a discovery of the blessings in bearing one another's burdens, and a deepened understanding of the identity and mission of the people of God.

Our experience with Care Team ministry is being replicated in many areas of the nation. Our early written work about AIDS ministry[13] and presentations at 35 local conferences and national meetings helped promote the Care Team concept, in general, and AIDS Care Team ministry, in particular. We seeded AIDS Care Team projects in Beaumont and Corpus Christi, Texas, approximately 90 and 200 miles, respectively, from Houston.

Our belief that the concept and model of ministry did not depend upon our personalities was vindicated through Associated Catholic Charities in New Orleans, Louisiana. Following a request for consultation with us in 1988, Associated Catholic Charities proposed to the Robert Wood Johnson Foundation a replication of our AIDS Care Team project in major urban centers, smaller cities, and rural towns in Texas, Louisiana, Arkansas, Oklahoma, and New Mexico. With multiyear funding from the Robert Wood Johnson Foundation, a Regional AIDS Interfaith Network was created with the conviction that the Care Team model could be duplicated in other areas of the country.[14] We learned at the first national meeting of AIDS Care Team ministries in Atlanta (November 1997), funded by the Centers for Disease Control, that AIDS Care Team ministries were active in approximately 75 locations in more than 30 states.

We are convinced that Care Team ministry will become even more prevalent as congregations and interfaith groups respond to the opportunities for ministry created by an aging population and a continuing epidemic of HIV/AIDS. AIDS Care Team programs are slowly becoming more inclusive caregiving ministries. Community-wide Second Family Care Team ministries are being developed by church-related nursing homes, hospitals, social and family service organizations in Washington, Wisconsin, Ohio, South Carolina, Minnesota, and Corpus Christi, Texas, following consultation with us. Similarly, we assisted an Alzheimer's care facility in Abilene, Texas, to sponsor a Second Family Care Team program with an emphasis on Alzheimer's care, further demonstrating concern about the devastating impact of dementia. The partnerships in ministry being created between congregations and church-related health care and social ministry organizations are forging a new appreciation for the mission they have in common and the contributions that each may make to the other.

This chapter began with the unfortunate story of one young man. Jay's AIDS diagnosis started us on a journey that has not yet come to an end. Our effort to learn quickly about AIDS in order to better care for him as he died proved hasty. Jay lived with AIDS for four years and two months, vastly longer than the six months that we expected. We continue to mourn his death, but we celebrate the caregiving that has evolved from the profound exchange—"The campus doctor thinks I have AIDS" and "I'm on the way."

CHAPTER 5

AIDS CARE TEAM MINISTRY

The Care Team concept and model evolved from our relationships with people touched by HIV/AIDS. From the first official days of the AIDS epidemic in June 1981[1] until April 1985 when AIDS became personal to us, AIDS had become a major threat to public health and the social fabric of the United States.[2] Fear was a common and understandable response. Much about the retroviral cause of AIDS (HIV or human immunodeficiency virus) either was poorly understood or unknown. Qualified scientific and medical statements often were seized upon by opportunists to advance a particular political, moral, social, or religious agenda. Rather than being subjects of compassion and care, people with AIDS more typically were condemned and neglected. Sex, drugs, disease, death and all of the strong feelings, beliefs, and judgments attached to them collided in a sensationalized AIDS crisis that tested the character of society and the identity of God's people.

The response of the church in general and individual congregations in particular to the opportunities for ministry created by AIDS during the first years ought not be criticized too harshly, in our opinion. It was impossible to know how long the epidemic would last or how many people would be caught in its grip. Typical American enthusiasm and an idolatry of scientific medicine prompted many to believe, or wish, that a quick "fix" would remove the threat. Questions about the transmission of HIV and the high cost to be paid if early assurances proved wrong gave pause to compassionate instincts. National and local religious institutions were torn between faith-based moral crosscurrents. It was difficult for many to determine how to be faithful to the commandment to love one another without compromising moral opinions about certain behaviors by which the AIDS virus is transmitted. While these and other issues were reviewed within the formal structures of faith, individual members tended to settle the issues for themselves. Most decided to sit this one out. A small but prophetic number began unrecognized ministries of sustaining presence primarily through volunteer service in secular organizations.[3] Perceptions of the church's early response to AIDS between 1981 and 1985 might be more favorable if the ministries of these individuals could be catalogued or if they had not been hidden from public recognition.

AIDS IN THE UNITED STATES

The epidemic to which AIDS Care Team ministry began to respond in 1985 is not the same epidemic on the eve of the twenty-first century. The needs of the typical person today with HIV/AIDS are markedly different in many respects from those the first AIDS Care Teams organized to meet. These changes have meant that AIDS Care Team ministry is a work in progress. The AIDS Care Team ministry that we created in 1985 is not necessarily appropriate for people with HIV/AIDS in 2000 or those who will follow within the next five years. It is impossible to confidently look beyond five years. Numerous factors could significantly affect the future course of the epidemic, including therapies, vaccines, drug resistance, virus mutations, demographics of the populations infected, social attitudes, government funding, and more. Nineteen years of experience with HIV/AIDS demonstrates that change is its only constant.

In some respects, there are reasons to have cautious hope that early worst case scenarios will not materialize. During the early years of the epidemic, the number of people being newly diagnosed with AIDS was increasing annually at a rate of 65% to 95%.[4] In 1996, the rising tide ebbed. New diagnoses of AIDS declined 7% from 1995. Deaths among people with AIDS also declined for the first time, down 29% from 1995. The number of deaths declined even more in 1997—down 47%

from 1996 (16,865 vs. 31,130). These decreases in morbidity and mortality are attributable to successful risk reduction and risk prevention education campaigns (particularly among men who have sex with men), wider use of medicines that prevent some of the AIDS-defining and life threatening diseases secondary to HIV infection, and combination anti-retroviral drug therapies that include protease inhibitors.[5] People with HIV/AIDS today generally are living longer and healthier than their predecessors. It is estimated that between 650,000 and 900,000 Americans are now living with HIV and AIDS. Approximately 40,000 new infections are estimated to occur each year and approximately 50,000–60,000 people with HIV disease annually progress to an AIDS diagnosis. HIV/AIDS is the second leading cause of death among adults aged 25-44.

HIV/AIDS is very much a local phenomenon. National data provide important information about the magnitude of the public health threat and a demographic picture of those who primarily bear its burden. These data, however, do not necessarily describe HIV/AIDS in Houston or any location. As of December 31, 1998, the Centers for Disease Control and Prevention report 688,200 cumulative AIDS diagnoses of which 52% were in four states (New York, California, Florida, Texas) and nearly 73% when the next six states or territories are included (New Jersey, Puerto Rico, Illinois, Pennsylvania, Georgia, Maryland). The ten most affected cities account for 43.3% of cumulative cases (New York City [109,050], Los Angeles [38,670], San Francisco [26,332], Miami [21,502], Washington, D.C. [20,121], Chicago [18,776], Houston [17,585], Philadelphia [16,123], Newark [15,426], and Atlanta [14,217]). HIV/AIDS is not evenly distributed geographically across the nation.

HIV/AIDS similarly is not evenly distributed demographically. AIDS was popularly associated with young, urban, self-identified gay men during the first years of the epidemic. Men who have sex with men[6] have accounted for the largest number of AIDS cases annually through 1997. However, the proportion of the cumulative total that this transmission route represents has been declining steadily for years reaching 33% of total adult (men and women) AIDS diagnoses by the end of 1998. This means, of course, that the number and proportion of new AIDS diagnoses due to other risks have steadily increased.

Injection drug use and heterosexual contact with an injection drug user accounted for 32% of new AIDS cases in 1997. This probably understates the actual percentage, since people tend to admit illegal behavior reluctantly. It is likely that the percentage of cases attributable to drug-related contact will increase as more of the "risk not reported or identified" cases (18% for 1997) are determined. Moreover, these shifts among newly diagnosed AIDS cases reveal in 1997 changes in the pattern of HIV infection that occurred years earlier. The time between HIV infection and AIDS diagnosis may be 10 or 12 or more years. It is widely believed that people are more able to modify sexual practices to reduce risks of HIV infection than to modify drug-use behavior. If this is true, AIDS will continue to become a disease more associated with the drug culture than the subculture of "young, urban, gay men."

HIV/AIDS has always been primarily an epidemic of young adults. Nearly 80% of all AIDS diagnoses have occurred among males and females between the ages of 13 and 44. Children under age 13 account for only 1.2% of cumulative cases. The actual and proportionate number of pediatric AIDS cases should continue to decline as more pregnant HIV+ women take advantage of medical protocols that significantly reduce a child's risk of perinatal HIV infection. This encouraging news overall, however, is tempered by recent studies of infection rates among young women. It is estimated that nearly half (44%) of new HIV infections between January 1994 and June 1997 in 25 states were among females aged 13 to 24. The majority of perinatally acquired AIDS cases continues to occur among African American and Hispanic children.

The burden of AIDS among African Americans and Hispanics is not limited to women. AIDS is becoming a disease of color, one of a synergy of plagues threatening poor urban neighborhoods. For the first time in 1996, African Americans accounted for more new AIDS diagnoses than whites, even though African Americans constitute only 13% of the total population. Of all new AIDS cases among adults and adolescents in 1997, African Americans accounted for 45%, whites 33%, and Hispanics 21%. Of cumulative AIDS cases from 1981 through 1998, 43.9% have been among whites, 35.8% African Americans, 14.9% Hispanics, and 5.4% other minorities. New AIDS diagnoses appear annually to be declining among whites, level among Hispanics, and rising among African Americans. African American women and children are being disproportionately affected representing 60% of all women reported with AIDS in 1997 and 62% of reported pediatric cases. The disproportionate future place of African Americans in the AIDS epidemic is foreshadowed by reports of new HIV infections. From January 1994 through June 1997, African Americans accounted for 57% of all HIV diagnoses in 25 states. Among people aged 13 to 24 diagnosed with AIDS between January 1994 through June 1997, 64% were African American. It is estimated that 1 in 50 African American men and 1 in 160 African American women are infected with HIV. AIDS is the leading cause of death for African American men and women aged 25 to 44.

Most AIDS Care Team ministries began during phases of the HIV/AIDS epidemic when the face of AIDS was white, male, young; and sexual contact was the means by which infection occurred. Gay enclaves were the urban centers of the epidemic. Treatments were few and relatively ineffective, death rates were high, and social services sparse. Care was callous. Abandonment and stigmatization were common social reactions. Institutional attention focused elsewhere. People literally were dying alone, scorned by a society whose moral light had dimmed. AIDS was publicized sensationally, and people with AIDS were stereotyped. The prospect of a protective vaccine was too distant to offer any hope for relief. AIDS Care Team ministries became a sustaining presence in the world of AIDS and the world beyond, demonstrating for all with eyes to see that God's place is among the broken.

Nearly two decades after the first cases of AIDS in the United States were described, much has changed. Improved treatments are enabling people with HIV/AIDS to live better and longer, if they can access the drugs, comply with the treatment protocols, and tolerate the side-effects of medications. Death rates are down. Government funding for medical research, treatment, and social services is in place, but lobbyists anticipate reductions from current levels in future years. Laws prohibit discrimination against people with HIV/AIDS. Fear of infection from casual contact has abated. Secular and religious institutions have adopted policies and developed programs to respond to the challenges of HIV/AIDS. Compassion has become more commonplace and visible as stereotypes have eroded following disclosures by celebrities and more extensive personal contact with a diagnosed person about whom one cares. Media attention is more restricted and restrained. AIDS is no longer the disease du jour. The first trials of candidate AIDS vaccines to determine efficacy are under way. But all is not well. The face of AIDS is still young but disproportionately darker, increasingly female, and linked to the drug culture (that is, infection due to intravenous drug use, exchange of sex for drugs or money to buy drugs, or sex with a partner who uses drugs).[7] The urban epicenters now are minority neighborhoods besieged by a synergy of plagues (HIV/AIDS, poverty, homelessness, joblessness, drugs, hopelessness, and more). AIDS Care Team ministries today are a sustaining presence among people even more marginalized and vulnerable than gay men were during the first decade of AIDS. The time for AIDS Care Team ministry has not passed, but its forms change as the epidemic changes.

AIDS CARE TEAM MINISTRY

Some of the care and support that AIDS Care Teams routinely provided in the early years is not needed now in many instances. The advent of government funding for social services available only to people with HIV infection has generated a dedicated and parallel social service system unique to AIDS that is the envy of most other disease groups. Private funding has provided for additional services and research. In urban areas, people with HIV infection typically are eligible for assistance with transportation, housing and rent assistance, food, medications, counseling, substance abuse treatment, home nursing care, attendant care, homemaker services, social work case management, medical care (if indigent), private medical insurance premiums, child care, day care, legal services, utility subsidies, hospice care, training to return to work, and more.

Many of these services were not available in 1985 and the years immediately following. AIDS Care Team members routinely provided transportation in their own cars, food from the church pantry, financial help from the church benevolence fund, basic bedside care or attendant care, help with chores in the home and yard, meal preparation, child care, respite care, service of an attorney in the congregation, emotional support, care of family and friends, nonproselytizing spiritual support, lay case management, advocacy, presence and comfort during the terminal event, sacramental ministry, and more. Care Teams were often the only resource available. The Care Team members were present because they felt called to be there. Their service could not be purchased. Their compassion was a gift and witness to the abiding love of God for broken humanity of every description.

Care Team members today may provide all of the care and support that their predecessors did. Public resources may not be sufficient to meet all care partner's needs, may not be available for other reasons, or may not be offered with compassion and respect. However, our experience is that as public resources provided by paid personnel increased, the range of Care Team ministry decreased. Care Team members serve care partners when they are available and free from other responsibilities. This means that they tend to be more available at nights and weekends, since the profile of most AIDS Care Teams consist of young men and women who work outside the home. Many of the needs of people with HIV/AIDS must be met during working hours when agencies and clinics are open. The availability of paid personnel and services to address these needs requires less intrusion into schedules of Care Team members.

The forms of care and support that are typical of Care Team ministry today continue to be classified as social, emotional, spiritual, and, at times, physical. Whereas Care Teams were accustomed to provide bedside care early in the course of the epidemic, such care now tends to be met by home health care agencies. Although Care Team members are grateful for the advances in treatment and the availability of resources, they tend to feel less needed. The sense of satisfaction for some also is less when ministries are less intensive because the care partners are more physically able to perform activities of daily living without assistance. The experience of physically caring for people wasted by disease, too weak to lift a glass of water is remarkably different from sharing social time with those fully able to meet all of their personal care needs. Nevertheless, social, emotional, and spiritual support and care are valid forms of ministry in which Care Team members experience reward because these are needs defined by care partners that add to their growth and enhance their sense of personhood.

Friends and family of some people with HIV/AIDS now are more willing to be present and supportive than in the 1980s. Relationships tend not to be severed as readily or irrevocably when a loved one or friend discloses his or her HIV infection. The social context of AIDS has changed enough to render faithfulness from family and friends less socially risky. It is rare now for a family to refuse to take a member home to be buried or to reject any involvement during a loved one's illness and death. This sort of abandonment and estrangement that scarred the early years of AIDS appears much less frequent currently. This is not to suggest, however, that relationships are unaffected when HIV/AIDS becomes a factor. People tend to relate differently under the shadow of HIV and an uncertain future. A new and unwelcome ingredient alters a relationship such that it can never again be the same as it was. Given the changes that may occur when disclosures are made, people with HIV/AIDS may keep their diagnoses secret. Secrecy requires an investment of energy to explain any HIV-related change to some other reason. Secrecy also has a moral cost when it entails deception. Feelings of betrayal of trust and remorse about dishonesty wound a person's integrity, as well as undermine relational intimacy.

People with HIV/AIDS may seek Care Team support in order to establish relationships that are not burdened by secrecy or fears of disappointment. Social activities with Care Team members who know the diagnosis are liberated from the burden of deception to be spontaneous and fulfilling. The relationships are safe, and so are the communications that attend them. Social support of people with HIV/AIDS tends to consist of simple pursuits and pleasures. Sharing conversation, window shopping, playing games, gardening, enjoying a meal, telling stories, listening to music, reading poetry aloud, discussing literature or politics, watching video movies, going to the theater, or any other activity may be a means to deepening relationships. The specific activity engaged in by a Care Team member with a care partner with HIV/AIDS is less important than the contribution that activity and the relationship that undergirds it makes to the growth of the parties.

Emotional support typically encompasses social support. While engaging in some activity, conversations tend to occur that reveal a person's emotional state. There may be subtle or overt expressions that include anger, sorrow, hurt, rage, grief, fear, regret, hope, joy, pleasure, contentment, anxiety, peace, and more. HIV/AIDS remains a disease of decline and recovery, although recent therapeutic advances have improved and prolonged the recovery cycles. Both positive and negative feelings accompany these changes. Being present to a care partner with HIV/AIDS, listening to his or her story, hearing his or her feelings are forms of emotional support. Care Team members are not counselors and neither are they responsible for or capable of fixing a care partner's problems. Care Team members are laypeople, responsible and able to be a sustaining presence through a care partner's journey with HIV/AIDS. They may do this, in part, by being faithful, present, compassionate, patient, attentive, nondirective, and nonjudgmental as they are entrusted with the intimate feelings of the people they serve.

A Care Team's spiritual support of a care partner with HIV/AIDS is nonproselytizing. It is rare that a Care Team's faith tradition corresponds with that of a person it serves. Most of the care partners our Care Teams have served have not been active in a church or synagogue at the time Care Team support was requested. Their congregation of childhood may have been inhospitable to the person they discovered themselves to be or intolerant of behaviors by which the stresses of life are sometimes escaped. Our experience is that people with HIV/AIDS may be separated from the church or synagogue but not feel alienated from God. Care Teams from churches or synagogues can be bridges by which care partners and their worshiping communities are reconciled. Care Team members may arrange a pastoral visit upon the request of a care partner. Spiritual support consists of supporting a care partner's spiritual journey along whatever paths it takes to whatever ends it seeks. No one can judge another person's relationship with God. We frequently suggest to AIDS Care Teams that if a care partner lives and dies with a sense of grace and peace because of the team's loving, nonproselytizing witness, they will have done well all that they can. Anything else is beyond the calling or power of Care Team members and in God's merciful providence.

Physical support continues to be part of a Care Team's ministry, although this type of care is much less intensive and frequent due to the availability of paid services and personnel. The physical support and care that an AIDS Care Team may provide is restricted to tasks appropriate for laypeople to perform. These may be simple forms of assistance, such as holding an arm while walking, bracing a care partner as he or she moves in or out of a chair, moving a care partner into a more comfortable position in bed, and other tasks that may be competently and safely performed by laypeople with a minimal amount of instruction and training. Care partners in locations where dedicated HIV services are not available or are limited may need physical care more than those in large urban centers with abundant services. It should be remembered that Care Team members are expected to engage only in ministries that are comfortable to them after appropriate instruction, including guidance about infection control.

As noted above, the scope of ministry provided by AIDS Care Teams has changed as services have proliferated. This does not mean, however, that Care Team relationships are restricted to prayer, sacraments, and funerals. Relationships between Care Teams and care partners continue to be rich experiences that contribute to the growth of the parties. The challenges faced by AIDS Care Teams today are different from those encountered during the 1980s. For example, many of the characteristics and intense needs of a certain segment of current care partners preexisted their HIV infections. Poverty, homelessness, addiction, criminal conduct, psychiatric problems, prostitution, and manipulation as a primary method of relating already were challenges that anyone faced when trying to provide support, care, or assistance. In many instances, these problems are as intractable as HIV infection. Alone or in combination, these tend to be complex and interrelated needs more appropriately addressed by experienced professionals than by inexperienced laypeople whose efforts to care will likely be ineffective. In short, it may not be in the interest of some people with HIV/AIDS to be assigned to an AIDS Care Team. Conversely, it may not be in the interest of Care Team members to attempt Care Team ministry with people whose needs are beyond their competence.

An appreciation for the changing environment of AIDS ministries helps us to avoid oversimplifying these special ministries or minimizing the multiple, major, interrelated problems that confront many people touched by HIV/AIDS and their caregivers, including AIDS Care Teams. Neither should a sober view of AIDS tempt us to think that the time for AIDS ministries has passed. It may be that the urgency for the church to befriend and defend people touched by HIV/AIDS is greater now than it was in the beginning. For example, consider the respective populations. When AIDS was so closely associated with gay men, the church faced a series of issues. Most notably, the church had to come to terms with its call to love and its propensity to condition compassion on assessments of moral merit. Teachings regarding homosexuality were regularly debated by 1981 when the advent of AIDS complicated the discussion. Scholars and laypeople on both sides of the issue engaged one another, sometimes in true dialogue and at other times in mutual harangue. God's regard for people who identify as homosexual, the morality of same-gender sexual relations, and conditions for church membership or leadership were routinely examined from the perspective of any discipline that might shed light on this rending issue.

One consequence of these discussions was that there were people inside the church who were kindly disposed toward gay and lesbian people. Many had concluded teachings that excluded gay and lesbian people were inconsistent, or even wrong. For these proponents of inclusion, people with AIDS were no different from all others stricken by disease in constituting a claim upon the church's compassion. The fundamental moral question about AIDS was the church's response to the command to love the neighbor, not judgments about the conduct by which HIV infection occurred. We are not taking sides in this debate. Our point is that there were advocates for gay and lesbian people in the church who extended their arguments to include a moral duty of compassion for people who are ill, even if they are gay, and even if the disease is AIDS. Nearly twenty years after the announcement of the first cases of AIDS, the church's turmoil over sexuality remains unsettled. If anything, positions have hardened on both sides. The church's compassion for people touched by HIV/AIDS has grown. Countless ministries and programs on local and denominational levels are tangible demonstrations that God's people may have trouble finding their way when faced with something new, but that God's spirit of love, mercy, and justice will lead those with eyes to see and ears to hear to a redemptive response.

The challenge to the church by AIDS during the 1980s was different from the challenge the church faces today. Where are the advocates inside or outside the church for people who inject or ingest drugs? Drug users are perceived to be morally weak, undisciplined, and responsible for many crimes against property and people. Seldom does one hear a sympathetic or informed word about them. Drug users seem easily characterized as "them," in contrast to "us" who enjoy greater favor with God. At least many in the church knew a gay or lesbian person, which provided some basis for extending compassion to gay men with AIDS. Few people, however, are aware of friends, family, or colleagues who rely on drugs to meet certain personal needs. Few have any basis in relationship to stimulate compassion for people whose HIV infection is related to the drug culture. Perhaps only child molesters are more reviled than people caught up in the drug culture. The truer test of the church's identity and mission with respect to the HIV/AIDS epidemic as its history grows longer may be its response to the new population most heavily burdened by AIDS. The test of the church's character may be more stringent when the matter of race is added. Will the church continue its commitment when the populations most burdened by HIV/AIDS is predominantly related to drugs, African American, and Hispanic? Will the segregated character of Sunday morning worship portend disregard for people who are out of sight, beyond intimate knowledge, and burdened by AIDS? The prophetic call to befriend and defend those whom scripture denotes as the "poor" takes on new meaning as HIV/AIDS enters a third decade in the United States.

In 1987, we were deeply involved in calling the church to compassionate and prophetic ministry as HIV/AIDS was sweeping across the nation leaving a path of human devastation in its wake. Through personal presentations and publications, we urged the church and God's people to remember and be faithful to their rich history of rising above ambivalence to affirm God's compassion for the oppressed, ostracized, marginalized, and defenseless in our midst. We recognized then, as well as now, that not all in the church are called to or graced by God to share ministry with people touched by HIV/AIDS. Neither is it the calling of every congregation to sponsor an AIDS Care Team ministry. We suggested several prerequisites to congregation-based AIDS ministry that remain appropriate more than a decade later.[8] Although the commentary may be different due to changed circumstances, the distinctive characteristics of AIDS ministry warrants careful consideration and preparation by a congregation considering AIDS Care Team ministry.

We suggested that preparing for AIDS ministry begin with individual and corporate self-examination. Risks remain part of AIDS ministry. The risks for HIV infection certainly are better understood today. Prudent conduct greatly reduces this risk for AIDS Care Team members. During 14 years of ministry to 1,850 people with AIDS by 3,800 members of AIDS Care Teams in our program, no single Care Team member has become infected. Appropriate orientation, training, and continuing education, coupled with good judgment, are critical for safe Care Team ministry.

The risk of AIDS Care Team ministry in a congregation is less about infection and more about perception. Through an AIDS Care Team ministry, AIDS becomes part of the congregation. All members of the congregation may not favor this special mission. Attitudes, feelings, judgments, and different priorities may contribute to resistance or opposition to an intentional and public embrace of people touched by HIV/AIDS. The fellowship of the congregation may be strained. Members touched by other diseases and needs may feel that a preference for AIDS implies indifference to other disease-related needs. These concerns may be addressed by appeal to Israel's prophets and Jesus who identified with those who had no one in a position of power to cry out on their behalf. Commitment to people with AIDS does not imply lack of concern for others impaired by other diseases or disadvantaged by other circumstances, nor does it elicit support of or antagonism to any lifestyle. Other ministries in the church may demonstrate the congregation's compassion and concern for needs unrelated to HIV/AIDS. An Alzheimer's Care Team or Second Family Care Team ministry may be one special part of a congregation's care of people burdened by illness. Multiple Care Team ministries in a single congregation provide an opportunity for people who feel called or particularly drawn to one category of need to be involved in a dedicated ministry consistent with that call or personal interest.

Care Team ministry by definition entails being present to people whose bodies are weakened or wasted by disease and where death is a common visitor. Ministry with the sick or dying is a calling that requires gifts that all do not have. Being with people whose lives are drifting away may be a stressful experience. The physical, emotional, social, and spiritual aspects of a Care Team ministry of sustaining presence may be as exhausting as they are rewarding. These features of Care Team ministry—AIDS, Alzheimer's, or Second Family—ought to be recognized and contemplated to determine if one can bear the pain and provide an effective ministry.

There may be discomfort of another sort in AIDS Care Team ministry. It remains true that few people served by one of our AIDS Care Teams are active in a church or synagogue. Their circumstances, living conditions, and lifestyles tend not to conform to a stereotypical portrait of church folks. AIDS Care Team members must be able to enter into these unfamiliar or offensive situations without judgment or condescension, entering into their experience, learning about them, loving them, and sharing their grief. All people engaged in AIDS ministry should meet on level ground: one person loved by God meeting another person loved by God; one person of inestimable value to God meeting another person of inestimable value to God; one vulnerable and mortal person meeting another vulnerable and mortal person. This encounter of persons, not stereotypes, is essential to a valid and effective ministry. Entering into the experience of others, as Jesus learned, may place one in uncomfortable or threatening surroundings. The command to love one's neighbors admits no exceptions. It may require courage to go there and to stay there, especially when being there places one in the presence of pain, suffering, death, and social stigma.

Courage and commitment are two sides of the same coin. Courage that lacks commitment may be too weak to redress injustice or too superficial to comfort and console. As people with HIV/AIDS live longer due to therapeutic advances, the relationship of an AIDS Care Team with a care partner similarly lengthens. The rapid cycle of introduction, multifaceted care of a weak and dependent person, and witness to a life prematurely ended is becoming less common. Caregiving relationships that were measured in weeks or months now may be measured in years. Establishing relationships apart from the coercion of near or total dependency presents different challenges to commitment for AIDS Care Team members. The sense of personal reward may be less intense when the threat to the care partner seems less tangible or immediate. These changes in the character and content of caregiving relationships suggest that a Care Team member's commitment to AIDS ministry should be more open-ended. Less frequent contact, less intense needs, and less turnover of care partners, within the total population of people with HIV/AIDS who are appropriately served by AIDS Care Team ministry, suggests that more time and personal dedication to this ministry may be required to forge bonds and secure relationships comparable to those rapidly established in the early days under the duress of critical need. The commitment required today includes an additional nuance that was missing in the past.

One's commitment to AIDS Care Team ministry will be tested sooner or later through one experience or another. Being part of an AIDS Care Team does not necessarily mean staying the course until the end of AIDS. After sharing ministry with one or many persons with HIV/AIDS, Care Team members may discover that their gifts for ministry would be better exercised elsewhere. No disgrace or failure is implied by this recognition. The Holy Spirit instructs and leads in discovering personal gifts and talents for ministry. Discipleship is a journey that may take many paths. Similarly, congregations are called to ministry in a particular place at a particular time. The gifts of a congregation may equip it to effectively serve one segment of the population with HIV/AIDS, but not others. And the season for AIDS Care Team ministry in a congregation may begin and end. Stewardship of a congregation's talents and openness to the leadership of the Holy Spirit guards against self-righteousness among AIDS Care Team members and ministries.

Caregiving is one form of a church's advocacy for people touched by HIV/AIDS. By being present, entering into relationship, and providing hands-on services, congregations proclaim the value, dignity, and personhood of people with HIV/AIDS. This example of compassion and respect reminds other institutions in society of the claims for compassion and justice of any disadvantaged member. Redemptive and prophetic Care Team ministries promote healing and reconciliation in a society fragmented by an AIDS-based fear, judgment, and estrangement. They represent God's will that the burden of oppression, in whatever form it takes, be lifted wherever it exists. This advocacy centered around the relief of suffering and estrangement summons individuals to compassion and institutions to justice. The presence of the church in the midst of AIDS sustains and heals by uniting factions in society separated by disease. An AIDS Care Team ministry promotes healing as people who may share little in common affirm each other's value, discover each other's inherent dignity, and experience the inclusive love of God. Servant ministry can be a powerful form of advocacy.

Confronting the discomfort that leaves people uninformed and at greater risk for HIV infection is another form of advocacy that an AIDS Care Team ministry may pursue based on personal experiences of meeting face-to-face the potential effects of ignorance and poor judgment. A congregation's AIDS ministry may include HIV risk avoidance or risk reduction education. Prevention is the best offense against the HIV/AIDS epidemic. Churches are positioned to communicate moral teachings about conduct by which infection may occur, as well as provide factual information about AIDS that includes guidance regarding risk avoidance or risk reduction strategies. Youth generally are thought to be most tempted to engage in behaviors that may result in infection. The disproportionate number of infections during adolescence that progress to AIDS in young adulthood supports this presumption. But curriculum planners should recognize that HIV infection among seniors is rapidly rising. Denying the threat to youth, accepting misleading stereotypes about seniors, or refusing to acknowledge the diverse repertoire of behaviors within any demographic group may have devastating consequences. Infectious disease is like a beacon in society that illuminates the private lives of its members and corrects stereotypes. Discussing AIDS and conduct that places people in jeopardy for infection may provoke controversy, but a price of silence may be death. Surely congregations can work through the concerns of all interested parties to find ways to care for one another through education that helps people to make informed choices about personal conduct.

Sharing one's story with AIDS may be one way to help people understand the broad swath HIV disease has cut across American society. AIDS Care Team members may recount their experiences with people they have served and the impact these relationships have had on their understandings of God and their lives. Members of the congregation not serving on an AIDS Care Team may find the courage to reveal how AIDS has reached into their families or circles of friends. Sharing these stories of personal encounter with AIDS will not occur if the congregation called to hear them is perceived to be inhospitable or indifferent. These are likely to be heart-rending stories of personal journeys marked by confusion, anger, bewilderment, pain, suffering, loss, and grief. They are likely, as well, to contain heart-warming anecdotes of joy, purpose, comfort, ecstasy, grace, and peace. Apart from the stigma attached to HIV/AIDS, the stories are not much different from those of others in the grip of any debilitating or life-threatening illness. They are stories of people confronted by vulnerability and mortality. They are stories of people capable of growth in the midst of decline. They are stories of grace in the presence of evil.

STORIES OF AIDS CARE TEAM MINISTRY

As we periodically review our encounter with HIV/AIDS, we feel sadness of unspeakable depth and joy of indescribable height. We are inspired by the love, compassion, servanthood, selflessness, tenderness, and humility of Care Team members whose discipleship lessens the burden of disease. We are saddened by the waste of life, the loss of relationships that contributed to our growth, and the human propensity to distance rather than embrace broken humanity. Stories in which we had a role and stories reported by others involved in our AIDS Care Team ministry illustrate the range of experiences, profound and trivial, that give content to the human condition. While Sunderland wishes that all of these stories had been collected and preserved in order to document the grace and growth that have been experienced, Shelp does not regret this omission in our history because the joyful aspects more easily overshadow the painful aspects when not confronted by them in print. Our first effort to humanize people touched by AIDS chronicled the stories of some of the people we met as we entered this arena. As initial experiences, these were formative and compelling encounters that helped to shape our understanding of the epidemic and the challenges it presented to the church and to individual believers. All of the people with AIDS whose stories we included in our first book are dead. One of us was with many of them when they died. From our personal ministries and those of Care Team members, we illustrate AIDS Care Team ministry.[9]

Andrew was representative of the first wave of people with AIDS. He was a young adult, white, gay, educated, employed, and personable. He attended church with his family while he lived at home in another city. When he moved to Houston to pursue his career and enjoy the company of other gay men, church and family were left behind. It wasn't that he didn't care about them. He felt unwelcome, even condemned, in a church that claimed he was beyond the love of God as long as he claimed his homosexuality. He was isolated from his family who were hurt and embarrassed by a son who, in their words, "defied God." His longing for God and his family persisted throughout his illness. The AIDS Care Team sponsored by a synagogue tried but failed to reconcile Andrew and his family. They were successful, however, in demonstrating God's love for him as they were present during his final hours.

The Care Team served Andrew for about a year before he entered his terminal phase. Their relationship consisted of social outings and light conversation more than bedside care and theological inquiry. A spiritual agenda was never introduced by Andrew in any direct way until he lay dying. He was a Christian, regardless of the judgment of his home church. The Care Team members were Jews. He never doubted their compassion. He enjoyed their company. He learned to trust them, respect them, and care for them. Perhaps he feared that talking about Christian faith with them would be pointless or offensive, even though he felt the presence of God in and through them. Suddenly his condition worsened. Gone were the days of merriment. But the delight the team and Andrew found in one another persevered. Andrew's elderly parents who lived in another city were alerted to his imminent death. They were physically unable to be present. They were deeply grateful for the commitment of the Care Team with whom they had spoken by phone many times during the course of their relationship with their only child.

Andrew's belief in God's faithfulness, presence, and love was vindicated by several team members who kept vigil by his bed as life slipped away. Narcotics eased his pain and induced peaceful sleep. He awoke periodically to be greeted by people who had become family to him. On one occasion, he asked the two team members who were present to read to him from the Bible. A Gideon Bible was found in the bedside table. The team members were not very familiar with the New Testament, but in respect for Andrew's faith, they randomly turned to one of the Gospels. Providentially they read passages from Luke, including the parable of the prodigal son. Andrew soon appeared to fall asleep again, but they could not be sure. So they kept reading. His reach toward God would not be frustrated by them. They were quite comfortable to be God's instruments of grace, even if grace was mediated through a tradition they did not embrace. They continued to read until Andrew breathed no more.

Nancy and Ned are 7-year-old twins. Ned is HIV+. Nancy is HIV-. Ned knows that he is sick, but he doesn't know the name of his disease. He receives care at a specialty clinic for children. He is doing remarkably well physically except that he is not growing as fast as his sister, and he doesn't learn as quickly. Ned was infected at birth. His mother has been absent for much of his 7 years of life. She has been in and out of prison for drug-related offenses and bad check charges since the children's birth. Short-term stays in drug rehabilitation programs seem to have no lasting effect. The twins' father is not known. Ned and Nancy live with Mary, their 78-year-old maternal grandmother in a two-bedroom, spotlessly clean duplex in a low-income neighborhood. She loves them deeply. Mary has a strong, simple faith. She knows that God has left her on earth to take care of these precious children. They are a gift, not a burden.

Mary, Ned, and Nancy have been served by an African American AIDS Care Team for two years. The team members look forward to every visit. They have become close friends with Mary. The children are delightful. Ned and Nancy love their Care Team friends. The team members marvel at Mary's energy. She is very involved with the children. She walks them to and from school each day. She helps as she can with their homework, always encouraging them to work hard and to be good Christians. Church is a big part of their lives. Mary takes Ned and Nancy to church and Sunday school every week. If there is an activity appropriate for them at church, school, or in the community, she has them dressed, scrubbed clean, and front and center. Mary wishes she could give them more. Her limited, fixed income affords the family few luxuries. Her husband is dead. Her other child, a son, is alcoholic. He helps Mary and the children as he can. Offers from the Care Team to obtain from the church financial help with utility payments are graciously declined. Mary is a proud African American woman, independent, and protective of these children. She doesn't worry about her future. But in private moments with Care Team members, her determination will yield to her private worry about what will happen to the children if the good Lord calls her home before they are able to be on their own. But then, her optimism and faith gain new strength. There is too much to do to waste time fretting about God's timetable.

Four members of the Care Team relate to Mary, Ned, and Nancy. The team members feel that they are "family" to them. They visit about once each week, often accompanied by their own grandchildren who play with Ned and Nancy. The family needs more than they will accept from the Care Team. If an offer is for the kids, Mary graciously accepts. If it is for her benefit, she graciously declines. A new school year brings new needs for clothes, supplies, and money. The team members gather uniforms from children in their extended families that will fit Ned and Nancy. Mary insists that Ned and Nancy's clothes that have been outgrown are exchanged so that those who gave also receive. Surely Mary would get by on her own, she has that strength of character and will. But life is better for her and the children because of the comforting presence of the Care Team who share her dreams for the children and her private worry. The team knows the family's secret, and it is safe with them. The team has fun with Ned and Nancy. Movies, McDonald's, parks, games, church socials, parties, and other activities that delight children fill their time together. At times, Ned is sick. Play is suspended. The Care Team's attention increases. They care for Nancy while Mary stays with Ned in the hospital. They visit Ned and reassure Mary of their faithfulness. In good times and bad, Mary, Ned, and Nancy are not alone. They feel the strong embrace of God's people. And God's people who are blessed to share life with Mary, Ned, and Nancy feel empowered to face their own uncertain futures because Mary, Ned, and Nancy have shown them how.

Robbie's world is quite different from Ned's. Robbie is 11 years old. He hasn't been told that he has HIV disease. He only knows that he's sick. Like Ned, his mom is in prison for selling drugs. His father is absent. No one ever speaks of him. The home in which he lives is "filthy." His 63-year-old fraternal aunt Beverly can't seem to keep it clean. She has her own medical problems, including morbid obesity. Beverly is disabled. Her income is low. Beverly's 82-year-old mother lives with her and Robbie. Other people stay in the home for a while and then they go. Some house guests are family, others are not. The home also is shared with dogs, cats, fleas, and roaches. In many ways, Robbie is on his own in a crowd.

Beverly is not very introspective or responsible. She tends to be pre-occupied with her troubles. Robbie is only one burden among many. But, Beverly is a survivor. The family has many needs unrelated to Robbie's diagnosis, but Robbie's diagnosis opens to them a world of opportunity for help. Beverly is very adept at manipulation. Almost every month Beverly will tell each of the Care Team members that she doesn't know how she will pay the overdue rent or utility bills. According to her, the family is only a day away from being on the street. Early in the team's relationship with Beverly and Robbie, they came to the rescue several months with funds from the church. The team learned quickly that Beverly is good at working the "system." Her interest in others turns on whether she can get something she wants from them. She trusts no one. Conversely, the Care Team no longer relies on her. The team is willing to help Robbie and his family, but they are not willing to be used. They invest most of their effort on Robbie. He is an active fellow in reasonably good health. He has learned to take his medicine without being monitored. He enjoys school, even though learning is difficult. Robbie relates to friends well, including his friends on the Care Team who spend time with him about twice each month. They take him to the park, the zoo, the Children's Museum, ice-cream shop, and his favorite restaurant—Dairy Queen. His face lights up when a team member asks if he'd like to go for a burger. Robbie has a big smile, a gentle spirit, and an uncertain future. One man on the team has developed a special relationship with Robbie. He has become the only stable man in Robbie's life. They enjoy "guy" talk—sports, cars, music, and more. Because they are not certain that their care and support is not misdirected by Beverly, the team regulates what they do, limiting most of their support to that which will directly benefit Robbie. For the team, Robbie is trapped and has few good options. They know that they cannot change his situation. They also know that if they terminated their relationship with Robbie, his good options would be fewer. So they persevere amidst the filth and stench, seeking nothing more than to see Robbie's big, warm, smile.

Susan and her 17-year-old daughter, Sandy, live in a county adjacent to Houston. Susan is 38 years old. Life has not been kind to this divorced mother. Susan has AIDS complicated by diabetes, pancreatic disease, alcoholism, and a history of drug abuse. A man lives with her. There is no evidence that Susan has lapsed back into drug or alcohol abuse since the Care Team has known her. She is no longer able to work. She has become a little woman, weighing only about eighty-five pounds. Despite routine fatigue, her days are filled by spending time at an activity program for people with AIDS about 30 miles one way by bus from her home. She has been served by an AIDS Care Team for about two years. They have watched her condition worsen. They also have watched Sandy's life spiral downward.

Sandy's behavioral problems have deteriorated in parallel with Susan's condition. Sandy seems unable to follow the rules or take responsibility for her life. She won't help Susan around the house. She prefers to hang out with her friends. Efforts to help her come to terms with Susan's disease or to prepare for her future are rebuffed. Nothing seems to satisfy her. When team members take her to a movie, lunch, or any outing, it is never quite right. She manages to find something wrong or unsatisfying. Accepting affection and being grateful for the kindness of others seem out of her reach.

Susan's home is similarly unacceptable to Sandy. Sandy runs away frequently, stays with friends or lives on the streets for extended periods, and tried unsuccessfully to live with her grandmother who is in poor health. Sandy has more or less raised herself. Discipline was lacking. Her self-esteem is low. She is overweight. She is withdrawn. She doesn't like going to school. If she has an opportunity or whim to do something else, she won't go to class. Learning is hard for her. Her relationship with Susan is so chaotic that Susan seems relieved when Sandy takes leave. The Care Team helped Sandy gain admission to a church-related home for troubled kids in another city. She ran away twice, refused to follow the rules, and finally was dismissed back to her mother.

Sandy acts out her feelings. She appears to have little appreciation for the consequences of her conduct. Occasionally Sandy will say something that suggests she is disturbed about her mother's diagnosis and not prepared for her death. The way she expresses her fear and frustration highlights her vulnerability for the Care Team members who try to work most closely with her. Sandy swallowed a bottle of Tylenol one night while at home. Her mother called the paramedics and the Care Team who met them at the hospital. This episode was greeted by Susan as one more attention-getting behavior by Sandy. Sandy's mother manifests a level of irresponsibility as well. She refuses to plan for Sandy after she dies. At some level she recognizes an early death as a possibility, but the affective threat is too remote to prompt any action.

The Care Team members who relate to Susan and Sandy have their hands full. Two members, in particular, have become quite attached to the daughter. They feel very sorry for her. They fear that she is incapable of protecting herself away from home. They foresee her being raped, drifting into prostitution, or drug addiction. Their instinct is to rescue Sandy. The team works monthly with these two about attachment and boundary setting. Without the discipline of the team, they would become overly involved, assuming responsibilities inappropriately, and attempting what may be impossible—taking control of Sandy's life. The team supports Sandy and Susan in several ways. They provide transportation when Susan goes to the doctor. They have helped identify and access social services in a county with limited resources. They visit both of them. Developing close relationship with either is problematic. The team members share little in common with Sandy and Susan, except that they are all white. Weekly contact generally consists of visits and social outings. They would like to develop a closer relationship with Susan, but she prefers to keep the team at arm's length. Any relationship with Sandy is difficult and perhaps not possible. Nevertheless, the Care Team is dedicated to Susan and Sandy. They can be relied on to keep their commitments to be present and compassionate to the degree they are allowed.

Carlos is 33 years old. He has been in the United States illegally for

19 years. He speaks enough English for basic communication but not conversation. Before becoming ill, he did the sort of work that others refuse to do at wages citizens refuse to accept. He has family in Mexico and a sister in Houston. Carlos has a taste for beer, and sometimes something a little stronger. Without a job, Carlos has no income. Without income, he has no place to stay. He has lived for short periods in several AIDS designated housing facilities. He doesn't follow the house rules and ends up being evicted. His sister sometimes talks her husband into letting Carlos stay with them when Carlos has no place else to sleep. His brother-in-law doesn't like having him around because he has AIDS. It usually isn't long before Carlos is on the street again.

Being homeless isn't Carlos's only problem. He is undocumented. Not being in this country legally disqualifies him from receiving services that are a safety net for other people with AIDS. Having a relationship with Carlos is a challenge. Communication is complicated unless one is fluent in Spanish. Some members of the Care Team assigned to Carlos speak Spanish well. Others who serve him communicate as best they can. Carlos calls his Care Team members on a social worker's phone at the clinic. He will arrange to meet the Care Team at a designated place and time. As often as not, Carlos doesn't keep the appointment. The bus will be late, or he'll miss it altogether. He'll call again, especially when things are going very badly and stay at the clinic until Care Team members arrive to respond to his urgent need, usually transportation to a service provider or to follow up on a strong lead for housing. When he connects with the Care Team, they enjoy spending time together. Food is a big part of their relationship. English language movies for entertainment are less feasible.

Carlos really opens up to the Spanish-speaking Care Team members. He talks to them about feeling alone in the United States. He has pulmonary tuberculosis. As long as he takes his medicine, he does well. When he is on the street, his medical compliance drops, he gets sick, and he becomes an infection threat to others. He is afraid that if his TB worsens, he will have to return to his mother in Mexico. She would take care of him, but there would be no treatment available for his HIV. He thinks he would die quickly. Carlos feels hopeless most of the time. Coping with all of his problems seems beyond his capacity. Getting drunk is a temporary escape. His world is beyond his control.

He tries to assert some control over his life by telling the Care Team leader which members of the team he wants assigned to him. When he is told that this choice is not his to make, his sense of impotency intensifies. He truly is an alien in a strange land with no one to cry out in his behalf. Nevertheless, Carlos holds onto his dignity. He has pride in himself and his appearance. By means that are not clear to the Care Team, he always meets them in clean, perfectly pressed clothes. Carlos is representative of a growing number of undocumented people who travel across the southern border. Unfortunately, his encounter with AIDS has made him a captive here. Fear of discovery and deportation haunt him. Trusting anyone is risky. His relationships with team members are still developing. He knows that they are trustworthy. They will not report him to the authorities. They help him in limited ways. Their friendship confirms the self-esteem that he maintains, represented by his meticulous attention to being clean and pressed.

Mark is married to Linda. They have one son. They live with Mark's parents in an exclusive suburb of Houston. Mark is 34, Linda is 22, Jeff is 2. Mark was matched with a Care Team late in the course of his disease. Linda is HIV+ but her disease has not progressed to an AIDS diagnosis. Jeff escaped infection. Mark's parents hid his diagnosis. They did not want to draw attention to their home by a variety of strangers coming and going. Absolute secrecy was required of the Care Team (a requirement easy to meet since confidentiality is a basic principle of Care Team ministry). This white upper-middle-class family were practiced at hiding a lot. They said little to the team members when they visited. When the team members arrived, they left.

Caring for Mark was a "strange" experience for the Care Team. Linda seemed in total denial. The advanced stage of Mark's disease seemed beyond her comprehension. She talked about how she and Mark had to keep going in order to raise Jeff. Her own weight loss and chronic fatigue were never connected to her HIV infection. She seemed to cope best with what was happening in her life by escape to her own fantasy world. As a consequence, Linda was always cheery, upbeat, chatty, and forward looking. The team members looked forward to their time with Linda. Their attitude toward Mark was a different matter.

Mark acted like a spoiled child. Relationships with him were going to be on his terms or not at all. Prior to becoming homebound, he attended an AIDS support group where he heard about the great relationships others were having with their AIDS Care Teams. Mark wasn't to be denied anything. He wanted one too. His anger and abuse were disproportionate to his wasted state. When the team met Mark, he weighed eighty pounds, was severely jaundiced, and very weak. He yelled at people as much as he talked to them. In his mind, he was doing the team a favor by letting them come. At times he would demand that the visitors stay in the room with him. Next time he would require them to remain downstairs. He wanted only one team member to be in the home at a time. Manipulation is easier this way. He was expert at making people feel sorry for him. Abiding by the team's rules for service was impossible. He wanted to set the rules, and they were constantly changing. The only thing predictable about Mark was his unpredictability.

He was assigned one of our best teams, probably to his dismay. Mark was accustomed to people explaining away and excusing his narcissism and self-absorption. He apparently was never held accountable in his life. He expected everyone to respond to his whim. Linda and Mark's parents excused his behavior because he was sick. Team members tried to overlook his abuse, too—after all, he had AIDS, despite the desire of everyone in the home not to acknowledge this fact. Another fact was unspoken. Mark was a substance abuser. It began in high school when the drug of choice was alcohol. Other oral and injected drugs came after. His life was so erratic that he couldn't keep a job. Dad and mom paid his way. Mark's addictions were just more dust to be swept under the carpet. The Care Team tried to continue their care, in part, because they had grown fond of Linda and Jeff and, in part, because they did not want to be defeated. Some team members tended to excuse Mark's continued abuse of drugs, prescription and off the street, while he was so sick. Finally, one night Mark directed the Care Team members to remain downstairs. He didn't want to see them. The phone rang. It was for Mark. He was heard to say that he would be at the open garage door. The team members watched him meet a person there, make an exchange, and return to his bedroom. The team members looked at one another and said, "We just witnessed a drug deal." It would have been easy to dismiss this incident. After all, he's dying, what can it hurt. But saner heads prevailed. This became the last time the team tolerated its care being abused. The team terminated their service. Within two weeks, Mark died. The team went to the funeral in support of Linda, who subsequently returned to live with her parents with whom she had a good relationship.

Caring, more accurately trying to care for Mark, was a learning experience. He was a user of drugs and people. He knew exactly how to manipulate people. He consumed a lot of the team's resources. Ten members were assigned to the family. Visiting in pairs, they would be present in the home two or three times each week for three hours. After it was all over, the team still is not sure that they weren't Mark's final scam.

In contrast to the bewilderment experienced by Mark's Care Team, consider the sense of accomplishment felt by another Care Team. Trish is a 26-year-old single mother of three children. She has known that she has AIDS for two years. No one is certain how Trish was infected. She says it doesn't make any difference. Trish and her three children, Sharon (age 5), Jason (age 4), and Jack (age 8), live with Trish's parents, both in their 60s. All of the children are healthy and HIV-. This is a low-income white family that barely gets by. Household income per month is slightly more than $600 from Social Security and food stamps. Trish's mother knows that Trish has AIDS. Her father has not been told. Her mother doesn't think he would understand. He knows Trish is quite ill, but her illness doesn't have a name.

The lives of these adults are focused on the three children. They will sacrifice anything and everything for their welfare. The Care Team is a safety net for them, albeit one with big holes in it. The team is pessimistic about Trish's future. She has lost a lot of weight. She is chronically fatigued. She is frequently ill with gynecological problems. Trish is intellectually limited. Keeping track of and following the complicated mix and dose of antiretroviral drugs is more than she can master. So she doesn't take them. Her parents are similarly incapacitated. None of the adults has had the advantage of an education. Much in life, not just a complicated medical routine, is too complex for them to negotiate. They live simply and lovingly together, asking for nothing. But for the children, they welcomed the Care Team into their lives. Trish's father thinks that they are just good church folks who want to help Trish because she is sick.

The team members who relate to this family have been proactive in propping up this crumbling family. They provide transportation to the clinic and social service offices. Food from the church pantry supplements their food stamp allocation and enables them to eat well all month. Small amounts of financial assistance are secured from the church benevolence fund in order to provide for the children. Otherwise the family will take something they own to the pawn shop. They help them to shop wisely. They entertain the children with movies and day trips to the beach. At Christmas, the team got the family adopted by a local grocery. A large fresh ham, frozen turkey, fresh fruit and vegetables, and bags full of canned, frozen, and dry food provided the best holiday meal they ever had and many more during subsequent weeks. These tangible forms of support, however, probably mean less to Trish, her parents, and her children, than the friendship and love that they experience so generously. Trish talks a lot to the team members. Away from her parents, she talks about her mistakes (unspecified) that resulted in her becoming infected. Her grief is less for herself than for her children and parents. She laments the lost experiences that too often are taken for granted: watching her children go to school, grow up, get married, have kids. She worries about what will happen to her children if her parents die or become unable to care for them. Will they be taken in by a good family? Will they be separated? Will they remember her? In quiet moments punctuated by tears, Trish pours out her heart to people who accept and care for her. There is no condescension. The Care Team and this family share a journey on a road leveled by AIDS and compassion. The team is grateful to know this family. They marvel at their resilience. They receive from people who have nothing else to give lessons about dignity, devotion, and love. Although they are grateful to be of such help to this family, they realize that when Trish dies their reason, as an AIDS Care Team, to maintain the relationships will end. They wonder what will happen to the children and the grandparents when they gently terminate their support. This certainty greatly motivates them to develop long-term solutions to the present needs that will persist. Then they can say good-bye and thank you with confidence that the hopes and dreams they all have for the children will have a better chance to be realized.

CONCLUSION

AIDS Care Team ministry now is more often family ministry than before. Ministry with single adults is not unknown, but it is less and less frequent. Care Team members are challenged to serve within family systems that are complicated. AIDS may be the precipitating need for relationship, but it is often interrelated to a variety of other social, emotional, and physical circumstances that draw Care Team members into broader supportive roles. Drawing distinct lines that separate AIDS-related needs from other needs is next to impossible. Ministry with a person with HIV/AIDS is somewhat akin to marriage—one doesn't only take on a spouse, one takes on the whole family.

Epidemiological trends suggest that the portrayals above will describe AIDS ministry during the next half decade unless therapeutic breakthroughs occur. The current cohort of HIV+ people is demographically different from the first wave of gay men. Their position in society is probably more marginal than that of gay men. The church remains obliged to be present with people touched by AIDS, but the outline of its ministries of sustaining presence may become more circumscribed without compromising the integrity of the ministry or the strength of the witness. A smaller segment of people with AIDS may be appropriately served by laypeople. This limitation may spur existing AIDS Care Team members to become more inclusive caregivers by evolving into a Second Family Care Team, which serves people with HIV and other frail adults. There are advantages to this evolution. First, AIDS Care Team members who are underutilized will have more opportunity to exercise their gifts for caregiving. Second, the congregation's Care Team may grow as members who feel no call to AIDS ministry but a call to caregiving are enlisted. Third, latent resentment in the congregation about preference being given to AIDS over other health-related support needs may be mollified. Fourth, members not sympathetic to AIDS may become so as they hear reports of other Care Team members. Fifth, Care Team members dedicated to AIDS are enabled to continue their specialized ministries within an enlarged support system.

We are not suggesting that a transformation of an AIDS Care Team into a Second Family Care Team ought to occur. Some congregations are located in neighborhoods where the burden of AIDS is growing heavier. An exclusive ministry with these families may be exactly what God calls them to create and continue. An AIDS Care Team ministry can be an effective mechanism for demonstrating a congregation's concern for the troubles that burden its neighborhood. This form of compassionate engagement reveals a congregation's prophetic and servant identity. And as the temptation grows among other societal institutions to turn away from AIDS, the faithful and prophetic presence and advocacy of congregational AIDS ministries will constitute a powerful witness for justice and mercy that cannot be silenced and is not governed by trends, prejudices, or public opinion.

CHAPTER 6

ALZHEIMER'S CARE TEAMS

As we began the expansion of the Care Team concept to assist caregivers of family members with dementia, our first inquiries were directed to the largest Houston congregations (the so-called megacongregations), since they would have the highest number of affected families as well as the greatest resource of potential Alzheimer's Care Team members. We began to recognize three trends. As our inquiries broadened, the impression that clergy and other congregational leaders lacked information about the nature and scope of dementia-related issues was confirmed. Second, as caregivers increasingly were overwhelmed by the growing demands of care for their disabled loved ones and all their energies were needed for these tasks, they had neither the time nor effort to spare for other commitments, including more than nominal congregational affiliation and attendance. Third, as we became aware of the course Alzheimer's disease typically takes and the response patterns of family caregivers began to emerge, other concerns were added to the story. We learned the impact of the disease on caregivers' lives, the unending torture evoked by their loved ones' declining awareness of reality, and their tendency to hide increasingly bizarre behaviors from public view. It was not necessarily that congregations failed to care. Many families were reluctant to disclose the deepening crises caused by the onset of a demential disease. Some families seemed to "hide" their afflicted members, were unable to identify their needs to others, declined help when it was offered, yet felt overwhelmed by their perception of being shut out and forgotten, even abandoned.

Becoming aware of the complex nature of the disease is the first step toward responsible and responsive pastoral care of dementia-afflicted families. Yet in 1991 when we began to explore the need for dementia-related Care Teams, we could not identify any clergy whose familiarity with dementia in general and Alzheimer's disease in particular had led to structured, congregation-based programs to minister to affected families. This was the case even in smaller, one-pastor congregations in which it reasonably could be assumed that the pastor and congregation knew the handful of families whose lives were shattered by dementia and shared their burdens by providing in-home support. In larger congregations, staff members questioned the need for such a program, since they knew of few families who would be served. They manifested little knowledge of the range of demential diseases, and assumed that any families so afflicted were receiving support. Our perception of the minimal roles of congregations and their clergy is borne out by the lack of references to either in Miriam Aronson's review of Alzheimer's disease, published in 1988 as "an in-depth, comprehensive guide" drawing on the combined knowledge of the Alzheimer's Association and 26 specialists. It contains no references to congregations as a resource and only 3 lines to clergy, including: "(Some) clergy may provide guidance and counseling in some cases."[1] Either response to the overwhelming nature of dementia was perceived as a complex, demanding task beyond their resources that evoked a sense of powerlessness on the part of congregations and clergy, or, on the assumption that there existed sufficient community resources to meet families' needs, there was no call for congregational action.

Nevertheless, some clergy agreed to assess the need in their congregations by announcing the possibility of forming Alzheimer's Care Teams, using pulpit and newsletter announcements to elicit inquiries. Responses were few and disappointing. The scarcity of responses from afflicted families seemed to confirm clergy assumptions that there was no problem, or that it was small and not urgent. Yet other inquiries by our staff contradicted these findings. Books and journal articles referred to the estimated number of 4 million dementia-afflicted families and chronicled their desperation. This was reinforced by interviews with caregivers referred to us by community agencies as news of the intended project spread. Many caregivers stated they felt their congregations had abandoned them, and some expressed outrage at the absence of support. They had given up hope for a positive response from the one source to which they believed they could look for help.

Gradually, the barriers to bringing together the resources of congregations with families open to receiving their care and nurture were overcome. Soon, Alzheimer's Care Teams were ministering to member families while expanding their vision to care for care partners in their neighborhoods who lacked congregation affiliation. Congregants joined Alzheimer's Care Teams for reasons similar to those reported by members of AIDS teams. We had learned that the people most likely to care for people with AIDS already had some idea of the nature and progression of HIV disease, usually because of direct contact with a family member, friend, fellow congregant, or colleague whose needs had struck a sympathetic chord. Similarly, members of Alzheimer's teams joined because of an awareness of the havoc the disease was wreaking in the lives of families and friends. Other members joined not from personal awareness of a family's needs, but because they had been looking for a place of ministry and responded when challenged by stories of the needs of these families.

ALZHEIMER'S AND RELATED DISORDERS (ADRD)

Dementing diseases are characterized by a range of functional impairments that include progressive loss of intellectual abilities, including memory, judgment, capacity for abstract thought, and other higher levels of activity that result in changes in personality and behavior. The 1980 revision of the Diagnostic and Statistical Manual (DSM-III) uses the term "organic mental disorder" to refer to suspected or diagnosed abnormalities of brain structure that result in loss or destruction of brain functions which may be short-term or permanent. Alzheimer's disease (AD) accounts for 38% of demential diagnoses, and is the most common diagnosis, followed by multi-infarct, or stroke-related, dementia (23%), nonspecific dementia (11%), Parkinson's disease (8%) and traumatic brain injury (8%). Six percent suffer from other degenerative diseases/disorders, including Pick's disease, ALS (amyotrophic lateral sclerosis or Lou Gehrig's disease), and Huntington's disease. In some instances, demential conditions result from clinical depression or from various medications, and is relieved when medication is discontinued or dosages are reduced.

Multi-infarct Dementia

An infarct or stroke occurs when the blood supply to an area of the brain is cut off and an area of tissue is destroyed. Strokes may be caused by arteriosclerosis ("hardening of the arteries"), when a blood vessel in the brain weakens and bursts, and when an embolus (a piece of debris from a clogged artery) breaks off and, if it reaches the brain, blocks a blood vessel. A series of small or large strokes that destroys a number of areas of brain cells may result in a "step-wise" loss of memory, ability to make decisions, and carry out simple instructions and tasks. Dementia increases with the cumulative effect of a number of these small strokes. Multi-infarct dementia must be ruled out before a group of symptoms can indicate an Alzheimer's-type dementia. Approximately 20 percent to 25 percent of dementias are caused by a combination of Alzheimer's disease and multi-infarct disease.

Parkinson's Disease

It is estimated that one million Americans, or approximately 1% of the population over the age of 55, suffer from Parkinsonism.[2] The common factor that leads to a diagnosis is the injury and gradual impairment of a particular set of brain cells in the substantia nigra, resulting from the depletion of a chemical substance known as dopamine. The onset is usually so gradual that both patients and family members are unaware of problems until a number of symptoms become difficult to ignore. Symptoms include trembling of the limbs, muscular stiffness, and slowness of body movements. Recent investigation indicates that some people with Parkinsonism develop dementia, although this condition may be due to medication, and often is relieved when medication or dosage is changed. Some patients exhibit symptoms of both Parkinson's and Alzheimer's diseases.

Huntington's Disease

An inherited disease, Huntington's is manifested in movement disorders characterized with frequent involuntary movements of all body parts. Dementia, when present, usually is found late in the course of the disease.

Less Familiar Dementias

Patients with Pick's disease often have behavioral symptoms that include social inappropriateness, such as loss of modesty and sexual acting out, although their memory may be only moderately impaired. The incidence of dementia in Binswanger's disease is low, and is always associated with hypertension. Similarly, sufferers from Creutzfeldt-Jacob disorder, an extremely rare disease that usually follows a two-year course, may also manifest symptoms of dementia. Dementia may also result from clinical depression or from various medications and may be relieved if dosages are reduced or discontinued.

It is usual to group all of these diseases under the term Alzheimer's and Related Diseases (ADRD), which is well established as the referent for personality and behavioral dysfunction described as dementia. This more inclusive term will be used throughout this chapter, except where reference is made specifically to Alzheimer's. Care Teams assisting caregivers of loved ones with ADRD diagnoses are referred to as "Alzheimer's Care Teams."

Alzheimer's Disease

Current research indicates the possibility of diagnostic tests that may facilitate diagnosis of Alzheimer's disease (AD) early in the course of the illness. Until this goal is achieved, diagnosis is confirmed only by examination of brain tissues during autopsy. At present, a diagnosis of possible (or probable) Alzheimer's disease is made only after other dementia disorders have been ruled out. A family member of an Alzheimer's patient described the disease as "a disease of exclusion: When someone begins to act strangely, confused, forgetful, he or she is tested to exclude what the problem is not!" What is left—what is—may then be Alzheimer's.[3]

Dementia refers to damage to the brain that results in the loss of thinking or reasoning capacity and, subsequently, in the ability to make sense of what the patient sees or hears, or to remember what was said or done as recently as the previous few minutes or hours. As the process of communication between the brain's nerve cells breaks down, nerve cell dysfunction, loss of connections between cells, and death of some nerve cells follows. Typical indicators of Alzheimer's disease include memory loss, loss of cognition and related behavior, and increasing dependence. Often people in the initial stages of AD think less clearly and forget names of familiar people and common objects. Later in the course of the disease, they may forget how to do simple tasks like washing their hands. As short-term memory is lost, the ability to perform familiar tasks falters. As the disease progresses and language and reasoning faculties fail, the patient's judgment is impaired. In some instances, emotional outbursts and disturbing behaviors, such as immodesty, wandering, and agitation, may occur. In the most severe cases, the ability to recognize close family members or to communicate at all is destroyed. The person becomes totally dependent on others for care. Finally, the disease becomes so debilitating that patients are bedridden and likely to develop coexisting illnesses. Most commonly, people with AD die of pneumonia.

SYMPTOMS THAT INDICATE THE
PROGRESS OF BRAIN DYSFUNCTION

Forgetfulness   Memory Loss
Inability to handle everyday tasks
Tendency to forget where items are placed
Tendency to forget names

147

	Changes in personality
	Withdrawal from social contact
	Neglect of appearance or housework
Confusion	Forgetfulness increased
	No recall of recent events
	Rapid mood swings
	Distress when unable to communicate
	Inability to perform routine tasks
	Agitation, weeping
	Stubbornness, resistance to requests
Dementia	Inability to recognize sensory stimuli
	Inability to recognize oneself, spouse, children
	Continued repetition of movements, tasks, and words
	Incontinence
	Catastrophic reactions
	Occasional loss of consciousness[4]

Alzheimer's disease (AD) is the fourth leading cause of death among adults, with 100,000 deaths annually. It affects primarily people aged 65 years or older, but may strike as early as the mid-30s. The prevalence of AD doubles every five years beyond the age of 65, until by 85 years, approximately half of this group has symptoms of dementia.

AGE GROUP	65-70	70-75	75-80	80-85	85+
INCIDENCE	3-4%	6-7%	12-13%	25%	50%

The threat represented by these data is apparent in the expected increase in the number of people who in the next century will live beyond 85 years. Now approximately 4 million, the number of Americans aged 85 and older is expected to total 8 to 9 million by 2030, according to the Bureau of the Census. Some demographers think the number will be much higher. The U. S. Department of Health and Human Services, through its National Institutes of Health, stated in 1998: "AD is a major health problem and expense for the United States. Until researchers find a way to cure or prevent AD, a large and growing number of people, especially those who live to be very old (85+), will be at risk for AD. Providing and financing the care of this growing older population will increase the strain on our already burdened health care system."[5]

Disease progression may take from 2 to 20 years before death occurs; on average, patients live for 8 to 10 years after they are diagnosed. Estimates of the number of people who suffer from a dementia-related disease vary widely. The 1995 Progress Report on Alzheimer's Disease published by the National Institute on Aging referred to a current estimate of 4 million Americans diagnosed with ADRD, that is, 1 in 70 of the population.[6] When Alzheimer's disease is differentiated from other types of dementia, estimates range from 2.4 to 3.1 million.[7] This estimate correlates with a 1988 study in which R. Brookmeyer and others estimated the prevalence of AD in the United States at 2.32 million. Of these individuals, 68 percent were women, twice the rate for men. The proportions do not signify that women are more prone than men to develop AD; the higher numbers of women reflect the higher proportion of women at older ages due to lower mortality rates. Brookmeyer demonstrated that age-specific incidence rates of AD rise steeply in the seventh and eighth decades of life, with a mean of 4.3 percent between 75 and 79 years to 28.5 percent over the age of 90 years. Approximately 43 percent of individuals with Alzheimer's disease are 75 to 85 years of age. It is estimated that there are approximately 360,000 new AD diagnoses each year.[8] As an indication of the variance in estimating incidence of ADRD, Evans and others reported rates in people over 65 years of age at 10 percent, rising rapidly with aging to 40 to 50 percent of people over 85 having symptoms of AD.[9]

Distressing as these data are, given the lack of readiness of most congregations to provide in-home care for ADRD-affected families, projections through 2050 are even more alarming: 8 to 14 million may be affected by dementia.[10] The effects of improving health care, exacerbated by the population bulge as baby boomers reach old age, will produce sharply increased incidence of ADRD as more people live into

149

their 80s and 90s. Statistical projections of population growth indicate dramatic increases in the number of people who will live beyond 85 years. Whereas the 1990 census recorded 31 million individuals aged 65 or older, including more than 3 million over 85 years of age, it is predicted that within two generations there will be 60 million over 65 years. Of this elderly population, 8 to 13 million will be 85 or older, and over one million people will reach 100 years, compared to approximately 36,000 in 1990.[11] (NOTE: Readers will note discrepancies in estimates of cohort sizes and target dates in this chapter and again in chapter 7 because projections of the number and characteristics of age groups in the American population vary from researcher to researcher. Differences illustrate the imprecise nature of the methods employed, but do not undermine the reliability of the major conclusion, namely, that based on present trends, the proportion of the over-65 population will increase dramatically.)

On the basis of the National Institute on Aging estimate of 4 million people with ADRD, approximately 40,000 people are affected in a metropolitan area of 3,000,000 such as Houston; or a city of 300,000 would include 4,000 families struggling to care for loved ones with dementia. To bring the issue closer to the local church, approximately 7 families may be afflicted in a congregation of 500 members, and in a "megacongregation" reporting over 10,000 members, as many as 140 caregivers may be faced with the daily burden of caring for a dementia patient. ADRD costs the nation approximately $80 to $100 billion per year. Since Medicare and private health insurance do not cover all types of care families need, most of the costs are borne either by Medicaid or by the families themselves.

Awareness of Alzheimer's Disease

Public awareness of the impact of a dementia diagnosis in the lives of patients and their families is growing slowly as the media portray the situations families face, books describing the disease and its consequences are published, and news stories provide accounts of research into dementia, its causes, and outcomes. The expansion of both daycare and residence facilities in the last decade, particularly by the for-profit sector, indicates a growing societal response. Nevertheless, a continuing pervasive lack of awareness on the part of the general public is characteristic not only of the clergy but even of many segments of the health care system. Rochelle Lipkowitz noted that many health care personnel have at best a fragmented approach to meeting the needs of either patients with dementia or their caregivers.[12] Lydia Greiner and David Snowdon report that 15 to 20 percent of family members fail to recognize the symptoms of dementia in individuals whose diagnosis was confirmed by cognitive and memory tests, and a slightly lower percentage reported dementia in family members for whom that diagnosis was subsequently excluded. Their finding that registered nurses familiar with dementia symptoms failed to recognize dementia in approximately 20 percent of the patients they examined is disturbing.[13]

THE DAUNTING TASKS FACED BY CAREGIVERS

Illness or disability of a family member inevitably affects the entire family as members' routines are changed to accommodate the ill or disabled loved one and concern grows as medical or physical status worsens. This is especially the case for family members who become primary caregivers and assume the bulk of responsibility for care. From this perspective, dementia differs from other disorders only in the degree to which it becomes an affliction of the *family*. That is, the case can be made that ADRD-affected families experience additional and more intense suffering because the usual illness-related concerns are exacerbated by the complication of neurological changes of dementia.

Accepting the Reality of the Diagnosis

As with any substantive loss or change, the realization of a loved one's mental deterioration is accompanied by grief. In essence, the marriage relationship "dies" as the impaired spouse is unable to contribute to the building of the relationship and to return the love the

151

caregiver offers. In the case of an adult child caring for a parent, child-parent relationships are impaired, then lost, as the roles are reversed: adult children fill parental roles, relating to parents as dependent children who no longer are capable of the familial relationships to which they have been accustomed. L. W. Morris and others studied the impact of an Alzheimer's diagnosis on healthy spouses who now serve as caregivers. They stated that acceptance of the diagnosis is often so emotionally painful that many spouses choose to ignore or deny the reality of the loved one's deepening dementia. Each day holds unexpected challenges and losses of personal control that are added to the problems that are anticipated in the light of the patient's known mental and behavioral deterioration. For the remainder of loved ones' lives, caregivers' physical and emotional health are at risk. Once the diagnosis has been acknowledged, caregiver depression and stress are highly correlated with caregivers' perceptions that the situations they are facing will continue and may be expected to affect all areas of their lives. The study is significant in that the researchers found that depression and strain were significantly correlated with caregivers' perceived lack of control over their own emotional reactions as well as over the dementia sufferers' behaviors.[14]

Role Captivity

Deterioration of patients' mental states results inevitably in the loss of the ability to relate at a cognitive level to ADRD-affected individuals, whose growing physical and emotional needs create a prison in which caregivers are captive to their responsibilities. Bryan and Geoff became the sole support of their father, Vic, after their mother deserted her husband when his Pick's disease symptoms could no longer be ignored. Vic had been a brilliant architect whose creative designs were visible in many of the buildings in the city. They grieved the loss of his intellect and creativity, but grief was forced into the background by the daily grind of his care. They placed him in a daycare center in order to continue working, but his wandering behaviors became their biggest concern. They juggled their work schedules in order to take him to and from the center, but his disruptive sleeping schedule was a more urgent threat. He could still manipulate the door locks despite his confusion, and on two occasions had left the house during the night and become hopelessly lost in the neighborhood where he had lived for forty-three years. Their only solution was to place a mattress across the front door, sleeping there in turn so Vic could not wander away. They had become their father's keepers, and had changed their lifestyles accordingly, imprisoned by his illness.

Caregiver Resentment

Caregivers' loss of independence, accompanied by frustration due to the impaired family members' behaviors, may lead to periods of irritability that can deteriorate into anger. Such responses can be evoked by the most trivial of incidents. For example, when Jill was asked how she might use opportunities for respite, she replied: "I really need help for just two hours each month. Harold stands at my shoulder from the moment he is dressed until I put him to bed. Can you imagine what it is like to have your spouse standing right at your shoulder hour after hour, day after day! That can get pretty wearing, especially when I go to the bathroom. I can never close a door against him—he either whines, cries, or recently, hammers on the door with his fists till I open it. I miss my privacy. When I sit down to write the checks for the monthly bills, Harold sits beside me, notices the check book, and snatches it, scrawling on the check form. I try to be patient, taking the book from him to continue, only to have it snatched from my grasp. I guess he has some vestige of memory from the time he always paid the bills. By the time four or five check forms have been trashed, I throw it across the room and shout at him. If I had some help for two hours at the end of each month so I could shut the door and get my checks written, perhaps I wouldn't get so angry with him." The Care Team's commitment to Jill began with two visits each month, but grew quickly to two per week as she realized the benefits of the respite the team afforded her. Jill's care of Harold was more considerate, and she became more patient with him as respite breaks from his care relieved much of her stress.

153

Caregiver Guilt

The inability to sustain an attitude of care following outbursts at impaired family members often results in bouts of disabling guilt. Aware that patients have few if any inhibitions—the previous restraints on behavior have dissolved with the growing severity of dementia—and their behaviors are not directed with the intentionality of rational adults, caregivers struggle with conflicting emotions. Caregivers who are ashamed because their irritability or anger is out of control may decline offered respite because they are ashamed of their behaviors and believe they do not deserve periods free from their impaired family members. With this self-punishment, the anger and the guilt multiply.

Caregiver Loss of Control

Few ADRD caregivers are able to afford the types of support that would free them, even if briefly, from the burden of their responsibilities. Apart from the high cost of nursing-home placement, even one or two hours per week of daycare may be beyond a caregiver's resources. In such instances caregivers either are relieved by other family members, or must carry the entire responsibility unaided. Julie was the sole support of her mother and father, Elizabeth and Frank. Elizabeth's health deteriorated because of the stress of caring for Frank, whose Alzheimer's was now well advanced. Dependent on public transport, Julie sought the help of neighbors to sit with her parents in order to keep her own clinic appointments. If she was unable to obtain a sitter, her appointments had to be deferred. When Elizabeth developed symptoms that her physician said required hospitalization, she informed him that it would need to be delayed—her daughter could not care for Frank and still tend to her three children. It would be three weeks before a distant family member could arrive to care for her husband. The loss of control experienced by caregivers forced to resign from their employment in order to care for family members, or to defer their own medical care because they have no alternative, is likely to be enervating, exacerbated by the fears that their financial resources and their health may not be sustained.

Caregiver Isolation

As with families caring for members with other chronic and terminal diseases, ADRD-affected families not infrequently experience loss of socialization opportunities due to abandonment by family members and friends. Susan Sontag points out that many chronic and terminal conditions have been so stigmatized that both the patient and the family are isolated from customary social supports. Writing in the late 1970s, she noted that cancer had displaced pulmonary tuberculosis (TB) as the "disease that doesn't knock before it enters." When diseases are mysterious or their causes are not understood and the ministrations of doctors remain ineffective, they are thought to be "insidious, implacable thefts of life."[15] According to Sontag, the metaphoric language used to speak of cancer and TB has a stigmatizing effect, serving to deter others from intimate contact with the family. The painful realization that they have been marginalized further immobilizes caregivers. Sontag's characterizations and families' experiences of isolation are equally true of ADRD. Anne, whose husband had advanced Parkinson's, said: "I was too humiliated to ask for a ride to church when no one offered to drive me. I felt an outcast."

Loss of Health

The effects of loss of control over one's life, autonomy, self-respect, dignity, relationships with peers and even family members, coupled with the growing sense that other people are too busy with their own lives to contribute time and energy, are cumulative. One result is often loss of emotional stability and physical health. Morton Lieberman and Lawrence Fisher surveyed the effects of chronic and persistent stress, exacerbated by concomitant decrements in personal health and well-being, experienced by caregivers of family members with ADRD.

They determined that for spouses of dementia sufferers, the more severe the illness, the higher the spouse's levels of anxiety and depression, and the lower the caregiver's sense of well-being. Among the accompanying losses and changes, high levels of perceived burden, a disrupted family life, financial burdens, and psychological problems that included depression, disturbed sleep, severe fatigue, anxiety, and feelings of hopelessness about the future abounded.[16] Predeceasing the ADRD patient becomes one of the greatest fears of spousal caregivers, further adding to their sense of insecurity, loss of control, and dread.

Depression

Caregiver depression is a constant theme running through all research into the emotional problems faced by ADRD caregivers. C. G. Shields found that nearly 50 percent of the incidence of caregiver depression could be traced to responses of anger and sadness of extended family members expressed towards primary caregivers.[17] E. Morrisey, J. Becker, and M. P. Rupert reported that whereas caregivers responsible for the full-time care of a dementia-impaired spouse evidenced a negative impact of the patient's disability level on the caregiver's marriage and recreation, the reverse was true when caregivers continued employment outside the home. Employment was the only life area in which the availability and mobilization of coping resources affected caregivers' levels of depression. This result was confirmed by later research indicating that "while mobilized coping resources (social activity level and homemaking activity level) were correlated with depression among homemakers, none of the indicators of mobilizing coping resources was correlated with depression among those who continued working."[18] The fact that working caregivers had significant interests and outlets outside the home suggests one explanation, according to R. A. Pruchno and N. L. Resch. Problems begin to emerge for those caregivers who lose this outlet in order to care full time for the dementia sufferer, if they cannot afford paid in-home assistance with activities of daily living and have no other source of respite. When caregivers' health begins to decline, or worse, declines rapidly, or when emotional investment is linked with greater spousal impairment and/or reduced availability of assistance with homemaking tasks, the likelihood of depression rises significantly.[19]

Impact on the Marital Relationship

It is not surprising that the quality of the marriage relationship is affected by the onset and steady deterioration of mentation due to ADRD. L. K. Wright found that, compared with a control group of "healthy married couples," caregivers of Alzheimer's patients differed with respect both to companionship and marital quality. Only 27 percent of the Alzheimer's-affected couples versus 82 percent of the well couples were sexually active. Sexual activity was especially problematic for female caregiver spouses. Seventy-five percent reported lowered interest and activity since their husbands developed symptoms, but they were able to adapt more effectively than male caregivers.[20] Pruchno and Resch also found significant relationships between the asocial and disoriented behaviors of impaired spouses and caregiver stress associated with caregivers' reported levels of depression and burden, mental health problems attributed to caregiving, and the extent to which caregivers sacrificed aspects of their own social life.[21] Finally, P. P. Vitaliano and others investigated the relationship between levels of caregiver distress due to exposure to stress coupled with measures of vulnerability and access to psychological and social resources. They found that caregivers with high vulnerability and low levels of resources had higher burden scores than caregivers with other combinations of these variables.[22]

CAREGIVER AMBIVALENCE

Caregivers are faced with the task of keeping ambivalent feelings in balance, usually a difficult and demanding process at the best of times. When both husband and wife, or adult child and parent, are struggling to come to terms with early symptoms of dementia, the balancing act is even more difficult, as denial vies with fear, frustration with patience, dependency with autonomy, or resentment with affection, and the care-giver swings between holding on and letting go. Caregivers describe their experiences as a roller-coaster ride which never pauses to allow them to alight. Resentment may begin to suffocate affection.

Denial Versus Foreboding

Denial is an effective coping mechanism. We use denial to hold pain and foreboding at bay. Few people enjoy being in pain, particularly psychic pain that challenges core elements of personality, and loved ones' dementia taps into caregivers' deepest fears of separation and abandonment. It is more comfortable to pretend symptoms are a pass-ing phase and to reshape reality by denial, even as fears build and threaten to overwhelm. The caregiver is like a lifesaver struggling to stay afloat with the victim's struggles to drown them both. Conflicting feelings evoke frustrations and impatience.

Frustration Versus Patience

In ambiguous situations that remain unresolved, the accompanying ambivalence tends to dissolve into bursts of irritation that all too easi-ly can explode into anger, even rage, feelings that are fed by an over-whelming sense of helplessness. As patients feel the ground shifting under their feet and strive desperately to retain their grip on reality, caregivers must begin the task of making decisions alone, while cop-ing with the day-to-day frustrations that arise from their loved ones' confusion and growing dependence.

Dependence Versus Autonomy

As the Alzheimer's sufferer grows more dependent, caregivers must learn to tolerate growing intrusions that rob them of privacy, freedom, and "space." Patients become increasingly dependent at the same time that spouses or adult children must learn to plan and act independently. Simultaneously, added responsibilities become burdens as they are deprived of opportunities for social outlets.

Isolation Versus Companionship

Dementia is an isolating illness. Patients are increasingly isolated within the shell of forgetfulness and confusion, moving from "the real world" into a world of their own, while caregivers lose loved ones' companionship and may lose relationships with peers and even other family members. Social contacts with friends and colleagues may be reduced or lost either because others withdraw or because caregivers choose to isolate themselves. At the moment caregivers are losing friends, they are also "losing" their loved ones.

Letting Go Versus Holding On

The patient-caregiver relationship, once so strong, becomes one-sided. As a husband's dementia worsens, he struggles to hold on; but he feels things are slipping from his grasp. The responsibility to maintain the relationship rests on his wife as caregiver, who feels her husband is slipping from her grasp into a world she cannot enter. If she places her husband in a nursing home, she surrenders her role as his full-time caregiver to strangers. Even depending on part-time help in the home, or rallying other family members to her support, means giving up some of her identity as wife and partner. It is sometimes difficult to avoid "blaming" the loved one for these changes and losses.

Resentment Versus Affection

The growing dependence of the Alzheimer's patient adds new burdens to caregivers' daily routines that eat away at the affection they have known in the past. There is little time now to enjoy memories that are lost under the burdens of dressing, feeding, toileting, bathing, exercising, restraining, protecting. It is difficult to be unfailingly affectionate, always "up." Caregivers' isolation, loneliness, and grief are enervating feelings that crowd out patience, joy, peace, even affection.

Love, laughter, and joy need not be irretrievably lost. Many caregivers learn to fuse humor with their sadness. When Allison's father became too impaired to live alone in his small Oklahoma community, she brought him to live with her family in Houston. Despite the problem behaviors that disrupted her family's life, it was a satisfactory solution until it became necessary for him to be checked medically. She laughed as she described his resistance to her efforts to persuade him to visit her doctor. She tried patiently to understand his refusal to see the physician, but he doggedly insisted that he wanted to see his own doctor. But his former doctor practiced at the Indian Hospital near his former Oklahoma community, and that was too far for regular visits. When her father became disturbed as she attempted to gain his acceptance, she put him in her car to give him the sensation of acceding to his demands to drive him to Oklahoma—she had found, as many caregivers find, that distracting the confused person is one means of ameliorating his distress.[23] She drove around the city for 40 minutes, then headed back to their neighborhood. She pointed out familiar places: "Look, Dad, there is the mall where we walk. . . . There is First Church. . . . Dad, isn't it nice to be home again!" Her father replied: "It sure is. But why did you need to drive so fast?"

If the daunting tasks faced by ADRD caregivers appear overwhelming to onlookers, that is exactly how they are experienced by the caregivers themselves. Our experience with Alzheimer's care partners indicates that, whereas many spouse caregivers manage their daily responsibilities with patience, compassion, and frequent expressions of the love that have enriched their marriages (or, in the case of adult children, their relationships with their now-disabled parents), their burdens and stresses exact a heavy toll on the most caring and loving family members. The more previous spousal and adult child-parent relationships have been fractured, the greater the difficulty caregivers face in sustaining their own spiritual, emotional, and physical well-being, so that they may more effectively care for their impaired loved ones. One only has to hear at first hand the stories of Alzheimer's caregivers, or read accounts such as those of Nancy Mace and Peter Rabins to feel the overwhelming nature of dementia-related concerns that threaten to destroy caregivers' lives.[24] Our growing realization of these stresses led to development of Alzheimer's Care Team ministry.

THE ANGUISH OF ALZHEIMER'S-STRICKEN FAMILIES

As the public becomes more aware of Alzheimer's disease and its ramifications, the veil of anguish is slowly being drawn aside. Caregivers are hesitantly telling their stories, and we are learning as we listen. A Presbyterian pastor spoke of his losses in personal terms. One of his emptiest feelings is going to bed alone. They stopped attending concerts because of her shouting in the middle of performances. She had served alongside her husband for 17 years in Japan, where they raised their two daughters. "Now she doesn't know them or her two grandsons, aged 3 and 1. . . . Some days I think she knows who I am, some days she doesn't. It's hard because she was a brilliant woman. But that's all been wiped out. In her mind, she's probably living back in her childhood. It hurts, but that's the reality of this disease. This is certainly not the cup I chose."[25] The founder of the ADRD Association described Alzheimer's as "the funeral that never ends."[26]

Howard Rice describes the onset of probable Alzheimer's in Veronica, his mother-in-law, and his bewilderment when she would put food on her fork, raise it to her mouth, but remain unsure what it was and what she should do next. When the family attended a dinner-dance, Veronica's daughter asked her father to dance. Veronica became distressed, mumbling that her husband was having an affair with a stranger. She deteriorated quickly; it seemed only weeks ago that she attended a grandson's wedding when she was more coherent. Her son-in-law added: "If I had known it would be like this, I would have said 'I love you' more often. I would have said good-bye."[27]

Mace and Rabins illustrate the range of emotional reactions caregivers often experience. Anger and frustration can be the most difficult feelings to cope with, because patients' behaviors can be aggravating and, in public, often embarrassing. They cite caregivers whose anger surged when they felt helpless, trapped in a situation they could no longer control. Feeling that other family members did not appreciate their daily misery, they reverted to yelling and arguing with loved ones whom they knew were not responsible for their behaviors. Feelings of guilt for losing their tempers, the way they had behaved to their loved ones in the past or had felt embarrassed in public, can leave caregivers immobilized. Caregivers' responses indicate the range of feelings:

"My mother's illness ruined my marriage, and I can't forgive her for that."

"I lost my temper with Dick and slapped him. Yet I know he is sick and can't help himself."

"I never liked my mother and now she has this terrible disease. If only I had been closer to her when I could."[28]

While new medications may relieve some symptoms temporarily or may slow the rate of progression, Alzheimer's disease remains insidious and irreversible. The grief that accompanies the deterioration of an Alzheimer's patient may be overwhelming. The initial attempt to maintain hope is suspended as it becomes clear the condition is irreversible. The sadness is flooded with anguish with recognition of the onset of the disease, especially if the person is aware of the diagnosis. How does one "prepare" to suffer from Alzheimer's or, as caregiver, stand by while a loved one attempts to cope with the onset of early dementia? As the disease progresses, patients' awareness of their situation is submerged by the destruction of areas in the brain as they fall deeper into the confusing world of dementia. As their worlds collapse, the sadness of family members deepens. Judah Ronch notes that as patients lose a clear awareness of themselves as discrete personalities, they drift further away from a vantage point in the life cycle where a sense of generativity and/or integrity may be maintained. "This loss of self threatens the patient with unavoidable feelings of stagnation and despair."[29]

The stresses faced by caregivers of loved ones with Alzheimer's do not differ significantly from those of other people who support terminally and/or chronically ill family members, though at some points the anguish may be sharper and the grief more intense. Caregiver burdens include feelings of stigma occasioned by the symptoms of dementia, including immodesty and inappropriate language that evoke feelings of embarrassment. Guilt may be a consequence of irritation, frustration, or anger with the impaired person. Grief is an inescapable feeling as the patient drifts inexorably into the abyss of dementia and is unable to return expressions of love and companionship that have been so much a part of a relationship now reduced to mundane acts. With the never-ending regression of the patient, many caregivers experience a deepening level of isolation.

Families bear most of the burden of caring for patients, and primary caregivers, if not well spouses, are usually daughters or daughters-in-law. Over 70 percent of ADRD patients are cared for in the home, and with day or night wandering a complication of the disease, 24-hour-care is necessary. That is, there are always at least two victims—the person stricken with dementia and the primary caregiver. Caregivers' attempts to alert other family members to the growing problems are often rejected, and even when acknowledged, caregivers are often abandoned to their tasks. Further, attempts to assume the primary care-giving role are often at the cost of caregivers' own health. Gelman and others found that as patients survive but progressively worsen over a period that averages 10 years but may reach 20, caregivers suffer an ordeal that has been compared to watching an endless funeral. In a way, the victim ceases to exist but continues to live. "You go through episodes of wanting to be relieved of it, the horror that goes on day after day, night after night," says a 66-year-old Brooklyn, N. Y., high school principal. "You often feel a desire that the person die—and then you feel like a monster for entertaining such thoughts."[30]

Caregivers' feelings of isolation and pain are tangible, captured by the story of one Alzheimer's caregiver. Gwen[31] had begun to note changes in her husband's behavior, manifested by forgetfulness, mild confusion, and inability to recall scheduled arrangements and familiar words and phrases. Stan's behavior became more erratic, and included use of epithets and inappropriate language Gwen could not associate with her previously modest, mild-mannered husband. As Stan's condition became more severe, Gwen withdrew more and more from her customary routine. At first, she tried to retain aspects of her schedule, leaving Stan alone at home while she attended her weekly Women's Circle or Sunday worship. The alarm of neighbors who discovered Stan wandering dazed and bewildered in the neighborhood one Sunday morning put a stop to Gwen's efforts to maintain some semblance of normality. She dropped out of her Circle meetings, and attendance at worship became spasmodic.

From her congregation's perspective, the situation could not have been more tragic; as her attendance at worship and other church activities became less frequent and finally ceased, Gwen was not missed! With her two sons living out-of-state, she had no access to family support, and either no one in the congregation realized Gwen's mounting trauma, or each person assumed someone else was in touch with Gwen. The result was the same. Gwen and Stan had dropped through the cracks. We tell Gwen's story in these terms to identify our initial assumption: that a degree of carelessness (a care-less response) on the part of the congregation's pastoral staff and Gwen's peer group had left her unsupported. Yet that was not the entire story: While Gwen's congregation seemed unaware of Stan's condition and the burden his care was placing on Gwen, she did not know how to bring her growing needs to the attention of her congregation. In her growing isolation, Gwen faced her caregiving tasks alone and without assistance to unravel the ambivalent feelings she felt towards her situation in general and Stan in particular. Yet she failed to bring the growing stress she faced to the attention of her pastor and her peers in the congregation. *She had not learned how to ask for ministry.*

On the other hand, some congregations and their pastoral staffs *are* careless and insensitive. A nurse told of tending to an Alzheimer's patient who had been a resident in a full-care facility for two years. As she finished feeding him, she noticed a letter from his congregation lying open on his bedside table. The letter noted that he had not attended worship during the previous two years, and the writer wondered if he wished his name removed from the congregation's membership!

THE IMPACT OF THE DIAGNOSIS ON THE SUFFERER

As one step in orienting to the care of Alzheimer's patients, Alzheimer's Care Team members may observe them relating to the staff of a daycare center. During one of these orientation sessions, Tim, a new Care Team member, tells of sitting in the lounge, waiting for the morning's activities to begin. Patients were being dropped off by family caregivers. Some did not want to stay, as their caregivers checked them in and exited from the building; others were seemingly unaware of their whereabouts, though they were regular "members" in the program. Tim was joined by Phil, who introduced himself as a newly diagnosed Alzheimer's patient: "I was at the doctor's last week, and she confirmed to my wife and me that I have probable Alzheimer's. Beth — my wife — and I had talked about my not being able to remember things, and I told her that if it was Alzheimer's, I wanted to know. This is my third visit here, so I am getting a pretty good idea of what lies ahead. I know I will be like the others. It is sad." He wandered out into the activity room, where the members were being gathered by the staff. Tim joined the circle as an observer to the process, and watched Phil as he joined in the activities. He reported his feelings to the Care Team during the ensuing meeting, wondering aloud how he might respond if he were faced with the same diagnosis.

Clinicians differ as to whether patients should be informed of the diagnosis of dementia. Some believe strongly the information should not be disclosed to patients, while others state just as emphatically that patients who ask for full disclosure have a right to know. V. Cotrell and R. Schulz report that individuals with Alzheimer's are often relegated to the status of object, as if they have no further contribution to make regarding either the disease or their own treatment.[32] Such neglect is often justified on the grounds that the nature of their cognitive disability precludes them from being able to communicate their feelings and the experience of their cognitive impairment. Yet during the early manifestations of symptoms that signal the slow, insidious loss of memory and mentation, ADRD patients deserve not only our sympathy but the readiness of caregivers and clinicians to continue to treat them as full participants. Their anguish as they face the unrelenting loss of rational thought and memory is difficult for the well onlooker to grasp. Our fantasizing about how we would deal with the threat if it were unavoidable is painful enough! The principal reason for nondisclosure may be the clinical discernment that some patients wish to be protected from the knowledge physicians and other clinical staff are gathering. On the other hand, disclosure of the diagnosis enables patients and their caregivers to make rational choices about finances and future care, and may obviate family dissension.[33]

Naomi Feil asserts that the "reality orientation" from the 1960s in which caregivers must constantly correct the disorientation of the affected individual has proved ineffective in communicating with Alzheimer's sufferers. Such an approach requires that a 90-year-old woman who remarks that she needs to visit her mother should be told that she is in reality 90 years old, and her mother died many years ago. The approach also proposes that orientation to time and place brings the individual back into reality. In its place, Feil argues for "validation therapy," based on the values of respect and empathy, which accepts the worldview of the AD-affected person and does not attempt correction. For example, if the individual thinks the lamp shade is a hat, the caregiver should not contradict this. Feil believes that anxiety and related behavioral difficulties can be ameliorated when the caregiver is an empathic listener who accepts the disoriented person's view of reality—a view frequently rooted in the person's distant past—after orientation to time and place is lost. In contrast to correction of the individual, which can lead to irritation and confrontation, rephrasing, close eye contact, a clear and loving tone of voice, mirroring the person's motions and emotions, and touching the person gently on the shoulder are recommended aspects of validation that evoke trusting and genuine relationships having a quieting effect on an otherwise combative individual.[34]

THE ROLE OF THE RELIGIOUS COMMUNITY

Carly Hellen supports Feil's thesis, rejecting the medical term *patient* because it carries the notion of passivity and medication. Claiming that people with dementia are often more capable that either they or their caregivers realize or expect; caregivers therefore should try to do less "for" or "to" and more "with."[35] Hellen believes that disoriented individuals' spiritual experiences and recollections can be mobilized for their well-being: Persons with Alzheimer's disease continue to respond to their faith and inner needs through long-remembered rituals that connect them with the present. Prayers and hymns are still familiar in many cases, especially if regular exposure is maintained.[36] Sunderland, while serving as interim pastor to a small, rural congregation, was accustomed on one Sunday each month to visit a nursing home in which many of the residents suffered from dementia. As the choir members circulated prior to the brief service in the home, residents with dulled eyes stared ahead with no acknowledgment of presence or greetings. It was only when hymnbooks were distributed, and childhood hymns sung, that eyes came alive and faces were wreathed with smiles. Few opened the hymnbooks—they sang from memory!

According to Stephen Sapp, "the way in which people deal with Alzheimer's disease is greatly influenced not only by theological beliefs but also by the nature of this particular illness. . . . One should not downplay the horrors associated with any illness. But Alzheimer's and other dementias are particularly pernicious."[37] Other illnesses deprive a person only of the present—one is sick, is treated medically or surgically, and recovers—or with other terminal illnesses, one loses both present and future. As sufferers from Alzheimer's are robbed of their present and the future, they also lose their past, as memory of people and events are lost in the confusion of the disease. Because the Western religious traditions are based on the belief that the eternal has actively intervened in time, the concepts of time, memory, and history are central in any theological consideration of Alzheimer's disease, of those who suffer from it, and of caregivers who bear the brunt of the anguish. Sapp notes that those interventions constitute a sacred history of the marvelous deeds of God, which lie at the heart of the faith Christians affirm.

Sapp cites author Oliver Sacks (*The Man Who Mistook His Wife for a Hat*) who quotes filmmaker Luis Buñuel's remarks about memory: "You have to begin to lose your memory, if only in bits and pieces, to realize that memory is what makes our lives. . . . Our memory is our coherence, our reason, our feeling, even our action. Without it, we are nothing."[38] Sapp does not concede that we are really nothing without memory—we do not consist of memory alone. He cites another author, A. R. Luria, a researcher known for his work with amnesia patients, who states that humans are moral beings with feeling, will, and sensibilities, matters that neuropsychology cannot address. Where human psychology fails us, other ways can be found to touch Alzheimer's sufferers and change them. Sapp suggests ways in which Western religious tradition can help guide people through what many individuals with Alzheimer's disease and their caregivers experience as, if not a dark night of the soul, a dark night of the mind. Certainly, caregivers can be sustained by the parable of the good Samaritan, and both are implicitly included in the list of those who received care in Matthew 25.

A short reflection on Sapp's essay does not do it justice, and we commend the entire piece to readers. Sapp notes that even after a person ceases to be aware of her life story, the story continues—manifested in the sheer physical existence of the person—interpersonally, in however limited a manner, and socially, because the person still occupies a place in the community. Even when a person's rational capacities fade or fail completely, "the 'I' that consists of much more than those capacities continues to exist—diminished, to be sure, but still worthy of the dignity and respect due to all those who are created in God's image." The patient's memory is a part of the collective memory of the people of the book. That is, it is not just the memory of the person with Alzheimer's that matters. The memory of the community of faith has been central to believers' self-understanding, and at points in history, was probably more important than any sense of personal identity. A broader, more corporate understanding of memory, Sapp suggests, may help us to relate to those individuals who may be losing (or have already lost) their own. Ancient Israel respected the "elders" highly because they were the depositories of the memory of the covenant people. Israel bore another responsibility—to produce offspring and convey to them the memories of the people, including the memory of those elders and their role in the history of Israel. The role of the faith community, then, is not only to remember its members when they are no longer here but also to remember for them when they can no longer do so for themselves.[39]

Thus, through the ministrations of Care Teams, congregations can offer both care and the gift of "a kind of immortality" by recalling for others around them what people with Alzheimer's disease no longer can recall, in order to strengthen the community's recollection of them and keep their roles in the story of the community alive. For example, instead of becoming irritated at the repetition of their stories from the

past, Care Team members need to listen carefully and record the stories, since, as Sapp suggests, "many of them . . . concern times when
[team members] were not around, and if they are allowed to be lost
with the fading memory of the person with Alzheimer's disease, then
that part of the family's and the broader community's history is gone
forever."[40]

And the stories are rich in meaning and in love, stories like that of
Mike and Helen.

Mike and Helen, married 41 years and their two sons happily married,
looked forward to retirement with more time to travel, especially to visit
grandchildren. Mike planned to teach his oldest grandson fly-fishing
during the next school vacation. Mike sang in the choir of the congregation in which he and Helen were founder members. Helen was a member of a women's circle that met in members' homes. Mike had been
concerned for some months that Helen had become forgetful, on one
occasion dressing to attend the circle meeting, which was not until the
following week. A week later, she left to drive to her meeting, but never
arrived. When one of the members phoned him to ask about Helen, he
drove around the neighborhood anxiously until he found her sitting in
her car, seemingly lost. A visit with their physician led to a series of tests
which resulted in a diagnosis of possible Alzheimer's disease. The doctor suggested that Helen should not drive alone in the future.

Mike turned away offers from Helen's friends to pick her up on their
way to meetings. He was embarrassed at the turn of events; he did not
want Helen's friends to see her in her confused state. Plans for his
retirement activities were put on hold. It was weeks since he had even
thought of playing his weekly game of golf. With Helen now requiring
full-time oversight, he first resigned from the choir, which had been
one of his greatest sources of satisfaction and fulfillment, then from the
men's Bible study group of which he had been a founding member. His
whole life now revolved around Helen's protection and comfort. He
rejected offers to sit with Helen—he reminded his pastor that he had
committed to love and honor her "in sickness and in health," and he
meant to keep that pledge.

It was only with great reluctance that, months later, he agreed to
accept the assistance of the Care Team his pastor had been pressing on
him. The team was composed of the members of Helen's former

women's circle, who quietly co-opted their husbands to invite Mike to join them at golf while they sat with Helen. The partnership between Mike and the Care Team members grew, as Mike acknowledged their contribution had lifted one burden from him. The burden of Helen's deteriorating mental state they could not lift. But at least he could rejoin the choir, because two of the women met him in the narthex each Sunday before worship and sat with Helen. If she became restless, they quietly left the sanctuary and met Mike after the service. Soon, Care Team members were picking Helen up, driving to the nearby shopping center, and "walking the mall" with her. As stores opened, they would open the shopping list Mike had given them and assist Helen to purchase the items, for which she drew cash from her purse. She enjoyed these outings, clearly relishing her "shopping trips." Care Team members, now comfortable being with Helen in public, invited Helen and Mike to join a Tuesday brunch group. The result is that Mike is fully resocialized, surrounded by members of the congregation, enjoying the respite opportunities the team provides, and, importantly, persuaded by his pastor that Mike's acceptance of Care Team support is a theological statement about what it means to be a member of the community of faith. When Helen dies, his bereavement will be shared by his Care Team members, as they have shared his grief over the long course of her illness.

CARE TEAM MINISTRIES

Caregiver Respite

Respite is the measure of support most frequently requested by caregivers of loved ones diagnosed with ADRD, and is at the heart of the Alzheimer's Care Team program. Caregivers who have overcome their reluctance to welcome team members into their lives and overcome the guilt some feel about taking "time off" from caregiving responsibilities experience the pleasure of quality time away from their loved ones. Fred, one of the first caregivers to take advantage of his team's offer, did just that! He had missed his weekly golf outings with fellow retirees from the plant. He met the Care Team members at the door with his golf bag over his shoulder, pointed to the den where his wife sat, and dashed to his car, returning five hours later! The team, expecting to provide Fred a two-hour spell, learned quickly that they needed to have a clear understanding with caregivers about how long they could stay. Boundary setting became an important negotiating point during intake interviews and is maintained by review of agreements for care at teams' monthly meetings.

Community daycare facilities provide some respite for harried caregivers, but costs usually begin at $40 per day, and there are few subsidized centers that can reduce those rates. In any case, some families are unable to afford even one day per week, while others lack transportation and will not use public transport for their dementia-affected loved ones. For those caregivers who are able to use day-care, transportation has become an important aspect of Care Team services. One team that began by busing care partners to a center two days each week now provides daily transportation. Another team developed its own version of "Alzheimer's Day Out," providing a twice-monthly Alzheimer's Gathering at the church. Four hours of activities include games, sing-a-longs, outings, and a nutritional lunch—a service valued by caregivers, who find that impaired loved ones who will refuse balanced meals at home will eat what is served at the Gathering! Team members who care for in-home patients while caregivers sleep, shop, or attend worship and other congregational activities become adept at "entertaining" ADRD care partners, learning new rules for card games and dominoes that may vary from visit to visit!

Empathic Listening

Care Teams offer more than companionship through "friendly visits," important as those gifts are. One of the most important gifts team members bring is their capacity to listen empathically to caregivers as they verbalize their frustrations and anxieties. One of the advantages of Care Team members visiting in pairs is the opportunity of one to visit with the care partner while the other team member talks with the caregiver. Team members who perceived their visit as a respite opportunity to enable the caregiver, Ross, to leave the home to shop, or keep an appointment, were surprised when he did not take advantage of the opportunity. Ross chose to stay and talk, and he confided shyly that he could devise ways to get out of the house—what he really appreciated was the chance for a conversation with other adults who were interested in him. Ross verbalized his sense of loss—his wife's return to her childhood, his loss of her companionship, of his marriage! The Care Team members making the visit also picked up a deeper yearning for appreciation for his care of his wife that she was unable to offer.

Affirmation of Caregiver Devotion

Affirmation of the quality of caregivers' support of loved ones is a treasured gift. Despite documented burdens and stress experienced by caregivers, teams see firsthand the tenderness and patience with which by far the majority of family members care for their loved ones. Their acknowledgment of such care is an important contribution to the well-being of caregivers. The opportunities to disclose their frustrations, the healing effects of catharsis experienced by caregivers, coupled with the degree to which their commitment is recognized by others, can enable them to continue their responsibilities refreshed and renewed. Caregivers' unsolicited expression of heartfelt thanks is one of the most rewarding aspects of the Care Team program. Care Team members are constantly reminded that their presence has returned joy and hope to lives that seemed empty and hopeless. A caregiver stated: "I realized early on that, as much as I wanted to, it would not be possible for me to go down this long, dark path alone. Ben and I are so blessed that God guided us to the Care Team. I started to see a light at the end of a very dark and frightening tunnel. The Care Team members assisting us are wonderful, caring, compassionate people. We are so thankful to them." Robert, writing to his Care Team, spoke from the heart: "I just wanted to drop a line to thank you for your friendship at a time in my life when I really need it most. You have been really wonderful and caring and I want you to know how much I appreciate it. I look forward to your visits. As you know, I have no family members here to help me care for Joan, and you have become my family. Thanks for being there for me, and I look forward to your next visit."

IMPACT ON THE LIVES OF CARE TEAM MEMBERS

Equally significant is the impact on the lives of team members, who refer to the personal and spiritual growth they derive from their ministries. Reflecting on the experience of seeing dementia care partners enjoying a social event, team member Norma recalled Al, a former Navy officer. Tall, still slim, he seemed fixated on not being able to see his wife, who had left after dropping Al at the church. The group was seated, singing "golden oldies," when Al suddenly stood, and with his fist waving, shouted "Beat Army!" The group responded by singing "Anchors Away," and Al resumed his seat, grinning broadly. In telling the story the Care Team member reflected on the meaning of her ministry with Alzheimer's patients. "I look at them, and think what they used to be. How do I feel about being with our care partners? I am where I am supposed to be. It is usually the little things, the brief moments, like when Al shouted 'Beat Army,' that make it worth while. It is a fulfilling experience." Bryan expressed the same thought: "I participate in the program because I know I have an aptitude for this ministry. I certainly don't do it for self-gratification—but I am aware that I feel valuable, and that I get more out of it than I can possibly give. Tom, one of our care partners, fell and broke his leg, and we were with Donna while he was in surgery yesterday. I will drop by to see Tom while he is in the hospital. He may not know me, or remember that I was there, and Donna may not know. But I will know! It is important to me."

CHAPTER 7

SECOND FAMILY CARE TEAMS

The replication in 1992 of the Care Team model to provide pastoral support for families caring for loved ones with dementia proved effective. The next step, taken in 1994, was its extension to other frail elderly people. Our empirical research indicated that, at best, elderly members might receive friendly visits and phone calls, but few congregations were organized to provide continuing in-home, hands-on care for chronically ill members. We were also aware of the growing body of literature reporting the escalating needs of the old, especially the oldest old, and warning of the rapid increase in their numbers as more survive into their 80s and 90s. If congregations were providing inadequate support for frail adult members in 1994, the situation will be much more intense as the projected increase in the number of frail elderly materializes in future decades. Our goal for Second Family Care Team ministry paralleled that for Alzheimer's teams, namely, to facilitate congregations' ministries to frail adults whose needs are so intense and so extensive that they overwhelm both frail seniors living alone or family caregivers of frail adults and their congregations' customary one-to-one pastoral ministries.

The initial Second Family Care Team was soon fully occupied supporting Joyce and her Parkinson's-afflicted husband, Max, and Eleanor, an 80-year-old legally blind widow living alone. Joyce and Max, in their mid-70s, accepted in-home support for Max so that Joyce would be free one day each week to volunteer in a nearby hospital! The arrangement met their need for the comforting presence of Care Team members, as well as providing Joyce the opportunity to have quality time out of the house.

The second care partner, Eleanor, was thankful for the companionship that team members provided. As friendships with Eleanor deepened, her mini-team expanded to eleven members spanning five generations. A young married couple with two toddlers brought young children into her life. Three junior high students were assigned to call on Eleanor once or twice each week to ascertain whether there was something she needed read, such as a utility bill or letters from out-of-state grandchildren. A middle-aged couple picked Eleanor up from her apartment and assisted with shopping. Her apartment was 150 yards from a busy thoroughfare lined with strip-malls, but with no sidewalk between her home and the shops, she was forced to use the roadway, a perilous walk given her lack of sight. Her support was rounded out by two women of Eleanor's age who drove her to church on Sunday, and the trio enjoyed lunch after worship. These two care partners' stories cut to the heart of the Care Team concept.

THE AGE WAVE

The urgency of developing broad, community-wide responses to meet the needs of frail seniors is apparent from the 1990 census data. Sam Roberts observes that "a society that reveres virility and reflexively attached the adjective *young* to the noun *nation* is growing older." He urges the nation to "get ready for the debut of sixty-something and a grandparent boom." Life expectancy, which at the beginning of the twentieth century was 49 years, increases to 75 for children born between 1990 and 2000. During this century the likelihood of surviving until the customary retirement age of 65 has doubled to 80 percent.[1] The population aged 65 and over is expected to more than double from 20 million in 1990 to 40 to 50 million early in the next century; nearly one in four Americans might be over 65 then. The first baby boomers will just begin to turn 85 in 2030. By midcentury, at present rates, the number of people 85 and over will, for the first time, exceed the number under age 5. The 85-and-older group will swell to nearly 13 million, or 5 percent of the population.[2]

One group among the frail elderly portends a further complication. Since the U. S. Public Health Service estimates the probability of dementia-related illness at 40 percent for individuals aged 85 or over; and if there is no breakthrough in dementia-related research, there may be as many as 6 to 7 million dementia cases in their mid-80s by 2050. The total number of dementia-related cases of all ages may be two or three times that number. And dementia is only one health problem confronting the frail elderly! Newspapers and magazines tend to sensationalize these data. *The Washington Post* reported that more American families will consist of four instead of two or three generations as more people live into their 80s and 90s. As a consequence, more people will face the concern and expense of caring for their very old, frail relatives, since so many people already live long enough to face multiple, chronic illnesses.[3] It all sounds challenging, and to some, threatening, not only for the "sandwich" generation of parents raising their own families while at the same time tending to elderly parents—or grandparents—but for the seniors themselves, who fear the dreaded words *nursing home*. Moreover, the fragmentation of extended families often leaves elderly people separated from adult children, who become distant caregivers less able to monitor personally the medical needs and well-being of parents.

The majority of people aged 65 years and above live in the community. It is estimated that approximately 5 percent of frail elderly are in nursing homes. The number who require long-term care, however, is much higher. The Center for Health Policy Studies in Washington, D.C., reported in 1988 that approximately 7 million elderly persons, that is, nearly one quarter of the total elderly population, needed some long-term care. About 22 percent of the elderly long-term care population reside in nursing homes and other institutions. Approximately 40 percent of dependent elderly live with spouses, 30 percent live with others, and 30 percent live alone.[4] The functional status of ill or disabled individuals is defined by the terms "Activities of Daily Living" (ADL) and "Instrumental Activities of Daily Living" (IADL). ADL measures refer to personal care: bathing, dressing, transferring (e.g., from bed to chair), toileting, and eating. IADLs refer to household tasks such as cooking, cleaning, and shopping. Approximately 30 percent of the elderly who need long-term assistance have limited dependencies and require only IADL support. Twenty percent are almost totally dependent and need assistance with every ADL and IADL. Approximately 76 percent of all elderly people are fully independent, that is, just being "old" does not equate to the need for long-term care. But this need rises exponentially with age: 13 to 15 percent of people between the ages of 65 and 69 need long-term care, whereas 55 percent of people aged 85 and older require assistance.[5]

A quarter of all women and 15 percent of all men aged 85 and over live in nursing homes, compared with only 1.4 percent of people between the ages of 65 and 74. According to Edward Campion,

> half the people over the age of 85 years experience impaired hearing; vision loss, falls, hip fractures, stroke, cancer, and cardiovascular disease are also common. Nearly a third of the very elderly have some degree of dementia. About 45 percent of those still living in the community require assistance with everyday activities, and 48 percent live alone. Half the men who are 85 or older live with their wives. Because wives tend to be younger than their husbands and have a longer life expectancy, only 10 percent of the oldest women live with their husbands.[6]

Because these data have received so much attention in the past decade, we should dispose of some of the myths of aging, the most common of which is that aging inevitably means descent into ill health. John W. Rowe and Robert L. Kahn contradict this myth. Their recent study funded by the MacArthur Foundation declares that most people age successfully.[7] Changes in life expectancy have been so dramatic that it is estimated that of all the human beings who have ever lived to be sixty-five years or older, half are currently alive. In 1900, approximately 4 percent of the United States population was aged over sixty-five. Today the percentage has jumped to 13 percent. More than 70 percent of Americans now reach sixty-five years, compared to about 25 percent in 1900. The life expectancy of children born in 1900 averaged forty-seven years. One of the most surprising of these demographic data is the increase in people living to 100 years. While centenarians in the United States were rare in 1900, their numbers swelled to 32,000 by 1982, 61,000 in 1998, and projected to be 600,000 to 1.2 million by 2050.[8]

Two reasons are advanced for increasing life expectancy. First, there has been a shift in the patterns of sickness in the aging population from infectious diseases, which led to premature death in the early 1900s, to chronic illnesses such as arthritis, hypertension and heart disease, diabetes, and disorders of sight and hearing, which in most cases are now amenable to therapies. Second, when seniors between the ages of 65 and 74 in 1960 are compared with the same age group today, there has been a dramatic decrease in disease due to high blood pressure, high cholesterol, and smoking. The former negative assumption that people grow older and sicker is now more difficult to defend: older people are much more likely to age well than to become decrepit and dependent.[9] The authors of the MacArthur Study similarly dispose of such other myths as "you can't teach an old dog new tricks," "the secret to successful aging is to choose your parents well," and "the elderly don't pull their own weight." The study is supported by other research that indicates a high correlation between good mental and physical health and maintaining a network of human relationships that are creative and supporting. Isolation, on the other hand, is a powerful risk factor for poor health, as is perceived loss of control that leads to loss of independence and self-esteem.[10]

So, every day and in every way are we all getting better and healthier? The future is not so rosy for every American. Advances in health care and medical science that undergird the health delivery system and enable many to look forward to a healthy old age are not accessible to many. Roberts' analysis of the 1990 census supports Campion's assessment. The census revealed that while about one in ten people between the ages of 16 and 64 said they had difficulty moving about or caring for themselves without help, more than three in ten people over the age of 65 required similar assistance.[11] Individuals and families living below the poverty line, including 20 percent of the elderly, eat less nutritious meals, receive less effective medical care, and single mothers and the frail elderly especially, are prone to defer seeking medical care until forced to do so by deteriorating health.

Rowe and Kahn place part of the responsibility for the notion that to grow old is to become frail on the relatively new profession of gerontology, with its preoccupation with disability, disease, chronological age, and underemphasis on healthy aging. But while data indicate that

178

the majority of people are aging successfully, as many as 30 million people are undereducated, receive marginal health care, and, because they are also poor, are politically marginalized. Their concerns need to be identified and understood, and they need voices to speak for them. Regardless of efforts by secular interest groups to speak to these issues by supporting the claims of low-income elderly, the Judeo-Christian community is obligated to do so. The prophets continually warned of the punishment that would befall those who turn aside the needy from justice (Isa. 10:2; Jer. 7:5-7, Amos 5:24). We are required proactively to develop means to address the needs of the poor, including personal care and maintenance of independent living as long as that is prudent. But even as congregations make these efforts, the horizon is clouded by a further threat. It is unfortunate that, as many low-income frail elderly face an uncertain future as managed care reshapes Medicare and Medicaid, tension is increasing because of doubts concerning the baby boom generation's access to adequate health care when its members reach retirement and health needs escalate.

GENERATIONAL CONFLICT

Conflict between the generations is an unexpected consequence of the concern over the security of the baby boomers' future. We have already noted that within the first fifty years of the new millennium, more families will consist of four generations, and in some instances, five. Given the social milieu of the nineteenth and early twentieth centuries, one could expect a sense of family pleasure and satisfaction as the oldest generation experienced the birth of the fourth generation infants, who, in turn would grow up with their great-grandparents and learn to sing: "Over the hills and through the woods to great-grandmother's house we go!" But in today's economy, with perceived threats to Social Security, the tune is more somber. Many families already consist of four generations: the youngest, the "X-generation," parents of young families, the baby boomers, now also termed the "sandwich generation," and the "greedy geezers" whom the successor generation fear will deplete Social Security and diminish their retirement plans.

179

Judith Gonyea notes that needs of the oldest old, the fastest growing segment of the U. S. population, are diverse and considerable. In light of one projection that the oldest old will number up to 24 million by mid-century, public policy discussions have been spiced by phrases like "the graying of the federal budget," "fiscal black hole," and "apocalyptic demographic forecasts."[12] Peter Peterson warns the nation must avoid "generational warfare" between working age taxpayers and the exploding number of retirees whom they will be asked to support.[13] On one hand, "the long-held view of older people as 'deserving' has come into question," according to Gonyea. "In a typical example of the media view, the *New York Times* columnist William Safire (1995) writes of borrowing to fund the growing deficit as 'no longer . . . a gift to our old but a theft from our young.' " On the other hand, the needs of frail elderly are growing, and must be addressed. Gonyea notes that "by age 85, including those in nursing homes, . . . almost two thirds of the age group are functionally dependent," a finding especially important for older women, "who, if they are not the recipients of long-term care, are likely to be the caregivers for someone who is" (more than one-third of functionally dependent men in this age bracket are cared for primarily by their wives).[14]

In what Peterson describes as "the ultimate, here-and-now youth society," he asks whether America will grow up and confront the long-term challenge of its own aging before it is too late? He states that a majority of all thirty- to fifty-year-old wage earners (a) believe Social Security won't be there for them, (b) are not participating in any meaningful pension plan, (c) have a personal savings rate (and a household net worth) hovering near zero, yet (d) expect to retire early with an ample standard of living. "Early in the next century, Florida won't be exceptional. By 2025 at the latest, the proportion of all Americans who are elderly will be the same as the proportion in Florida today. America, in effect, will become a nation of Floridas— and then keep aging. By 2040, one in four Americans may be over sixty-five."[15] Helen Dennis and John Migliaccio suggest that boomers could and should be saving more for their future. In a worst-case scenario (the elimination of Social Security benefits), boomers would have to increase their savings almost tenfold to maintain their current standard of living. Boomers who do not meet their savings goals likely will have to delay retirement indefinitely or accept a lower standard of living.[16]

The challenge to expectations that were assumed to be firmly set and protected—access to adequate health care in old age, and the solvency of Social Security—has resulted in a sense of conflict that has begun to pit one generation against another, as noted above. One significant influence of the need for access to adequate care as baby boomers age is their assumptions about what they can and should expect as they enter older age. Both their physical and financial well-being are at stake. David Morgan agrees with this assessment and adds a second factor, namely, the demographics of both the baby boom and "generation X" which follows, "most notably the number of caregivers available to the younger generation relative to the number of people needing care in the older generation."[17] Elizabeth Kutza suggests that "the baby boom generation will face a very different policy environment compared to their parents' experience."[18] The financial situation relative to managed care and the stability of Medicare and its availability when needed introduce a level of uncertainty that is adding to the potential conflict already flaring between the generations. A further issue cannot be overlooked: While much of the attention is given to conflict between generations as cohorts of the total population, there is still the question of the relationships that exist and will always exist between younger, middle-aged, older, and the oldest old *in the same family.*[19] The pressure on the health care delivery system as the number of frail elderly explodes, together with the extent to which family caregivers will be able to shoulder their burdens, are the issues that underlie much of this chapter, as we examine congregational opportunities for ministry occasioned by these demographic trends.

CONGREGATIONAL CARE OF THE FRAIL ELDERLY

Second Family Care Team ministry was launched into these turbulent seas. A frail senior living alone who lacks family support needs a "second family." Overburdened caregivers of frail elderly need the support of a new "extended family"—a second family to share some of the burden of caregiving. Out-of-state, distant caregivers need the assurance of trustworthy people on the spot to provide the care they are unable to offer. Our goal was to mobilize congregations to identify and serve frail seniors whose marginal functional and health status and isolation conspired to further threaten their ability to enjoy old age, and to assist congregations to establish partnerships of care with individuals and families whose needs constitute a call for pastoral support.

Care Team ministry can make a critical difference in the lives of frail elderly living alone. Since meeting socialization needs diminishes the isolation that is highly correlated with increasing health problems, including depression, the companionship Care Teams provide is an important contribution to their well-being. Their "friendly visits" are just the first step in long-term care. Care Team members contribute to preventive care by keeping close contact with frail seniors, monitoring nutritional intake, encouraging them to seek medical attention, and providing transportation to enable them to do so. As team members take time to sit and visit older members, they receive from them stories of the congregation, its neighborhood, and developments older members have observed during their lifetimes. Since many elderly people have strong ties to their faith traditions, team commitments strengthen these ties by enabling them to attend worship and other congregational activities or at least keep in touch with their congregations. Church attendance and participation in the congregation's liturgies of worship and its social gatherings reinforce the sense that they are valuable and valued members of a community that cares.

Care Teams assist congregations to answer a question formulated by Henri Nouwen and others: "How can we creatively respond to Jesus' call, 'Be compassionate as your father is compassionate'?" Team ministry to the frail elderly provides a channel through which God's compassionate presence becomes visible in our everyday lives, entering into solidarity with our fellow human beings and offering them loving and obedient service.[20] According to the New Testament, the compassionate life is a life together. Compassion is not an individual character trait, a personal attitude, or a special talent, *but a way of living together*. It reflects a Pauline emphasis: "If then our common life in Christ yields anything to stir the heart, any loving consolation, any sharing of the Spirit, any warmth of affection or compassion, fill up my cup of happiness by thinking and feeling alike, with the same love for one another, the same turn of mind" (Phil. 2:1-2 NEB). Perhaps Paul had heard from Luke the words of Jesus: "Be compassionate as your Father is compassionate" (Luke 6:36 NEB). Nouwen suggests that we witness to God's compassionate presence in the world by the way we live and work together. Those who entered the first Christian communities revealed their conversion not by feats of individual stardom but by entering a new life in community, in which members show love by caring for one another, sharing each other's burdens, and so fulfilling the law of Christ (Gal. 6:2).

Trinity United Methodist Church, the oldest African American United Methodist congregation in the Texas Conference, ministers to two "congregations": the parents, now grandparents, who have remained in the neighborhood, and their families who settled outside the Third Ward and travel back to Trinity for Sunday worship. Trinity's Second Family Care Team was formed in 1994 to strengthen the congregation's care of its frail members. Trinity's is a typical Second Family Care Team story. Prior to the team's formation, pastoral ministry consisted mainly of phone calls, a few friendly visits by laypeople, and visits a busy pastor could fit into a crowded schedule. Care Team members more than doubled contacts with Trinity's large number of homebound seniors living alone. Transportation increased, not only to church events and worship, but to doctors' offices and clinics, and shopping. Companionship was so highly valued and anticipated that when it was impossible for a Care Team member to make a scheduled visit, the senior was on the phone to remind the member how much he or she had looked forward to the visit. A men's group that assisted frail seniors with minor home repairs was alerted by Care Team members when their services were needed. One of the first Care Team meetings reviewed care being offered to Joanna, a 93-year-old widow living alone. She had called her two Care Team members at 2:00 A.M. to ask them to come to her aid. She had fallen out of bed and was unable to move. While it was properly a 911 call, Joanna had called the only two people she trusted. The married couple debated whether they should dress and respond to her call. When they arrived at her home, they smelled gas and found that Joanna was semiconscious—she had left a gas jet open when she retired for the night. They literally had saved her life.

LOSSES INHERENT IN OLD AGE

Regardless of whether the elderly age successfully or are burdened by chronic illness, they experience losses that, if not worked through, may result in debilitating depression. Aging is both a physiological process and a state of mind. Many of us know people who feel and appear old at 65, or even at 55! On the other hand a 100-year-old great-grandfather resists exchanging his independent lifestyle in a self-contained cottage for assisted living in which he could have more intensive oversight. He justified his decision not to relocate on the basis of not losing his independence and privacy—losses so great that he would rather risk falling and injury. A retired pastor, he continues to preach once or twice monthly and protests that he really doesn't feel like a centenarian. In his mid-90s, he was accustomed to crossing a busy six-lane thoroughfare on foot, dashing to the median through a break in the traffic and then across the remaining lanes when the traffic thinned. He was finally persuaded to use the pedestrian crossing. When his arthritic ankle finally limited his dashing, he solved the problem by purchasing a motorized wheelchair.

The 65- and the 100-year-old may experience the same range of losses. *Material losses* may include loss of residence, driving privileges, and personal effects; where does one place a household of memories when moved to a nursing home? *The death of the first spouse* leaves the widow or widower not only bereft, but lonely in his or her grief. *Loss of relationships* also occurs as an elderly person moves from her residence in a distant city to be closer to her daughter, losing contacts with her peers and old neighborhood. Relationships may also be lost due to the deaths of peers, which are felt deeply. As children growing up, which of us was not puzzled when we realized our parents, on opening the daily newspaper, turned first to read the obituaries to learn who of their friends had died. *Loss of identity* as a spouse or a productive employee may be accompanied by *loss of self-*

esteem. Loss of ability for household and yard chores, and, worse, for *personal care* may be accompanied by *loss of accustomed roles,* partial or complete *loss of functional ability,* and restriction or *loss of mobility.* and in the majority of these cases, the loss is likely to result in chronic conditions that result in *loss of the former lifestyle. Loss of control* over core elements of one's life is connected inexorably with *loss of independence* and the *ability to manage one's affairs,* that may be as critical as loss of health itself, and may occur at the same time that an elderly person *loses a sense of being needed. Loss of sexual expression* may result not only from the death of the spouse, but may be concomitant with placement in a nursing home, or as pointed out in chapter 6, from the loss of the spouse to demential or other neurological diseases.

These losses are not placed in any special order, nor are they experienced with the same intensity by every individual, since we all age differently and our lives are shaped by the totality of our own experiences and situations. Regardless, losses in old age may be multiple and catastrophic, and may signal the need for emotional and spiritual support and understanding on the part of caregivers. Care Team members are trained to recognize and respond to indications of these needs. Such ministry appropriately takes the form of listening to seniors' accounts of their losses, in the course of visits that include practical assistance with ADLs and IADLs. Sensitive team members are always alert to affirm life's joys, and many Care Team visits are joyous celebrations of the stories care partners enjoy sharing.

STORY LISTENING

Care Team members who visit frail adults are particularly well placed to listen to care partners' experiences and to hear and respond to expressions of grief that arise from unmet needs and losses. Abraham Mazlow documented humans' basic needs, which, if not met, diminish quality of life and the maintenance of personal integrity. The elderly have needs for fulfillment and meaning, community and socialization, and, for those whose religious history has been a fulfilling part of their lives, opportunities to worship and continue relationships with their congregations. Other needs represent the counterpart to personal losses: need for a sense of being valued, opportunity to be as productive as limitations permit, relationships, a sense of security (physical and emotional), health, acceptable and adequate housing, mobility and transportation, privacy, independence, and in the case of frail elderly living alone, the practical issues of home maintenance: repairs like fixing leaking faucets and changing lightbulbs. It is situations and needs like these on which frail seniors focus their stories—and storytellers need story listeners.

Listening with care is a fundamental aspect of Care Team ministries, and careful listening to the elderly has a special quality because they have such a story to tell. Listening to another's story demonstrates that the listener cares, and that is one of the most enriching gifts one person can give another. Mr. Angus, a lay pastoral minister in his congregation, was assigned to visit Mrs. Ellis, a 91-year-old nursing home resident. After many months of patiently building a pastoral relationship with her, he gradually won her confidence sufficiently for her to invite him to enter her private bed-sitting room. She positioned him across the room, while she sat on a chair by the open door. During one of his visits, she suddenly began to share her life story of growing up on a dairy farm and later marrying a farmer. Some of her children had predeceased her, and others are failing: "If only my children could be healthy, I would gladly give up my health," she told her visitor. On the next visit, Mr. Angus reported,

> The first thing she asked me was my name, apologizing for not remembering, but thanking me for the visits we had together. When I left, she gave me a thank-you card to post. I knew she could have posted it in the nursing home, and I wondered if her action meant that she was beginning to place more meaning in my visits.
>
> I still visit her regularly, even though my time on the Board of Deacons has elapsed. Somehow, the pastoral ministry program is more than just a matter of responsibility for a given period. I feel I have a continuing ministry to members of the congregation. When I visit Mrs. Ellis, we mostly discuss politics, church, and, of course, her family. She has

186

told me much more of her story. *It is like a living history, and has meaning now, not only for her, but for me.*[21]

Elderly people are not alone in retaining stories that give meaning to their lives, but they may be more likely to dwell on those stories and enjoy retelling them, sometimes endlessly. They understand their stories when they are able to tell them to receptive listeners and the process is blessed. The caring listener who really wants to know another's story is one of the greatest gifts of life, because it is in the listener's attention that the storyteller discovers he has a story to tell in the first place. Nouwen proposes that "listening is a very active awareness of the coming together of two lives." The listener not only listens to a story but brings a story to the relationship. This makes listening a very active and alert form of care. After a story is heard and received with care, the lives of both storyteller and story listener have become different. "Two people have discovered their own unique stories and two people have become an integral part of a new fellowship."[22] But the development of such a relationship is not without risks.

HELPING WITHOUT HURTING

Underlying risks can surface in the intimate relationships that develop between team members and care partners. It is easy to become overly involved in care partners' lives, as team members listen to their stories and complaints. Team members must develop skills that enable them to keep an appropriate emotional distance in their relationships and to be alert to resolve problems that arise when a care partner begins to breach the boundaries that were set when the members accepted the assignment. Becoming overly involved, enmeshed, or entangled in others' lives and problems can be destructive for both Care Team members and care partner. We can hurt instead of heal. Wayne Dyer offers some commonsense counsel to people who want to help. For example, if we believe that feeling bad or worrying long enough will change a fact, we are living on another planet with a different reality system. Or, again, worrying, obsessing, and attempting to control others are illusions, tricks we play on ourselves; if we think we have the solution for this other person, and if only he or she would listen to *us,* he or she would be able to get out of the mess he or she is in! What are the risks, the dangers? People who are excessively preoccupied with or worried about a problem of another person may become so obsessed with the attempt to control others and to resolve their problems that they are unable to fulfill responsibilities to themselves or their families. They may become *reactors,* instead of being able to *act* responsibly in a situation of crisis or need, or may be seduced into thinking that they are responsible to fill the roles of caretaker, rescuer, or enabler instead of being a resource that assists care partners to identify, face, and resolve issues and problems.[23] According to Dyer, obsession with a person or problem is an awful state to be in! One can talk and think about nothing else. Some people's lives revolve around worrying about, reacting to, or, worse, trying to control others. Such people can be so focused on someone else that they become "shells of depleted energy" with little awareness of their own personal responsibilities. So how can such pitfalls be avoided? The alternative to a*ttachment* is *detachment.* That means releasing or detaching from a person or problem *with love.* We mentally, emotionally and sometimes physically disengage ourselves from unhealed (and often painful) entanglements with another's life and responsibilities and from problems we cannot resolve. Another way to make the same point is to state that a Care Team member must maintain enough distance from a care partner that is it "safe" to be close.

Detachment is based on the idea that each person is responsible for him or herself. We are doing well if we are making a reasonable effort to face our *own* issues, problems, and responsibilities! Most of us know that we cannot solve problems that are not ours to solve, and that worrying doesn't help or resolve the issue for the other! If we know what is good for us and for the care partner, we adopt a policy of keeping our hands off other people's problems and tend to our own instead. We strive to live our own lives. *Detachment does not mean we do not care!* It means we learn to love, care, and be involved without losing our ability to keep our balance. Sometimes, detachment even motivates and frees people around us to begin identifying and facing their own problems and seeking their own solutions. Is attachment always wrong? Of course not. How can we care without becoming attached out of compassion and friendship? But it is just this closeness that carries risks. That is why it is so important to take the warnings seriously and to maintain enough distance that it is safe to be close. When should we *detach*? When we cannot stop talking or worrying about someone or something, when our emotions are churning and boiling, when we feel like we have to do something because we cannot stand it another minute. A good rule to follow is: "You need to detach most when it seems to be the least likely thing to do."[24] Because that is sometimes difficult to accomplish, the monthly Care Team meetings are important opportunities to listen to one another and to sharpen the interpersonal skills that help to maintain an effective team ministry. Some of the most difficult and painful relationships in which to apply these skills are those in which the care partner is deeply depressed.

THE LINK BETWEEN DEPRESSION AND CHRONIC ILLNESS OR CATASTROPHIC DISABILITY

Henri Nouwen draws attention to the consequences of isolation and the loneliness and depression it breeds. While we all need opportunities for privacy, we were created to live in community.[25] Loneliness, one of the most universal sources of human suffering, is particularly stressful for frail seniors and accounts to some degree for suicide among the elderly. Our egoistic culture that cultivates independence and self-interest as opposed to an emphasis on group concern and self-sacrifice tends to produce anomie and isolation, according to Priscilla Ebersole and Patricia Hess. They point out that the classic research of Edward Durkheim into suicide has been confirmed consistently during the past 100 years; rates of suicide in the elderly are correlated with their degree of isolation, and increase concomitantly with age until 80 years, when rates for women decrease but those for men increase substantially.[26] Robert Binstock suggests that, even if anticipated, suicide is always a shock. The aging of the population and the fact that the elderly are more likely to kill themselves makes the matter even more urgent. Accurate data are difficult to establish because of the long recognized unreliability of death certificate data, "particularly when a cause of death is so encumbered with stigma and concealment as suicide."[27] Elders who feel separated from, even rejected by, their families and feel useless in a society that regards them as a burden are subject to depression that further weakens them. On the other hand, social integration, the extent to which a person is embedded in a social network, is health inducing.

It is not merely the need to have some interpersonal contact, though almost any is preferable to none! The quality of the relationship is a key factor. It is of interest that even when care and support is offered in the home, the quality of support varies according to the nature of the care-providing agency. Social research differentiates care provided by employed home health care aides or paid sitters from that provided in the voluntary relationship that characterizes Care Team ministry. A study reported by Catherine Harris found that trained volunteers, compared to paid providers, functioned as family surrogates, motivated by altruistic and substitutive needs. They were older, had more education, many including a professional identification, and spent considerable time interacting with the family caregiver before and after respite visits. Their nurturing attitudes and expressions had a beneficial effect on family caregivers. On the other hand, paid workers, though viewed as competent, creative, and nurturing acted primarily as an extension of family caregivers, yet did not manifest the initiative to move the family to a higher level of function. Harris concluded that volunteers play a unique role in the social support of caregivers.[28] While Care Team ministry eschews the term *volunteer* for theological reasons, our observations correspond to the study's findings. That is, paid workers function as they are paid to perform. However effectively they perform their tasks, their service is contracted, whereas those whose presence is a manifestation of their call to ministry are present for very different reasons, and specifically include care of family caregivers, supporting them in their caregiving roles, and contributing to their resocialization where social functioning has been limited. Care Team ministry offers the types of emotional and spiritual support that lighten some of the burdens caregivers experience and contribute to personal well-being of both caregivers and the frail elderly.

Attending to the physical and emotional needs of the old and the very old not only pays dividends in renewed meaning at the end of life, but not incidentally surely contributes to decreasing health-care costs by providing personal care that reduces depression and other health-related crises. But Second Family Care Team ministry is responsive to younger adults as well as seniors.

THE OLD DO NOT HAVE A MONOPOLY ON NEED!

While our first efforts were mobilized to address the needs of frail older people, some congregations had few such needs. Consisting of younger families mainly concerned with children and adolescents, the adults had healthy parents or were distant caregivers. In some congregations, the need was for care of *younger* frail adults. Bobbie, aged 41 years, is quadriplegic, the result of an auto accident. When her husband learned during her long convalescence that her disability was permanent, he deserted Bobbie, leaving her with three young children. Bobbie divorced him, and her mother moved in with the family to care for her. Each morning, Bobbie's mother lifts her from bed into her wheelchair, feeds the family, and departs for work, to return between 5:00 to 6:00 P.M.

When we visited her to discuss how a Care Team might ease her struggles, we learned that Bobbie was incontinent of bowel and bladder and concerned that she had to wait for care until her mother's return. Bobbie's Care Team, consisting of a group of women of her own age, now visits her in pairs each day at noon, lifting her to a standing position, changing her diaper, and reseating her in her chair. Team members frequently have lunch with Bobbie, providing her not only with physical support but meeting her socialization needs. A women's circle that includes members of her team began meeting in Bobbie's home each Wednesday, providing her with another link to her congregation. Team members take the place of Bobbie in carpooling the girls to some of their evening activities and to shop, offering a model of care as mentors and providing stability in lives that without their care would be much more seriously threatened. When crises of such depth strike individuals, they strike at the security of the entire family. In minister-

191

ing to Bobbie, team members are also ministering to her mother and her three children. Perhaps the biggest impact in the long run will be in the children's lives.

It had not been our intention to extend the Care Team model to families with chronically ill or disabled minors, but the pastor of Bobbie's congregation suggested we also visit with Brian and Pam Jenkins. Their only child, Brendan, then three years of age, had been born with multiple congenital anomalies, including a cleft palate that required more than 20 surgical procedures to repair tissue and bone. Pam had resigned from her employment to care for Brendan, who required full-time care at home — the risk of infection from other children kept him from both preschool and church participation. When asked how they could make use of a Care Team, Pam asked if it would be possible on occasions for members to sit with Brendan on Sunday morning, so she and Brian could worship together. A mini-team of four couples was formed, and with each pair sitting with Brendan at home one Sunday each month, Brendan's parents were able not only to worship together but to return to their adult Bible class. In a moving tribute to the care they were receiving from the congregation through its Care Team, Brian spoke at a morning worship service, attributing their stronger marriage to the support of the team.

HEALTH CRISES, SUDDEN OR CHRONIC, CATCH FAMILIES UNPREPARED

Diseases and disabilities which eventually may become chronic and long term can fall upon families unprepared for the ensuing crises. It is unusual for families to plan for such crises; few people include planning to deal with the crises of illness or disability in their long-range expectations of their future. While the marriage vows include commitments to care for each other "in sickness and in health," it is continued good health and prosperity to which they look forward. Few parents like Pam and Brian anticipate that their pregnancy will result in the birth of a catastrophically impaired infant. Parents of teenagers rarely plan for the eventuality of a son's spinal cord injuries due to a diving or auto accident. Nevertheless, while the prospect of caregiving is a fundamental aspect of family life and most family members expect that, if a loved one becomes chronically ill or disabled, they will bear that burden, few families anticipate that possibility or have a clear perception of what may be involved if called on to respond to such catastrophes. Thus, when a loved one becomes chronically ill or disabled, it is as if the crisis is thrust upon family caregivers without warning. Their roles may be assumed with varying degrees of willingness, disruption, resentment, and guilt; and when prolonged, caregiving may result in varying levels of emotional, physical, and spiritual exhaustion. Second Family Care Team ministry can have a sustaining role in these circumstances that call the congregation to manifest its nature as a *community* of faith.

We first met John in 1997, following a call from a hospital discharge planner. She informed the office that John, whose ALS disease was well advanced, had fallen and broken his leg, and when discharged, would need in-home support. Could he have a Care Team? Situated in the eastern corner of the county, with no Care Team in the area, we asked whether John and his family were members of a congregation. The reason for the inquiry is simple: If no Care Team is available in the area, there may be a congregation that could be challenged to develop a team in response to its member's need. In the case of John and Anne, there was. Their pastor was aware that John's condition was following the inevitable course of ALS, but his ministry was limited to serving John Holy Communion at home. Anne, employed at a travel agency, frequently worked ten-hour days, leaving John isolated, lonely, and constantly at risk for the type of injury he had suffered.

An introductory visit by our staff acquainted Anne and John of the ways in which a Care Team could contribute to their well-being, and they gratefully accepted the offer. John's primary needs include companionship—"the phone is a poor substitute for face-to-face relationships"—and a practical need: He was hoping for delivery of a motorized wheelchair. If he had an access ramp at the front door, he could get out of the house, once the summer heat passed. One of the benefits of a Care Team program coordinated by a central office is the ability of staff to connect congregations. The day one staff member visited with John, a second staff member had been offered a motorized

193

wheelchair a family had provided following the death of its user. The chair was available for as long as John could use it, when it would be "recycled" for use by another person who was physically challenged. In the meantime, Care Team members mobilized to build John's access ramp. One of the moving moments in the first interview with John centered on how he was facing his terminal condition. He described how, in a previous congregation, he had been a mentor for a junior high student in a Hispanic neighborhood; and his regret when he developed ALS symptoms was his inability to continue working with his young friend. Now, he said, he was on the receiving end—a role he had not ex-pected to fill. A discussion about the nature of giving and receiving care ensued, and John said with considerable feeling that his theology affirmed that it was just as important to receive care as to offer it: "That does not make it any easier to accept my situation, but it will make a big difference as I lose my strength."

THE BURDEN OF CAREGIVING

Few of us would wish to fill a caregiving role in support of a frail family member; after all, we all hope that our family members will remain healthy and not require such intervention. But when eventualities thrust upon us the responsibilities of responding to loved ones' chronic illnesses or catastrophic disabilities, and even though we accept the caregiving role with good grace, it is difficult to fulfill the role without periods of ambivalence that pit our desire to care against resentment at the loss of freedom and control over our lives. Caregivers who undertake their responsibilities in a loving, empathic, and unselfish manner may be hesitant to acknowledge to others that their activities are burdensome. Recent research into the nature of the caregiving relationship, however, makes it clear that caregivers face many burdens. The concept of burden, in fact, is inherent in caregiving and the focus of much of the literature on caregiving.[29] Care of the caregiver, accordingly, is a key element in Care Team ministry. If the team's sustaining presence shares enough of caregivers' burdens that they are able to continue their work, can defer or avoid institutional care of their loved ones, and can do so without becoming incapacitated themselves, their patients and they are more secure and the light at the end of the tunnel grows a little brighter.

Care Team members address caregivers' needs by showing they understand the stress of caregiving and the ambivalence it evokes. Feelings of frustration, impatience, anger, and grief are less threatening when they are shared with understanding team members. Caregivers are helped to reframe overwhelming feelings and to seek options that had been hidden under the blanket of their hurt and pain. Perhaps most important, Care Teams affirm the importance of the caregiving role and encourage feelings of satisfaction that these efforts are beneficial for both the caregivers and the care partners. The fact that Care Team members are part of the family's congregation maintains the family's links to its religious roots. In instances in which the care partner family has no congregational ties, the team's ministry is a powerful, though usually implicit, message that there is a religious community that cares. The Care Team's ministry is always nonproselytizing, but often evokes interest in the reasons why the team members choose to reach out to people with special needs. This is illustrated in the story of Eleanor at the beginning of this chapter. She was not a member of the team's congregation and described herself as a nominal member of another denomination. She elected to attend worship with team members and transferred her membership to the congregation during the team's second year.

THE FAMILY'S RESPONSE TO ITS CAREGIVING ROLE

Family responses to chronic health problems in adult members are shaped by many factors, one of which is a family's stage of life at the onset of illness or disability. A young adult, if married, is likely to become dependent upon her or his spouse. If the spouse is employed outside the home, and especially if there are young children, balancing competing demands and responsibilities may impose intense strains upon the caregiver. If chronic illness or disability occurs in middle years, the caregiver-spouse is likely to be challenged to provide emotional support to the ill spouse and to growing children, while being the sole source of the family's financial security. As noted above, the incidence of chronic illness rises with age, with the oldest old being most susceptible to this threat. Not only are spouses, if living, likely to be old as well—the circle of peers may include many with health problems that impair their ability to help their friends—they may have their own problems to face. Members of extended families also respond to the severity of chronic conditions. Chronic but comparatively mild conditions may still tax caregivers, but the stresses may be ameliorated by periodic relief from other family members. As health problems become more severe and demanding, caregivers' levels of stress also increase, and resources are stretched. The number of family members able to assist the primary caregiver, the integrity and degree of cohesion within the family, and members' readiness to share caregiving burdens also come into play. The strength and quality of previously existing relationships between family members and the extent to which the family as a whole as well as individual members are embedded in a social network will play a part in determining the shape of each member's behaviors and attitudes.[30]

The nature of the health crisis, including the duration of its onset and the ability and motivation of individuals to manage their own activities of daily living, will also play a large part in how other family members respond to the situation. When onset is gradual, for example, a dementia-related condition, a slowly growing malignancy, or pulmonary-related illness such as emphysema, family members may have an extended period in which to adjust to growing physical and emotional dependency. Caregivers, particularly primary caregivers, may "ease into" their caregiving roles. The readiness and ability of either caregivers or patients to recognize and acknowledge growing impairment may complicate this process. A husband may have difficulty accepting the reality of early symptoms of amyotrophic lateral sclerosis (ALS, or Lou Gehrig's disease) or muscular dystrophy; an adult child may deny that a parent's forgetfulness and occasional confusion may indicate the onset of a demential disease when symptoms are pointed out by other family members. The sudden onset of disability due, for example, to vocational or automobile-related trauma evokes different types of responses. Bobbie's story of a husband who was sympathetic and considerate following his wife's accident but became emotionally distant and finally deserted her and their three children, illustrates the toll such an event can have in a family's life. Even in a family in which members ultimately are able to adapt to the unexpected crisis, the accompanying shock initially may be severe and render adaptation difficult. Feelings, which in the case of gradual onset may be worked through one-by-one, now must be faced in a vortex of ambivalence—loving concern may vie with anxiety, numbness, and panic.

The manner in which caregiving roles are learned also contributes to the ease of adapting to the role. Individuals who experienced family caregiving responsibilities early in childhood may have felt so deprived by the level of attention and care an ill or disabled member received that they retain negative images of caregiving. They may resent being trapped in later life in a primary caregiving role, whereas other individuals enter adult life with very different perceptions of the same role. On the other hand, children who acquire positive images and memories of caregiving from sensitive parents or other adults who serve as mentors may carry these influences throughout their lives. Elizabeth Midlarsky notes that "a precondition for altruistic motivation is, first of all, the concern for others." Asking when the concern for others emerges, she underscores that altruism may develop throughout the life span. Participation in diverse helping roles, including parenting, may increase empathy, altruistic motivation, and subsequent altruistic behavior. Moreover, education, occupation, and caretaking experiences as adults may form and shape moral judgment, and likely assist in the development of positive attitudes toward caregiving.[31] She points to Erik Erikson's later work in which, adding to his conviction that successful resolution of the "mid-life crisis" results in a broadening of concern for others, he posits a ninth developmental stage in which caring and contribution are extended to all of humankind.[32] Our experience in developing intergenerational Care Teams corroborates Midlarsky's findings, but adds a further dimension of particular importance to congregational caregiving, namely, the impact of Care Team participation on children and adolescents who are members of Care Teams.

INTERGENERATIONAL TEAMS

David Morgan states that the ability to define a generation "depends on making comparisons across multiple generations." The separating out of a particular set of birth cohorts such as the baby boom, and labeling that set a generation, requires the location of a "watershed," those events and patterns that mark this generation as different from those that precede and follow it. He states that no one generation stands alone.[33] From the outset, AIDS Care Teams included families that introduced children to the possibilities and challenges of caregiving relationships. Similarly, some Alzheimer's Care Teams recognized the contribution quite young children can make to the emotional health of caregiver and care partner. The notion came into full flower with the development of Second Family Care Teams. The first team included two toddlers and three junior high students whose contributions were profoundly important to the team's care of Eleanor. The visits of the young family were anticipated because the parents' presence meant Eleanor could entertain the children. The students' visits also were particularly meaningful to her. On one occasion, when they inquired whether there was anything to read, Eleanor said she was waiting for them. Arriving after school, she asked them to read the pile of travel brochures on the coffee table. Eleanor told the girls some of her friends had persuaded her to accompany them on a European trip; and when she demurred, they reminded her that she could smell, hear, and touch, and they could describe the various sites! So, she told the girls, "I need to know what I am missing." They spent an hour reading the brochures and shared the story with the Care Team at its next meeting. The young mother of the two children listened to their account, then said: "I don't know why Eleanor would want you to read all the brochures. I had read them to her the day before!" The team members laughed, as they sensed what was behind their care partner's request: It was a way for Eleanor to gain another visit from "her girls." In turn, Eleanor shared the incident with her two older friends as she sat with them, waiting for worship to begin.

It does not take much imagination to realize that what is happening in the lives of children and teenagers who participate in their congregations' pastoral ministries will stay with them throughout their lives. Learning in childhood the skills and nuances of ministry, particularly from parents who model and mentor children, emphasizes that baptized members of the church are called to ministry. Indeed, some school districts require students to participate in community service as a requirement of graduation, and the Boy Scouts have institutionalized the gathering of merit badges amongst which are awards that recognize care of others. Why not as preparation for confirmation? If we take seriously the meaning of baptism as call to ministry, what more significant a step could children take than to learn the meaning of membership in the congregation as they prepare for entry into adulthood! Apart from the values instilled in the lives of children, such a step may be an answer to the problems of congregations in which a minority of members pledge their financial support or join a small group such as an adult class or midweek circle.

A story from another Care Team illustrates the same theme. Eleven-year-old Robert and his two sisters were accustomed to visiting with their parents. They were assigned to Wanda and Bill Phillips, a childless couple in their mid-80s. Wanda's care of Bill following his recent stroke was taking a heavy toll on her, but she initially declined when offered Care Team support. Bill had been instructed he could no longer drive and had become morose and unsociable. She didn't think it advisable to introduce outsiders into their lives; she could not be sure that Bill would tolerate "church folks" kindly. Wanda agreed to a visit from Beth but suggested she should not bring the children. During a second visit Beth was accompanied by Robert and the girls. Bill did not appear; but on the third occasion, he stood in the den doorway, glowering. During the following visit, Bill sat down briefly beside Wanda, and as he rose after a few minutes to leave, Robert asked him if he really had participated in the D-Day invasion at Omaha Beach. Bill stopped in surprise and sat down. Yes, he had been there, he told Robert, who replied that he needed to write a term paper on America's contribution in the Second World War. He wondered if Bill would tell him what it was like to be in the Army. Bill responded with a few gruff sentences, but agreed to see Robert again. In the ensuing weeks, Robert called to talk with Bill on the way home from school, and a firm friendship developed between the veteran and the boy.

The story did not end with the writing of the term paper. Bill asked Wanda to drive him to the ballpark so he could watch Robert play baseball. Just before Christmas, Bill had Wanda drive him to the gift shop so he could purchase ornaments for the miniature trees in the children's bedrooms. He presented the little packages during the Christmas dinner to which the family had invited Wanda and Bill. The children ran to their rooms to place the gifts on their trees with Bill hobbling after them to enjoy their delight. As he left the room, Wanda told the parents that this was the first time Bill had bought a gift for a child—she could not believe the change they had made in his life—and her own. On Grandparents' Day, an annual event at the children's school, Wanda and Bill were present. When challenged by other grandparents that they did not have grandchildren, Bill said proudly, "Oh yes, we do."

NURSING HOME PLACEMENT

As in the case of Wanda and Bill, Care Team ministry is nearly always centered in care partners' homes. However, team support of caregivers does not end upon nursing home placement, though placement does change the kinds of involvement caregivers have with their loved ones. The decision to place an impaired or frail family member in a special facility is painful for many families. It may even represent failure and arouse guilt if a previous promise not to do so is reversed. The cost of nursing home placement has to be weighed against the family's ability to bear that cost and the increasing difficulty of providing adequate care in the home. The pain is exacerbated when family members cannot agree on the decision for institutional care. Conflict over the decision is not unusual. Care Team members do not participate in this decision, which can only be made by the primary caregiver in consultation with other family members. But team members, as in each other moment of care, can be effective listeners, a sounding board off which to bounce both options and feelings. Once the decision is made, it is customary for the team, which has been so closely involved in the in-home stage of care to continue the ministry of support and encouragement with the caregiver. A Care Team member describes one such relationship: Frances, diagnosed with cancer but in remission, cared for her husband, Gerald. Frances could call on her son who did what he could, but was hampered by her insistence on bearing the major responsibility for Gerald's care. The Care Team visited Frances and Gerald weekly, and responded to Frances' need for affirmation of her primary caregiving role; her care of Gerald was tender and loving, a joy to observe. When Frances experienced her first stroke, team visits were increased to three or four weekly. It was clear that her ability to care for Gerald was gravely compromised by her physical limitations and confusion. The team leader kept closely in touch with their son, who decided to admit Gerald to a nursing home. The team's support of Frances, increasingly distraught because of her separation from Gerald, helped her to deal with her grief and her stroke-related limitations. Team members continued their in-home support, including driving her to the nursing home each day.

We have emphasized throughout the importance of the mutuality of the pastoral caregiving relationship as a partnership in which those who care and those who receive care are both aware of their wounds and open to the healing gifts each brings. We are called as people of faith to care for one another and to extend our care to those who are harried, like sheep without a shepherd. We face two interlocking tasks as we enter the twenty-first century: (a) The role of the religious community. The rapid increase in number of the oldest old almost certainly will be characterized by a concomitant increase in the number of low income, medically dependent elderly. The religious community's traditional role as a prophetic voice for the marginalized—the "poor"—demands that church and synagogue speak out on behalf of those who do not have a voice that can be heard amidst the clamor of self-interested groups. (b) The tradition of a reconciling community. This tradition identifies the people of God as a reconciling community, calling people to live as a community the common goal of which is its members' care for one another. This identifying characteristic of God's people makes this people the firstfruits, a foretaste, of the community of which it is God's will all should be members. We are to be like a city set on a hill, a lamp held aloft. This community's care of its frail members must be a beacon for the wider community of which it is a part. The ministry that Care Teams offer their care partners helps to fulfill the church's role.

IMPACT OF CARE TEAM MINISTRY IN
THE LIVES OF TEAM MEMBERS

It is appropriate to end this chapter by recollecting the impact team ministry exercises in the lives of team members. When asked what keeps her committed to Care Team ministry, Mary said that now that she has retired from her nursing career, she needs to be doing something useful; and the team's care of care partners is a wonderful way to keep active. When pressed, she described how, when her children were young, she had been closely involved as a volunteer at their schools. Now that they are married, that service continues in her Care Team activities. Her gratification is a feeling of doing something worthwhile that keeps her challenged as it helps family caregivers continue their caring responsibilities with loved ones. Mary values the companionship she experiences in the close, intimate relationship she has with other team members and with care partners. Aware of her ambivalence, she is uncomfortable having people depend on her, yet her feeling of being needed makes the effort worthwhile. As so many Care Team members state, Mary receives far more for herself than she can offer to others. Shyly, she indicated that her husband has also benefited from her Care Team work. He doesn't contribute directly as a team member, but shares Mary's dedication to people with special needs. Mary continues her commitment with his support.

Lila talked about the lasting friendships she had made with care partners to whom she has ministered. Ministry to elderly members in her inner-city congregation expanded greatly when the Care Team ministry was introduced in 1994. During her three years as an active team member, she was personally in contact with more than thirty elderly members of her congregation, usually accompanied by a wheelchair-bound team member who, though physically limited, shared her ministry, visiting some care partners at least weekly and contacting others regularly by phone. Calls and visits were never over until news of the congregation was shared with homebound members. On days when she was unable to make a home visit, care partners phoned to ask why she had not come and to tell her they had missed her visit. Her active team participation was restricted following a stroke from which she is recovering. When her care partners learned of her hospitalization, they called to ask about her progress, always thanking her for her cheery visits. Many of these calls are still received daily. As Lila scanned the list of her team's care partners, she recalled more than thirty who had died since the team's ministry began and spoke of the gratitude family members expressed for care loved ones had received. Lila's greatest satisfactions are twofold. She experienced a "high" when the ministry began in her congregation, which she still feels every time a care partner calls. Second, she recalls Mrs. Thoms, a long-time member of the congregation who had traveled widely in the United States and shared her knowledge of their United Methodist tradition gathered during her travels. Lila stated: "I never would have known Mrs. Thoms but for the Care Team ministry. I have been truly blessed."

CHAPTER 8

A FUTURE FOR CAREGIVING

The journey that began in 1985 with our first Care Team continues in Houston and its neighboring counties serving people with HIV/AIDS, dementia, and other frail adults, with branch lines that lead to Dayton, Ohio; Columbia, South Carolina; Abilene and Corpus Christi, Texas; Oshkosh, Madison, and Appleton, Wisconsin; and Stanwood, Washington; and to more than 70 other cities in which our AIDS Care Team ministry has been replicated. The 1998 President's Service Award to the Foundation we created and lead emphasizes growing recognition of the national reach of the Care Team model. Our enthusiasm about the potential of Care Team ministry is based on our experience since 1985, the expanding experience of others, and the theological ground in which these ministries of sustaining presence are rooted. The comfort experienced by care partners, the personal and spiritual growth of Care Team members, and the renewal of congregational pastoral ministry that we have witnessed in Houston and elsewhere encourage us to explore even further how this model of ministry may meet human needs and contribute to the mission of the church. We continue to explore additional forms to which the concept can be applied. Two additional ministries of sustaining presence utilizing the Care Team concept are under development.

GRIEF CARE TEAMS

Beginning with the first AIDS care partner, Care Teams have ministered to people they knew were dying in their care. Also from the beginning, we promised care partners that they would not suffer and die alone. Care Teams have honored that pledge. From 1985 until September 1999, more than 1,184 AIDS care partners served by teams have died, and team members were present to support them and their families through end-stage disease and death. One of the duties of our staff, therefore, is to support Care Team members who experience multiple deaths and continuing grief. Care Team orientation, subsequent training during team meetings, and continuing education sessions address the grief process and support team members as they grieve care partners' deaths.

Careful monitoring of the grief of caregivers whose loved ones have died focused our attention on development of Grief Care Teams. The Open Society Institute's *Project on Death in America* was convinced the need existed and funded a two-year pilot program we designed to explore the feasibility of Grief Care Team ministry. The potential for grief ministry was evident. First, many congregations are as little prepared to minister to bereaved families during the course of their grief as they are to recognize and respond to the needs of chronically ill and catastrophically disabled members. The newsletter of the Association for Death Education and Counseling reported, based on a recent Gallup poll, that while a national sample of 1200 adults expressed a strong need for spiritual support, only 36 percent believed that such support could be found with clergy. The study concluded with a recommendation that steps be taken by appropriate and specific groups to alleviate the "all-too-common situation of people dying alone, feeling unloved, unforgiven by God, with little hope, and in physical, emotional, psychological, and social pain."[1] Second, while Care Team ministry addresses needs of the relatively small number of congregants who suffer from catastrophic illnesses, many of which are terminal, bereavement-related needs exist throughout the congregation and may be outside the scope of an existing Care Team's responsibilities. Moreover, the grief experiences of many families are unrelated to chronic illness or disability. Third, while it is desirable for congregations to supplement existing pastoral ministries by the formation at least of Second Family Care Teams, the same case can be made for establishment of Grief Care Teams. Congregations have a duty to minister to families caring for chronically ill members *and* to support families that mourn the deaths of loved ones.

We conjectured that one reason for the lack of adequate and effective ministry to bereaved families was a societal reluctance to confront dying, death, and grief concerns that pervades congregations.[2] We proposed a coordinated grief education and grief support ministry to congregations that participated in the grief project. Development of an effective bereavement ministry required that congregations and individual families comprehend the elements of the grief process and understand the course of "normal" grief and the concerns arising from "complicated" grief. A well-informed congregation would then have a foundation on which to build a comprehensive grief ministry. Initially, ten congregations participated in the pilot phase of the project. Congregations were offered four options from which to choose.

• All-age grief education, including segments for K-12 children and young, middle age, and older adults.

• Initiation of a grief support group.

• Development of a Grief Care Team that would provide continuing ministry to individual families at least throughout the first year of bereavement.

• Development of a Care Team to minister to families caring for terminally ill members. While in congregations that already had developed AIDS, Alzheimer's, or Second Family teams, this aspect of care could be referred to existing Care Team(s); the notion of a Grief Care Team may be developed in congregations in which that step has not been taken.

The concept of how a Grief Care Team may function was described by Sunderland in his book, *Getting Through Grief,* in which a blueprint was offered to guide congregations seeking to implement a coordinated grief education and support ministry.[3] The story of one congregation illustrates the value of implementing such a ministry. Epiphany of the Lord Catholic Community was established in 1981 and has grown quickly to a parish of 3,153 families. It is located in what formerly were rice fields in Katy, a dormitory suburb 25 miles west of

Houston. The congregation consists of younger, middle class families, most with young children and teenagers. By the early 90s, however, grief care was listed as a parish ministry.

Claire and her family moved to Houston late in 1997 when her husband was transferred to Houston by his company. He died suddenly within a month of settling in Houston, leaving Claire to care for three young children aged 1, 2, and 6 years. They had not yet unpacked their belongings. Claire, who had undergone a kidney transplant ten years earlier, was diagnosed with cardiomyopathy a few days after her husband died. Physicians determined that she needed a heart transplant. Due to the extent of her disease, Claire was so weak that she was unable to do housework, drive the car, and care for her two youngest children, who were placed in the care of Claire's sister in another city; she missed her children, adding to her distress.

Grief Care Team members rallied to Claire's assistance, unpacking boxes, hanging pictures and drapes, sorting clothes into drawers and closets, and running errands. Members coordinated the activities of other parish ministries, including the transportation committee to get Claire to clinics and doctors' offices, and a ladies group that is providing meals. The team also serves as Claire's ombudsman with her husband's company. Members were present when the medical social worker discussed with Claire the limits of her resources and stated that she was fortunate the congregation was standing with her—there were few other possibilities for support! In an extraordinary way, Claire became the team's "teacher." A faith-filled and amazing person (the team's description of Claire), she had always reached out to help others, had been active as a volunteer in community activities in other cities, but now was the person in need of care and support. She taught team members by her own sensitivity and grace. They learned from Claire what it means to be totally dependent on others—and team members learned the lesson that any one of them, perhaps without warning, could find himself or herself in such a position. We discussed with parish staff the stress evoked by the Care Team's support of Claire. Team members feel the depth of Claire's grief following her husband's untimely death and her own health crisis. Support of members of the Grief Care Team, including recognition and response to their own grief, is essential if members are to maintain their support of the family. It is both heart-warming and heart-wrenching to stand by the team as members stand by their care partner.

KIDS' PALS CARE TEAMS

The need of caregivers of chronically ill and severely disabled children for in-home assistance, especially respite, is as real as it is for frail adults and their caregivers, and led us to examine the application of the Care Team concept to support this population. Pediatricians, social service agencies, and researchers involved with these families speak of the urgency and scope of the need. Research indicates that divorce is from 2.5 to 10 percent higher in families caring for chronically ill or severely developmentally disabled children compared to other families, and up to 30 percent of mothers who remain at home to care for these children experience depression.[4] Although it is difficult to ascertain the full extent of parental divorce due primarily to birth and care of ill and disabled children, some families so stricken disintegrate due to the stress a child's catastrophic needs may exert on the parents. Mothers who are abandoned by husbands find it difficult to cope with the stress of daily, and often 24-hour, attention their children require, further endangering the family. Respite care for these parents is usually first on the list of stated needs.

With Care Team ministry so effective in response to the needs of families caring for loved ones with dementia, AIDS, frail seniors living alone, and other frail adults struggling with the distress of chronic illness or disability, it is reasonable to assume that it would be equally beneficial for families caring in the home for ill and severely disabled children. We are investigating the special considerations of ministry that would apply to ill and vulnerable children. Screening and supervision of Care Team members who work with children will entail background checks of Care Team members to comply with legal requirements if government funds are solicited in support of this ministry. We shall provide liability insurance, as we do for all Care Team members, to relieve team members' concern. Agreements for service may need to be more precise in contrast to the more informal oral agreements with adult care partners, specifically ruling out nursing procedures and including complete instructions for all supportive care. The special conditions that differentiate ministry with children with special needs from Care Team services with frail adults should be manageable. Ministries of Kids' Pals Care Teams will be supervised by staff with credentials and experience appropriate to the care of chronically ill and disabled children. As funds become available, Kids' Pals Care Team ministry will be initiated in a limited number of congregations as a pilot study, while procedures are tested and revised.

CONCLUSION

Our thesis that underlies this presentation of Care Team ministry is that pastoral care is too important to the identity, mission, character, and vitality of congregations to be left to chance. Structures for and practices of caregiving that served congregations well in the past may not be responsive to the intense and continuing support needs of members and others within social, cultural, and economic contexts undergoing radical change. One-on-one care is responsive to most pastoral ministry: a pastoral call or visit, the ministry of one member with another, a congregation's response to a crisis (accident, death, or other devastating event) will likely remain the norm for congregational pastoral care. But, as we have emphasized, this mode of pastoral ministry often fails to support members and their families whose needs are so intense and so extensive that this form of pastoral care is insufficient. Unfortunately, families experiencing this level of need may feel the congregation is not "there" for them, a far cry from a more vigorous experience of community described in the New Testament. Such needs simply are too great to be met consistently and effectively by single caregivers, no matter how dedicated or competent they may be. Moreover, alternate sources of support, such as home health care and other paid services, may be beyond financial reach, and even if accessible, do not address the need for continuing pastoral ministry. Community-based volunteer care and support may be similarly unavailable, and family support may not exist or other family members may be distant or unable for a variety of reasons to participate in their care. Friends and neighbors might provide some assistance, but few people may make the long-term commitment required in situations of dire need.

It is timely for the church to strengthen its heritage of community, particularly with respect to the care that members offer to one another. Care Team ministry is one means by which this recovery may be made. For situations in which the support needs are too great for a single caregiver to meet alone, a team response may make the difference that allows a person to remain at home rather than receive care in an institutional setting. From a theological perspective, the ability to remain in place adds to the benefits a congregation realizes by embodying the biblical concept of the family of God. Our experience with AIDS, Alzheimer's, and Second Family Care Team ministries suggests that congregational pastoral care can be enriched by adding in-home support of individuals and families with special needs to customary forms of care.

What we propose here and have demonstrated in our work since 1985 is not new. The theological roots of Care Team ministry reach into the lives of first-century Christians as described in Scripture. In addition, the organization and practice of Care Team ministry resembles the life of adult Sunday school classes, which have been an effective instrument of church growth, religious education, and pastoral care. The small group caregiving ministry of a Care Team demonstrates a congregation's commitment to each member. It provides assistance and support that may be desperately needed by members coping with adversity. It also provides a mechanism for ministry that efficiently and effectively utilizes the gifts of members for ministries of sustaining presence. The contemporary fascination with individualism appears to have penetrated the boundaries of the church at the expense of community, and familiar and intimate relationships characteristic of community. But, as Gareth Icenogle observes, "[w]here there is no community, there is no ministry. Where there is no ministry, there is no community."[5] Care Team ministries of sustaining presence are one means by which to recover, preserve, and enrich ministry and community.

Carl George, director of the Charles E. Fuller Institute of Evangelism and Church Growth, identifies needs the church must address in the future: "(1) the hunger for a personal touch, (2) the continual need for new options, (3) the need to have a place to interpret what's happening in the world, (4) a structure to help the church deal with rapid change, (5) a place for both women and men to lead in ministry, (6) a way to motivate every member in faith and ministry, (7) an organizational structure where people matter, and (8) a way for every member to receive personal care."[6] George argues that these needs are best met through small-group ministry structures. He may be fully correct about the utility and sufficiency of small-group structures. Although we find value in small-group ministries, we have not seen evidence to support George's claim that these needs are *best* met through small groups, other than in those situations where intense needs dictate a small-group approach to care such as Care Team ministry. Corporate activities within a congregation still appear to us to have a vital role and respond to different sets of needs. It is not an either/or question for us. Rather, there is obvious merit in small and large-group structures in doing the work of the church. This is not a matter that we need to settle in order to assert from our experience that Care Team ministry can, in fact, address some of the needs identified by George and others.

Robert Wuthnow's analysis of the church in the twenty-first century is instructive to consideration of Care Team ministry. Wuthnow suggests that one reason to reflect on the future is to provide room in the present to think about what we are doing. In our opinion, Care Team ministry can contribute very well to actualizing community within our churches and to providing pastoral care as a ministry of the *congregation* across a broader range of pastoral needs. If we look into the future, are we content for the church to forfeit its care of individual members and families entirely or settle for an impoverished substitute for community? If our answer is no, or "not exactly," then changes need to occur now in order to meet the challenges prompted by systemic and radical trends reshaping society in general, and health care and social services in particular.

A critical challenge for the church in the twenty-first century, according to Wuthnow, is the experience of the institutional church as community: "If the church is unable to provide community, none of these other programmatic concerns [finances, membership, missions, programs] will make very much difference, for the community above all, as Karl Rahner has observed, 'is the visible sign of salvation that God has established in this seemingly godless world.' "[7] The realization of community, therefore, is pivotal to the future vitality of the church and its primary embodiment in a congregation. Community is the way the church functions. It is basic to a person's Christian identity, which necessarily is developed in relation to community. One's search for community in a congregation is likely through participation in small groups, such as a singles group, choir, class, or other special purpose group, where meaningful interaction with others is more likely and the young are incorporated into a community of memory.

Hope for the church as community rests in the church's realization of *koinonia* or mutual support of every member's commitment to the faith and to each person's physical and emotional needs.[8] In theory and in practice, as we have described in the preceding chapters, Care Team ministry is one means by which *koinonia* may be actualized and the future of the church strengthened. The ministries of sustaining presence provided by Care Team members on behalf of congregations help make meaningful each member's Christian identification. If being Christian becomes meaningless, the church becomes irrelevant to God's redemptive purpose. We share Wuthnow's belief that the church retains power to make Christian identity and faith meaningful in its existence as *a community of memory*, in its *denominational structures*, and *as a supportive community*.

The church is a community of memory. It is constituted by founding events and perpetuated as its story or constitutive narrative is told and retold. It offers examples of men and women who have embodied and exemplified its meaning as community. Its tradition is forged on these stories, which contribute to the formation of one's identification with this particular community of memory. According to Henri Nouwen, "the first obligation of the apostle vis-a-vis the community—beyond founding it—is to make the faithful remember (the story) they have received and already know—or should know. So it is in keeping with the core of the biblical tradition to look at ministry in the context of remembrance."[9] Nouwen continues that the sustaining power of memory is most visible in God's revelation in Jesus Christ. Jesus reveals to the disciples that only in memory will real intimacy with him be possible, and only in that memory will they experience the full meaning of what they have witnessed.[10] Care Team ministry can have a strategic role in the formation of Christian identity by constituting and exemplifying *koinonia* and the practice of caregiving, which supports the spiritual, physical, and emotional needs of one another. The story of caregiving that accrues teaches succeeding generations about community and confers permission to create new ways to realize community as new situations unfold.

The contribution of denominational structure and identity to community is more indirect. Denominational ties and programs tend to be more significant to clergy than to laypeople. Clergy denominational responsibilities and professional perceptions of clergy as spiritual guides or personal witnesses to what it means to be Christian may relegate pastoral caregiving to a lower priority. Nurture of the congregation and caregiving may become merely one task among the many with which clergy are confronted daily. A pastor's participation in denominational activities brings the global mission of the denomination to the local congregation, and the local congregation participates in that mission through the representation of the pastor and contributions to the denominational budget. This sort of pastoral activity has an impact on community and Christian identity. Wuthnow suggests that people relate to a particular denomination less out of loyalty and more because they like the pastor, people, building, location, or activities. Congregations in which pastors have responsibilities beyond the local church may have a heightened lay involvement by members who shape the identity of the congregation and give life to community. Lay caregiving may become a ministry of the congregation consistent with the biblical precedent. Care Team ministry may be a structure by which this ministry of the congregation may be implemented, Christian identity defined, and community realized.

Finally, Christian identity is conferred through the church as a supportive community. Traditional support systems are undergoing significant change. Families are more fragmented and dispersed than ever before. Parenting consists stereotypically of soccer, Scouts, and school more than teaching caregiving or the moral virtues. The larger size of congregations and an accompanying impersonality may erode a congregation's capacity to augment the identity-shaping tasks of family with adult role models and social support. Small groups within congregations, however, may redress this shortcoming by providing opportunities for intimacy, ministries that actualize community, and

213

times for transmitting the story from one generation to another. Care Teams that have intergenerational memberships including whole families is one means for the church to be a supportive community that perpetuates and validates its constitutive narrative.

Care and compassion are ethical ideals central to the church's identity and mission. Through stories of caregiving as well as participation in caregiving ministry, the value of caring may be learned. Through the example of ordinary people, caring is seen as within reach of every person. By being cared for in a time of sorrow, loss, or crisis, one may be more motivated to offer relief to another in a time of need. And in extending oneself to another, one learns important lessons about oneself. The dynamic of caregiving and the routine of seemingly trivial expressions of care and support help people to appreciate that small deeds are acts of compassion central to the Christian gospel. Wuthnow observes that "the stories of caring that we experience in our own lives are an epiphany. They become part of the gospel message. When they are related to the biblical tradition, they take on a larger meaning, an added historical and sacred significance. When they are told in community, their power is amplified."[11] As Care Team members visit with care partners, their presence embodies God's presence; and when they leave a home, they leave behind as a gift to their fellow members awareness that their presence is also a reminder that God is present in that home. As the story of Care Team ministry grows in a congregation, it becomes a salient and defining feature of the congregation's story.

The Care Team story now is part of the caregiving identity and community narrative of many congregations in the United States. In Houston and elsewhere, Care Team ministry is helping congregations to strengthen pastoral ministry as a function of the congregation. It is providing an infrastructure for community to be actualized. It is contributing to the formation and meaning of Christian identity. Care Team ministry will be a lamp set on a hill, a sign that people of God care for those whose burdens leave them weary and heavy laden. Such sustaining ministries will strengthen and perpetuate the church's story of caregiving, reviving the servant and pastoral ministries of the congregation, and translating the concept of community into a way of living. By so doing, the church will be stronger and broken people will be sustained.

NOTES

Chapter 1. Congregational Caregiving

1. Merton P. Strommen, Milo L. Brekke, Ralph C. Underwager, Arthur L. Johnson, *Report of a Two-Year Study of 5,000 Lutherans Between the Ages of 15-65: Their Beliefs, Values, Attitudes, Behaviors* (Minneapolis: Augsburg Publishing House, 1972), pp. 40-42.

2. Robert N. Bellah et al., *Habits of the Heart: Individualism and Commitment in American Life* (New York: Harper & Row, Publishers, 1985), p. 50.

3. Ibid., p. 84.

4. See William F. May, *The Patient's Ordeal* (Bloomington: Indiana University Press, 1991), p. 153.

5. Andrei Simic, "Aging, World View and Intergenerational Relations in America and Yugoslavia," in *The Cultural Context of Aging: Worldwide Perspectives*, ed. Jay Sokolovsky (New York: Bergin and Garvey Publishers, 1990), p. 91.

6. Ibid, p. 94.

7. Ibid., p. 106.

8. Quoted in Bruce D. Marshall, "Why bother with the church?" *Christian Century* (24 January 1996): 74.

9. See, Earl E. Shelp and Ronald H. Sunderland, "AIDS and the Church," *Christian Century* (11-18 September 1985): 797-800.

10. Bellah et al., *Habits of the Heart*, p. 84.

Chapter 2. Pastoral Ministry

1. Bernard Cooke, *Ministry to Word and Sacraments* (Philadelphia: Fortress Press, 1976), p. vii.

2. The list of theologians includes H. Richard Niebuhr, Carroll Wise, Seward Hiltner, and James Fenhagen.

3. Charles Gerkin, *An Introduction to Pastoral Care* (Nashville: Abingdon Press, 1997), p. 92.

4. Cooke, *Ministry to Word and Sacraments*, p. 61, also pp. 62-64; 197-200.

5. Ibid., p. 5.

6. John T. McNeill, *History of the Cure of Souls* (New York: Harper and Brothers, 1951), p. 268.

7. Karl Barth, *Church Dogmatics* (Edinburgh: T. and T. Clark, 1962), IV, 3, p. 743.

8. Alan Richardson, *An Introduction to the Theology of the New Testament* (New York: Harper and Bros., 1958), p. 301.

9. The kingly role and function defined in Jewish scripture and manifested in the person of Christ is most fully expressed as servanthood exercised as pastoral oversight of God's people. Earl E. Shelp and Ronald H. Sunderland, eds., *The Pastor as Servant* (New York: The Pilgrim Press, 1986), pp. ix-xvi.

10. Hendrik Kraemer, *A Theology of the Laity* (Philadelphia: Westminster Press, 1958), p. 143.

11. Richardson, *Theology of the New Testament,* p. 304.

12. Lesslie Newbigin, "Four Talks on 1 Peter," *We Were Brought Together,* Report of the National Conference of Australian Churches, Melbourne, 1960 (Sydney: Australian Council of Churches, 1960), p. 101. See also Cooke, *Ministry to Word and Sacraments,* pp. 197 ff.; James Fenhagen, *Mutual Ministry* (New York: Seabury Press, 1977), pp. 123-26; James Fenhagen, *Ministry and Solitude* (New York: Seabury Press, 1981), pp. 16-18.

13. J. A. T. Robinson, *Layman's Church* (London: Lutterworth Press, 1963), p. 16.

14. Hans Rudi-Weber, *Signs of Renewal* (Geneva: World Council of Churches, 1957), p. 65.

15. Ronald H. Sunderland, "A Concept of Ministry Based on the Supervisory Process Developed by the Clinical Pastoral Education Movement" (Unpublished S. T. M. Thesis, Southern Methodist University, Dallas, Texas, 1968). Also "Lay Pastoral Care," *Journal of Pastoral Care,* XLII (summer 1988): 159-71.

16. Max Thurian and Geoffrey Wainright, eds, *Baptism and Eucharist: Ecumenical Convergence in Celebration* (Geneva: World Council of Churches Publications, 1983), pp. 3-4.

17. Oscar Cullmann, *Baptism in the New Testament* (London: S. C. M. Press, 1950), p. 31.

18. Fenhagen, *Mutual Ministry,* p. 21.

19. Fenhagen, *Ministry and Solitude,* p. 14.

20. Cooke, *Ministry to Word and Sacraments,* p. 198.

21. Ibid., p. 351.

22. Victor Paul Furnish, "Theology and Ministry in the Pauline Letters," in *A Biblical Basis For Ministry,* ed. Earl E. Shelp and Ronald H. Sunderland (Philadelphia: Westminster Press, 1981), p. 102.

23. Furnish, "Theology and Ministry," pp. 118-19.

24. Ibid., p. 132.

25. Richard P. McBrien, *Ministry: A Theological, Pastoral Handbook* (San Francisco: Harper & Row, 1986), p. 111.

26. Parker J. Palmer, *The Company of Strangers* (New York: Crossroad Publishing, 1983), p. 69.

27. Thomas W. Ogletree, *Hospitality to the Stranger* (Philadelphia: Fortress Press, 1985), p. 3.

28. Stanley Hauerwas, *A Community of Character* (Notre Dame: University of Notre Dame Press, 1985), p. 23; also p. 49.

29. Robert Banks, *Paul's Idea of Community* (Grand Rapids: Wm. B. Eerdmans, 1980), pp. 102-3.

30. Ibid., p. 111.

31. John Patton, *Pastoral Care in Context* (Louisville: Westminster/John Knox Press, 1993), p. 24.

32. Ibid., p. 27.

33. Cited by Ronald H. Sunderland, "The Character of Servanthood," in *The Pastor as Servant,* ed. Earl E. Shelp and Ronald H. Sunderland (New York: Pilgrim Press, 1986), p. 43.

34. William A. Clebsch and Charles R. Jaekle, *Pastoral Care in Historical Perspective* (Englewood Cliffs, N.J.: Prentice-Hall, 1964), p. 7.

35. Schubert Ogden, Personal communication; see Ronald H. Sunderland, "The Character of Servanthood," note 23, p. 126.

36. Sunderland, "The Character of Servanthood," pp. 42-45.

37. Martin Buber, *The Knowledge of Man,* ed./tr. Maurice Friedman (New York: Harper & Row, 1965), p. 71.

38. Texas Bix Bender, *Don't Squat with Yer Spurs On* (Salt Lake City: Gibbs Smith/ Peregrine Smith Books, 1992), p. 46.

39. Robert Wuthnow, *Acts of Compassion* (Princeton, N.J.: Princeton University Press, 1991), p. 8.

40. Ronald H. Sunderland, "Pastoral Care of Volunteers," in *Dictionary of Pastoral Care and Counseling*, ed. Rodney J. Hunter (Nashville: Abingdon Press, 1990), pp. 121-31. See also the entry "Lay Pastoral Care and Counseling," pp. 632-34.

41. McBrien, *Ministry,* p. 110.

42. Alan Keith-Lucas, *Giving and Taking Help* (Chapel Hill: University of North Carolina Press, 1972), pp. 60 ff.

43. Ibid., p. 47.

44. Henri Nouwen, "Care and the Elderly," in *Aging and the Human Spirit,* ed. Carol LeFevre and Perry LeFevre (Chicago: Exploration Press, 1981), pp. 292-93.

45. Keith-Lucas, *Giving and Taking Help,* pp. 70-88.

46. Ibid., pp. 70-88, 204-5.

47. James Wharton, "Theology and Ministry in the Hebrew Scriptures," in *A Biblical Basis for Ministry,* ed. Earl E. Shelp and Ronald H. Sunderland (Philadelphia: Westminster Press, 1981), pp. 27-28.

48. Ibid., p. 60.

49. Dietrich Bonhoeffer, *Ethics* (London: S C M Press, 1955), pp. 83 ff.

50. Wharton, "Theology and Ministry," p. 69.

51. Ibid., p. 71.

Chapter 3. Ministries of Sustaining Presence

1. Herbert Anderson, "The Congregation: Health Center or Healing Community," *Word and World* (Spring, 1989), pp. 123, 126-27.

2. Milton Mayeroff, *On Caring* (New York: Harper & Row, 1971), p. 45.

3. Robert Wuthnow, *Christianity in the Twenty-First Century* (New York: Oxford University Press, 1993), pp. 93-95.

4. Ibid., p. 70.

5. Henri J. M. Nouwen, Donald P. McNeill, Douglas A. Morrison, *Compassion: A Reflection on the Christian Life* (New York: Image Books, 1983), p. 4 .

6. James M. Gustafson, *Ethics from a Theocentric Perspective: Volume Two, Ethics and Theology* (Chicago: University of Chicago Press, 1984), p. 210.

7. Shelp's earliest work with metaphors and caring professionals was published in his study of moral perspectives and issues in neonatology. The metaphor of sustaining presence was applied to the role of neonatologists caring for severely impaired newborns in intensive care nurseries. Cf. Earl E. Shelp, *Born to Die? Deciding the Fate of Critically Ill Newborns* (New York: Free Press, 1986), pp. 92-98. The application of the metaphor to caregiving relationships, in general, and pastoral caregiving in particular, has been a continuing interest since this early work.

8. Gareth Weldon Icenogle, *Biblical Foundations for Small Group Ministry* (Downers Grove: Inter Varsity Press, 1994), p. 36.

9. Katherine Doob Sakenfeld, *Faithfulness in Action: Loyalty in Biblical Perspective* (Philadelphia: Fortress Press, 1985), p. 102.

10. James L. Mays, quoted in Sakenfeld, p. 103.

11. Walter C. Wright, Jr., "The Ministry of Leadership: Empowering People," in *Incarnational Ministry*, ed. Christian D. Kettler and Todd H. Speidell (Colorado Springs: Helmers and Howard, 1990), p. 212.

12. Mayeroff, *On Caring,* p. 4.

13. Ibid., p. 23.

14. Nel Noddings, *Caring: A Feminine Approach to Ethics and Moral Education* (Berkeley: University of California Press, 1984), p. 31.

15. Mayeroff, *On Caring,* p. 22.

16. Wendy Farley, *Tragic Vision and Divine Compassion* (Louisville: Westminster/John Knox Press, 1990), pp. 93-94.

17. Ibid., pp. 115-16.

18. Henri J. M. Nouwen, cited by Icenogle, *Biblical Foundations,* p. 180.

19. Stanley Hauerwas, *Suffering Presence* (Notre Dame: University of Notre Dame Press, 1986), p. 77.

20. Ibid., pp. 81-82.

21. William B. Oglesby, *Biblical Themes for Pastoral Care* (Nashville: Abingdon Press, 1980), p. 41.

22. Farley, *Tragic Vision,* p. 113.

23. Hauerwas, *Suffering Presence,* p. 78.

24. Ibid., p. 80.

25. Ibid., p. 35.

26. Robert Wuthnow, *Learning to Care: Elementary Kindness in an Age of Indifference* (New York: Oxford University Press, 1995), p. 44.

27. Farley, *Tragic Vision,* p. 81.

28. Ibid., p. 119.

29. Oglesby, *Biblical Themes,* p. 83.

30. Ibid., p. 83.

31. Michael E. Lodahl, *Shekhinah/Spirit: Divine Presence in Jewish and Christian Thought* (New York: Paulist Press, 1992), p. 141.

32. See Farley, *Tragic Vision,* p. 114.

33. The Sunday school movement began in the United States during the second decade of the nineteenth century because Sunday school classes proved to be an "effective instrument of evangelical values and a useful means for inculcating agreed-upon virtues." Martin Marty, *Righteous Empire: The Protestant Experience in America* (New York: Dial Press, 1970), p. 75. By the 1850s, increasing numbers of the poor prompted Sunday schools to cooperate with benevolence societies to address social needs, thereby extending their mission beyond the religious education of the faithful. Cf. Timothy L. Smith, *Revivalism and Social Reform: American Protestantism on the Eve of the Civil War* (New York: Harper & Row), pp. 163-67, and Robert Baird, *Religion in America* (New York: Harper Torchbooks, 1970), pp. 166 ff.

34. William A. Clebsch, *From Sacred to Profane America: The Role of Religion in American History* (New York: Harper & Row, 1968), p. 88.

35. See Constant H. Jacquet, Jr., ed., *Yearbook of American and Canadian Churches, 1990* (Nashville: Abingdon Press, 1990) and Kenneth B. Bedell, ed., *Yearbook of American and Canadian Churches* (Nashville: Abingdon Press, 1994).

36. Mark Chaves and James C. Cavendish, "More Evidence on U.S. Catholic Church Attendance," *Journal for Scientific Study of Religion* 33 (1994): 376-81; *Christian Century* (8-15 September 1993), pp. 848-49; C. Kirk Hardaway, Penny Long Marler, Mark Chaves, "What the Polls Don't Show: A Closer Look at U. S. Church Attendance," *American Sociological Review* 58 (December 1993): 741-52; C. Kirk Hardaway and Penny Long Marler, "Did you really go to church this week? Behind the poll data," *Christian Century* (6 May 1998): 472-75; and for a defense of self-reports see Michael Hout and Andrew M. Greeley, "The Center Doesn't Hold: Church Attendance in the United States, 1940–1984," *American Sociological Review* 52 (June 1987): 325-45.

37. "Church Attendance Hits Six-Decade Low," *Christian Century* (7 May 1997): 441-42.

38. Hardaway and Marler, "Behind the poll data," p. 475.

39. Donald A. Luidens, "Fighting 'Decline': Mainline Churches and the Tyranny of Aggregate Data," *Christian Century* (6 November 1996): 1078.

40. George H. Gallup, Jr., "Six Basic Spiritual Needs of Americans," in *Yearbook of American and Canadian Churches, 1992*, ed. Kenneth B. Bedell and Alice M. Jones (Nashville: Abingdon Press, 1992), pp. 15-16.

41. Robert Wuthnow, *The Restructuring of American Religion: Society and Faith Since World War II* (Princeton: Princeton University Press, 1988), pp. 123-25.

Chapter 4. Care Team Ministry

1. Cf. Earl E. Shelp and Ronald H. Sunderland, "AIDS and the Church," *The Christian Century* (11-18 September 1985): 797-800. Several of the themes that we developed in subsequent books were first articulated in this pioneering article. Our first book that examined AIDS from a pastoral perspective was *AIDS: Personal Stories in Pastoral Perspective* (New York: Pilgrim Press, 1986). Our colleague Peter W. A. Mansell, M.D., joined us as an author in this volume of stories. Other articles in theological publications and op-ed articles in newspapers preceded the first edition of our more complete examination of the subject: Earl E. Shelp and Ronald H. Sunderland, *AIDS and the Church* (Philadelphia: Westminster Press, 1987), revised in a second edition as *AIDS and the Church: The Second Decade* (Philadelphia: Westminster Press, 1992).

2. *Chronic Care in America: A 21st Century Challenge* (Princeton, N.J.: The Robert Wood Johnson Foundation, 1996), pp. 8-13.

3. Ibid., p. 57.

4. Ibid., pp. 62-64.

5. This discussion of biblical texts is drawn from Robert Banks, *Paul's Idea of Community: The Early House Churches in Their Historical Setting* (Grand Rapids: Wm. B. Eerdmans Publishing, 1980), pp. 54-111.

6. Ibid., p. 111.

7. Cf. Gary Gunderson, *Deeply Woven Roots: Improving the Quality of Life in Your Community* (Minneapolis: Fortress Press, 1997), pp. 24, 28.

8. William A. Clebsch and Charles R. Jaekle, *Pastoral Care in Historical Perspective* (Englewood: Prentice-Hall, 1964), p. 7.

9. Cf. Pearl M. Oliner and Samuel P. Oliner, *Toward a Caring Society: Ideas into Action* (Westport: Praeger, 1995). The authors make this point as follows: "Care . . . is more likely to occur when core participants within institutions assume responsibility for it and help shape it. In this view, an institutional structure supporting care comes only after an internal culture supports it; that is, after caring impulses are integrated and incorporated into the heart of institutional life" (p. 206).

10. Farley, *Tragic Vision*, p. 69.

11. The concept of autonomy, respect for autonomy, and the principle of autonomy are vastly richer ideas in moral theory than presented here. The right of persons to act as they wish is not unlimited. For a brief discussion, see Tom L. Beauchamp and James F. Childress, *Principles of Biomedical Ethics* (New York: Oxford University Press, 1979), pp. 56-62.

12. We frequently consult with church-related organizations that wish to develop and coordinate Care Team ministries as a service or gift to their communities or constituencies. The orientation that we provide during three days equips a sponsoring organization to initiate and sustain these ministries.

13. In addition to the books referenced in note 1 above, see Ronald H. Sunderland and Earl E. Shelp, *Handle With Care: A Handbook for Care Teams Serving People with AIDS*

(Nashville: Abingdon Press, 1990) and Ronald H. Sunderland and Earl E. Shelp, *AIDS: A Manual for Pastoral Care* (Philadelphia: Westminster Press, 1987).

14. Rebecca Lomax, Divisional Director, Associated Catholic Charities of New Orleans, personal correspondence, 18 November 1988.

Chapter 5. AIDS Care Team Ministry

1. Centers for Disease Control, "Pneumocystis Pneumonia—Los Angeles," *Morbidity and Mortality Weekly Report* 30 (5 June 1981): 250-52.

2. We restrict our discussion of HIV/AIDS to the United States. It should be noted, however, that HIV/AIDS is a pandemic that is devastating lives on every continent. Countries in North America and Europe have been better able to respond to the crisis than nations of the developing world. Infection rates appear to be stabilizing or declining in the United States, whereas a greater proportion of the population of many developing nations is becoming HIV+. Similarly, advances in treatment of HIV infection and its complications are restricted mostly to economically advantaged nations. These differences in the history of HIV/AIDS pose significant prophetic challenges to the church.

3. Although certain features of the HIV/AIDS epidemic in the United States are unprecedented, many social, cultural, political, and religious responses are familiar to students of the history of diseases. For our overview of this matter, see Earl E. Shelp and Ronald H. Sunderland, *AIDS and the Church: The Second Decade* (Louisville: Westminster/John Knox Press, 1992), chapter 1. We are not aware of a published history of the church and AIDS in the United States. An enterprising Ph.D. candidate or church historian would perform an important service by undertaking such a project even though the final chapter is far from being written. The end of AIDS is not in sight. The response of the church continues to evolve. A brief summary description of the impact of AIDS on the church appears in Albert R. Jonsen and Jeff Stryker, eds., *The Social Impact of AIDS in the United States* (Washington: National Academy Press, 1993), chapter 5. This book is the product of a panel formed by the National Academy of Sciences. It examines the impact of the epidemic on the selected institutions of public health, health care delivery and financing, clinical research and drug regulation, religion and religious groups, voluntary and community-based organizations, correctional systems, and public policies on children and families. Earl Shelp was a member of the panel.

4. All statistical data are drawn from reports by the Centers for Disease Control and Prevention in Atlanta, Georgia. Updates are regularly posted on the Internet. Semi-annual printed reports appear in *HIV/AIDS Surveillance Report*. Mortality data for 1997 were reported by Steven A. Holmes, "1997 AIDS Deaths Down by Almost Half in U.S. from 1996," *New York Times*, 8 October 1998, pp. A1, A 24.

5. Assessing the relative contribution of each of these factors to fewer diagnoses of AIDS is difficult. For example, during the year prior to the introduction of protease inhibitors, new AIDS diagnoses increased by 5%, vastly less than the rates in early years.

6. The phrase "men who have sex with men" is preferred over "gay" men to denote means of infection. "Gay" generally refers to a self-identification, which includes sexual preferences and also may have social, cultural, and political connotations. It is well recognized among researchers that there are men who have sex with men who do not self-describe as "gay." Some of these men may describe themselves as bisexual or homosexual.

7. Attention is generally focused on the role of injection drug use in HIV infection. There is evidence that other forms of drug use also have a role as cravings for drugs or diminished inhibitions secondary to substance use cause people to take risks. For example, the Centers for Disease Control and Prevention cite one study of more than 1,000 young adults in three inner-city neighborhoods that found crack smokers were three times more likely to be HIV+ than nonsmokers.

8. Shelp and Sunderland, *AIDS and the Church*, pp. 119-57.

9. In references to individuals and families in the care of teams throughout the book, names have been changed in order to protect privacy.

Chapter 6. Alzheimer's Care Teams

1. Miriam K. Aronson, ed., *Understanding Alzheimer's Disease* (New York: Charles Scribner's Sons, 1988), p. 216.

2. M. B. Stern, "The Clinical Characteristics of Parkinson's Disease and Parkinsonian Syndromes: Diagnosis and Assessment." In M. B. Stern and H. I. Hurtig, eds., *The Comprehensive Management of Parkinson's Disease* (New York: PMA Publishing Group, 1988), pp. 3-50. See also Roger C. Duvoisin, *Parkinson's Disease* (New York: Raven Press, 1991), pp. 1-5.

3. Howard M. Rice, "A Daily Hell in Living with Alzheimer's Disease," *The Houston Chronicle*, 12 December 1994, p. 19A.

4. Richard Schulz, et al., "Psychiatric and Physical Morbidity Effects of Dementia Caregiving: Prevalence, Correlates, and Causes," *The Gerontologist* vol. 35 [6] (1995): 771-91.

5. U. S. Department of Health and Human Services National Institutes of Health Publication, No. 99-3616, p. 3.

6. U. S. Department of Health and Human Services, Public Health Service; National Institute on Aging, NIH Publication, No. 95-3994, p. 2.

7. Schulz, "Psychiatric and Physical Morbidity," p. 772.

8. R. Brookmeyer, S. Gray, and C. Kawas, "Projections of Alzheimer's disease in the United States and the Public Impact of Delaying Disease Onset," *American Journal of Public Health* 88 (September 1988): 1337-42.

9. Denis A. Evans et al., "Prevalence of Alzheimer's Disease in a Community Population of Older Persons," *Journal of the American Medical Association* 262 (10 November 1989): 2551-56.

10. David Gelman, Mary Hager, and Vicki Quade, "The Brain Killer," *Newsweek* (18 December 1989): 56.

11. Sam Roberts, *Who We Are: A Portrait of America* (New York: Times Books, 1993), pp. 229 ff. See also Edward W. Campion, "The Oldest Old," *New England Journal of Medicine* 330 (23 June 1994): 1819.

12. Rochelle Lipkowitz, "Services for Alzheimer Patients and Their Families," in Miriam K. Aronson, ed., *Understanding Alzheimer's Disease* (New York: Charles Scribner's Sons, 1988), p. 199.

13. Lydia H. Greiner and David A. Snowdon, "Underrecognition of Dementia by Caregivers Cuts Across Cultures," *Journal of the American Medical Association* 277 (11 June 1997): 1757.

14. L. W. Morris, R. G. Morris, and P. G. Britton, "Cognitive Style and Perceived Control in Spouse Caregivers of Dementia Sufferers," *British Journal of Medical Psychology* 62 (June 1989): 173-79.

15. Susan Sontag, *Illness as Metaphor* (New York: Doubleday, 1978), p. 5. See also Irving Goffman, *Stigma* (Englewood Cliffs, N.J.: Prentice-Hall, 1963).

16. Morton A. Lieberman and Lawrence Fisher, "The Impact of Chronic Illness on the Health and Well-being of Family Members," *The Gerontologist* 35 (1995): 94-102.

17. C. G. Shields, "Family Interaction and Caregivers of Alzheimer's Disease Patients: Correlates of Depression," *Family Process* 31 (March 1992): 19-33.

18. E. Morrisey, J. Becker, and M. P. Rubert, "Coping Resources and Depression in the Caregiving Spouse of Alzheimer Patients," *British Journal of Medical Psychology* 63 (June 1990): 170-71.

19. R. A. Pruchno, and N. L. Resch, "Husbands and Wives as Caregivers: Antecedents of Depression and Burden," *The Gerontologist* 29 (April 1989): 159-65.

20. L. K. Wright, "The Impact of Alzheimer's Disease on the Marital Relationship," *The Gerontologist* 31 (1991): 224-37.

21. Pruchno and Resch, "Husbands and Wives," p. 159.

22. P. P. Vitaliano et al, "Predictors of Burden in Spouse Caregivers of Individuals with Alzheimer's Disease," *Psychological Aging* 6 (September 1991): 392-402.

23. See, for example, Naomi Feil, *The Validation Breakthrough: Simple Techniques for Communicating with People with Alzheimer's-Type Dementia* (Baltimore, Md.: Health Professions Press, 1993), pp. 27 ff.

24. Nancy L. Mace and Peter V. Rabins, *The 36-Hour Day* (Baltimore, Md.: John's Hopkins University Press, 1991).

25. Ken Walker, "One Spouse's Story: This isn't the cup I chose," Louisville: *The Western Recorder* (25 October 1994): 12.

26. Aronson, *Understanding Alzheimer's Disease*, p. 75.

27. Rice, "A daily hell," p. 19.

28. Mace and Rabins, *The 36-Hour Day*, pp. 200-6.

29. Judah L. Ronch, *Alzheimer's Disease: A Practical Guide for Families and Other Caregivers* (New York: Continuum Publishing, 1991), p. 23.

30. Gelman et al., "The Brain Killer," p. 55.

31. In references to families in the care of teams throughout the book, names of families and their congregations have been changed in order to protect privacy.

32. V. Cotrell and R. Schulz, "The Perspective of the Patient with Alzheimer's Disease: A Neglected Dimension of Dementia Research," *Gerontologist* 33 (April 1993): 205-11.

33. Lipkowitz, "Services for Alzheimer Patients," p. 201.

34. Feil, *The Validation Breakthrough,* p 130.

35. Carly R. Hellen, *Alzheimer's Disease: Activity-Focused Care* (Boston: Andover Medical Publishers, 1992), p. 2.

36. Ibid., p. 100.

37. Stephen Sapp, "Memory: The Community Looks Backwards," in *God Never Forgets: Faith, Hope, and Alzheimer's Disease,* ed. Donald K. McKim (Louisville: Westminster John Knox Press, 1997), p. 40..

38. Ibid., p. 41.

39. Ibid., p. 51.

40. Ibid., p. 54.

Chapter 7. Second Family Care Teams

1. Sam Roberts, *Who We Are: A Portrait of America* (New York: Times Books, 1993), p. 232.

2. Ibid., pp. 234, 254.

3. Barbara Vobejda, "Census: Elderly Population Growth Will Lead to 4-Generation Families," *The Washington Post,* 10 November 1992, p. A3.

4. William Scanlon, "A Perspective on Long-term Care for the Elderly," *Health Care Financing Review,* 10, 4 (Summer 1988): p. 7.

5. Ibid., p. 7.

6. Edward W. Campion, "The Oldest Old," *The New England Journal of Medicine* 330 (23 June 1994): 1819.

7. John W. Rowe and Robert L. Kahn, *Successful Aging* (New York: Pantheon Books, 1998).

8. Cited by Rowe and Kahn, *Successful Aging,* p. 6.

9. Ibid., p. 16.

10. Ibid., pp. 152-53.

11. Roberts, *Who We Are,* p. 235.

12. Judith G. Gonyea, "Age-based Policies and the Oldest-Old," *Generations* 17 (fall 1995): 25. Also Campion, "The Oldest Old," p. 1819.

13. Peter G. Peterson, *Will America Grow Up Before It Grows Old?* (New York: Random House, 1996), p. 19.

14. Gonyea, "Age-based Policies," p. 27.

15. Peterson, *Will America Grow Up,* pp. 13, 15.

16. Helen Dennis and John Migliaccio, "Redefining Retirement: The Baby Boomer Challenge," *Generations* 21 (summer 1997): 41.

17. David L. Morgan, "The Aging of the Baby Boom: An Introduction," *Generations* 22 (spring 1998): 8.

18. Elizabeth A. Kutza, "A Look at National Policy and the Baby Boom Generation," *Generations* 22 (spring 1998): 16.

19. See, for example, V. L. Bengston et al., "Generations and Social Change," in *Handbook of Aging and the Social Sciences*, 2d. ed., ed. P. L. Binstock and E. Shanas (New York: Van Nostrand, 1985).

20. Henri J. M. Nouwen, Donald P. McNeill, and Douglas A. Morrison, *Compassion: A Reflection on the Christian Life* (New York: Image/Doubleday, 1982), p. 49.

21. Ronald H. Sunderland, *Equipping Laypeople for Ministry* (Houston: Elm, 1997), pp. 5-8.

22. Henri Nouwen, "Ministry to the Aged," in *Aging and the Human Spirit,* ed. Carol LeFevre and Perry LeFevre (Chicago: Exploration Press, 1981), p. 294.

23. Wayne Dyer, *You'll See It When You Believe It* (New York: Avon Books, 1989), pp. 143-83.

24. Ibid., p. 162.

25. Henri J. M. Nouwen, *Reaching Out* (New York: Image/Doubleday, 1975), pp. 23 ff.

26. Priscilla Ebersole and Patricia Hess, *Toward Healthy Aging* (St. Louis, Mo.: C. V. Mosby, 1985), p. 596.

27. Robert H. Binstock, "The Final Reckoning: Suicide in Old Age" *The Gerontologist* 37 (June 1997), 418. See also, Heather Uncapher, et al., "Hopelessness and Suicidal Ideation in Older Adults," *The Gerontologist* 38 (February 1998): 62 ff.

28. Catherine Harris, "In-Home Respite Care: A Comparison of Volunteers and Paid Workers," *The Journal of Volunteer Administration* (fall 1991): 2-14.

29. Elizabeth Midlarsky, *Family Caregiving Across the Lifespan*, eds. Eva Kahana, David E. Biegel, and Mary L. Wykle (Thousand Oaks, Calif.: Sage Publications, 1994), p. 89. See also David E. Biegel, Li-Yu Song, and Venkatesan Chakravarthy, "Predictors of Caregiving Burden Among Support Group Members of Persons with Chronic Mental Illness," in *Family Caregiving Across the Lifespan,* 179-215.

30. F. Cohen, M. Horowitz, and R. Lazarus, "Panel Report on Psycho-Social Stress," in *Stress and Human Health: Analysis and Implications for Research,* ed. G. Elliott and C. Eisdorfer (New York: Springer, 1982).

31. Midlarsky, *Family Caregiving,* pp. 69-95.

32. E. H. Erikson, J. Erikson, and H. Kivnik, *Vital Involvement in Old Age* (New York: Norton Publishing, 1986).

33. Morgan, "The Aging of the Baby Boom," p. 6.

Chapter 8. A Future for Caregiving

1. Jack Gordon, President, Hospice Foundation of America, cited in *The Forum Newsletter,* Association for Death Education and Counseling 24 (September/October 1998): 11.

2. Ronald H. Sunderland, *Getting Through Grief: Caregiving by Congregations* (Nashville: Abingdon Press, 1993), pp. 12, 32 ff.

3. Sunderland, pp. 80 ff.

4. Personal communication from Dr. George Singer, Graduate School of Education, University of California at Santa Clara, Calif.

5. Gareth Weldon Icenogle, *Biblical Foundations for Small Group Ministry* (Downers Grove, Ill.: InterVarsity Press, 1994), p. 105.

6. Cited by Icenogle, p. 99.

7. Robert Wuthnow, *Christianity in the Twenty-first Century* (New York: Oxford University Press, 1993), p. 6.

8. Ibid., p. 33.

9. Henri J. M. Nouwen, *The Living Reminder* (New York: Seabury Press, 1977), p. 13.

10. Ibid., p. 41.

11. Wuthnow, p. 70. The prior discussion relies heavily on Wuthnow's analysis; see pp. 33-67.